Entangled Peace

Entangled Peace

UN Peacebuilding and the Limits of a Relational World

Ignasi Torrent

ROWMAN & LITTLEFIELD
Lanham • Boulder • New York • London

Credits and acknowledgments for material borrowed from other sources, and reproduced with permission, appear on the appropriate page within the text.
Published by Rowman & Littlefield
An imprint of The Rowman & Littlefield Publishing Group, Inc.
4501 Forbes Boulevard, Suite 200, Lanham, Maryland 20706
www.rowman.com

A catalogue record for this book is available from the British Library

Library of Congress Cataloging-in-Publication Data
Library of Congress Cataloging-in-Publication Data
Names: Torrent, Ignasi, 1987- author.
Title: Entangled peace : UN peacebuilding and the limits of a relational world / Ignasi Torrent.
Description: Lanham : Rowman & Littlefield, [2021] | Includes bibliographical references and index. |
Summary: "This book unfolds an exploratory journey intended to scrutinise the suitability of entanglements and relations as a mode of thinking and seeing peacebuilding events. Through a reflection upon the UN's limited results in the endeavour towards securing lasting peace in war-torn scenarios, Torrent critically engages with three relevant debates in contemporary peacebuilding literature, including the inclusion of 'the locals', the achievement of organisational system-wide coherence and the increasingly questioned agential condition of peacebuilding actors. Inattentive to the relational vulnerability of involved stakeholders, it is suggested that the UN seeks to secure a totalising modern distory, defined in the book as a story that undoes other stories. Whilst affirming the entangled ontogenesis of actors and processes in the conflict-affected configuration, Entangled Peace also delves into a cautionary argument about what the author refers to as entanglement fetishism, namely the celebratory, normative, deterministic and exclusionary projection of a relational world. Inspired by Alfred North Whitehead, Entangled Peace is an invitation to speculate over the peacebuilding milieu, and by extension the broader theatre of the real, as radical openness, in which events emanate from the collision of an infinite multiplicity of possible worlds"— Provided by publisher.
Identifiers: LCCN 2021020674 (print) | LCCN 2021020675 (ebook) | ISBN 9781538150764 (cloth) | ISBN 9781538150788 (paperback) | ISBN 9781538150771 (epub)
Subjects: LCSH: United Nations. | Peace-building. | International relations—Philosophy.
Classification: LCC JZ5538 .T67 2021 (print) | LCC JZ5538 (ebook) | DDC 341.5/84—dc23
LC record available at https://lccn.loc.gov/2021020674
LC ebook record available at https://lccn.loc.gov/2021020675

To Elena and our son Ignasi

Contents

Acknowledgements

This book is the result of a long journey along which I have been inspired and supported by numerous people, places, works, practices and modes of seeing the world. First and foremost, this book would have not been possible without the generous, tireless and caring assistance of my friend and colleague David Chandler, without whom the academia would be a darker, duller and squarer space. Also, as the present fruit admittedly originates in my doctoral dissertation, I also want to give credit to my former supervisors, Caterina Garcia and Josep Ibáñez, for their thoughtful and valuable advice.

Undoubtedly, the research exposed in the following pages on the notion of peacebuilding and particularly how the UN engages with it has critically benefitted from the priceless academic experiences I have had over the past few years in Pompeu Fabra University in Barcelona, the University of Sierra Leone in Freetown, the City University of New York and the University of Westminster in London. Memunatu Pratt, Samuel Allen, Ibrahim Tucker, Rebecca Nielsen and Tom Weiss, amongst many others, contributed one way or another to this project. I also want to thank all the anonymous interviewees who kindly addressed my questions and provided crucial insights that later informed some of the arguments developed in the book.

In addition, the thinking unfolded in the present text has been greatly influenced by countless encounters and conversations over the past years with friends and colleagues from the academic sphere and beyond, including Pol Bargués, Oscar Mateos, Albert Caramés, Itziar Ruiz-Giménez, María Martín de Almagro, Judith Nora Hardt, Itziar Mújika, Pablo Pareja, Harshavardhan Bhat, Pierre Parrouffe, Anthony Powis, Farai Chipato, Sara Raimondi, Cedric de Coning, Peter Finkenbush, Marta Íñiguez de Heredia, the crew from the New Materialisms Reading Group based in the University of Westminster in London, especially the after-hours at the Yorkshire Grey, Elisa Randazzo, with whom I co-authored an article that sets the basis for chapter 3, and the rest of my current colleagues at the Politics and International Relations department at University of Hertfordshire, Hannah Richter, Francesca Batzella and Ben Nutt. On top of all these, I want to acknowledge all the students that I have had over the past decade, from whom I have learned an invaluable amount of things. I apologise in advance to those who have remained unsaid and who should have been added to the list.

I also want to express my gratitude to the helpful support offered by the editors from Rowman and Littlefield throughout the whole process, Dhara Snowden and Rebecca Anastasi. I have partly published chapters 1 and 3 in the *Journal of Intervention and Statebuilding* and *Security Dialogue*, respectively. I thank their respective editorial boards for giving me permission to use that content.

I would also like to mention my closest friends, aka the top of the top, and my family, who, despite having a vague idea of what the academia is and entails, are always unconditionally there for me. Finally, and above all, this book is dedicated to my wife, Elena, without whom, literally, none of this would have ever been possible, and who brought to this world our most precious thing, our son Ignasi.

Introduction

The true relata are events.

– Whitehead (2006:24)

Over the past two decades, a proliferating number of academic disciplines as well as a broader set of human practices, including policy arrangements, techno-scientific advances and the arts, amongst others, have incorporated entanglements and relations as a guiding mode to be in, think and transform the world. The present exploratory journey delves into one more attempt to scrutinise the suitability of this more and more compelling framework by developing an in-depth dissection of peacebuilding events, meaning those societal processes aimed at recovery, stability and lasting peace that post-conflict milieus undergo, frequently assisted by external agencies. Notwithstanding indisputable analytical value, the book does not blossom into a celebratory experiment, a discovery or a revelation building up and invigorating what is hereby defined as entanglement fetishism, to be precise, the normative and emancipatory projection of the world as an all-encompassing, interconnected and autopoietic wholeness. Entangled peace refrains from claims of an entangled ontogenesis of all beings and processes so as to prompt an intervention in the world. It is not the object of entangled peace to unleash a saviour breakthrough or a liberatory venture towards a longed-for telos. Entanglements, relations, collisions, tensions, negotiations, frictions, entwinements, knots and so forth are not approached hereinafter as rigid and deterministic cuts that claim what the world should be like.

How would such an exclusionary version of entangled thinking surpass the hubristic, homogenising and universalising cosmovision in which modernity and other forms of violence are embedded? It would simply not. Constraining what the world is to the (entangled) human experience of it entails one more reductionist, egoistic and self-indulgent political formulation. Entangled peace attempts to modestly eschew this ontological elitism. By expanding the underlaying problematics of the peacebuilding undertaking, entangled peace unfolds a form of seeing the theatre of the real that atomises *ad infinitum* the possibilities of and with the world(s), from a particle coalescence scale to the clash of galaxies. Rather than delimiting the genealogy as well as the future of all earthly elements in the relational paradigm, the hereby worldview proposes to demystify entanglement fetishism and embrace the realm of experience as a composite of infinite colliding stories. Therefore, the book does stand by entangled ontological assumptions, but to the ultimate implications: entangled peace is an invitation to speculate over the world as radical openness, where events emanate from the clash of a multiplicity of possible worlds, experienced and non-experienced, entangled and non-entangled. In sum, entangled peace is a warm welcome to collapse, from the Latin 'falling together', as the very prime condition for possibility.

Arguably circumscribed in the area of inquiry of Critical Peace and Conflict Studies, the book critically reflects upon the manifestly limited results of United Nations (UN) peacebuilding engagements assisting war-torn scenarios in their path towards durable peace. Fundamentally, the text questions the hopes for enforcing, making, keeping and building peace as an essentialised, objectifiable and reachable 'out-there' order. While a substantial amount of critical peacebuilding literature singles out the ill-capacity of a given actor that sorrowfully fails in its peace endeavours, the text problematises instead that this peace-seeking actor is imagined as an external subject with intervening powers in the world. Rather, as suggested in the following pages, this subject, as well as the rest of beings, is materially entangled in a mutually co-constitutive mode with the rest of actors and processes in the conflict-affected landscape. The prime implication of affirming this entangled ontological formula, in which beings and processes co-emerge in relation, is acknowledging the weakness, vulnerability and dependence of the being. Accordingly, entangled ontologies fundamentally dispute the Cartesian hierarchical subject-object divide, for which the (human) subject stands from a higher and prominent position over the rest of the world, and on which the liberal Man has edified the 300-year fantasy of anthropocentric and colonising modernity. Unveiling the relational ontogenesis of the human ultimately questions its autonomous and purposeful agency, which is continuously hindered by generative negotiations with other beings and phenomena. This presumption invalidates any attempt by any actor to pursue peace in a teleological manner, as if events unfolded in a sequential Humean cause-effect scheme. On the basis of these underpinning assumptions, the book invites readers to think peacebuilding events, and by extension the broader world, as continuous and weird space-time framings that accommodate the ruins of convoluted modes of being and becoming.

In the words of the English philosopher Alfred North Whitehead, who should be credited as the largest source of inspiration in the present book, 'the experience of Peace is largely beyond the control of purpose'.[1] Peace is hence unattainable, thereby freeing peacebuilders from protracted anxiety and rendering efforts towards peace in a contentious and unsettling terrain. The author continues to elucidate how peace cannot then be a hope for the future, as it comprises an unreachable sense of infinitude, an appeal beyond classic space-time boundaries.[2] Foremost, to Whitehead, the comprehension of peace requires the recognition of its immanent entangled genealogy with surrounding processes, including soreness, war and tragedy. The notion of entanglement in entangled peace is envisioned alike: the affirmation of a relational world does not determine its ontogenesis as entangled in a normative and deterministic fashion; on the contrary, it is hinting at an eternal collision of infinite world-making possibilities, relational and non-relational. 'The meaning of Peace is most clearly understood by considering it in its relations to the tragic issues which are essential in the nature of things. Peace is the understanding of tragedy, and at the same time its preservation'.[3] From this account, peace and tragedy keep one another alive in ongoing knotted reinvention. Furthermore, tragedy is the disclosure of the possibility of peace: 'What might have been, and was not: What can be'.[4] At last, Whitehead thus associates the experience of peace with potential eventuality, generative force and adventurous creativity.

With these insights in mind, the monograph embarks on two major storylines. Firstly, through critically thinking with UN peacebuilding missions, with a focus on the cases of Sierra Leone, Burundi and the Central African Republic (CAR), it discusses the operational conceptualisation of peace as a phenomenon that can be known, captured, manipulated, managed and achieved from the outside through a goal-oriented, linear and progressive strategy. In this book, actors and processes in the peacebuilding setting are seen as ontologically composing each other, meaning that their very being stems from the complex and unpredictable relations with further actors and processes. Second, the book suggests that, disregarding the entangled ontology of actors and processes in the peacebuilding enterprise, the UN resolves to expand its own essentialising, exclusionary and uncaring distory, described in the following pages as a story that undoes other stories. Noticeably anchored in the pillars of liberal modernity, UN distories erase the possibility for vernacular and non-modern stories to thrive. For this discussion, the book critically engages with story-telling practices that invoke entangled modes of being and becoming, what Stengers calls non-hierarchical modes of existence.[5] Crucially, the text also exposes the limits and encumbrances of ethico-political disruptions attempting to materialise and preserve a relational (and solely relational) world. Entangled peace cautions that this intrusive mode of configuring the world risks reproducing the same exclusionary logics as other forms of violent distories, including the normative and universalising dreams of modernity. In this expansive version of entangled thinking, the non-relational seems to play the same role that the non-modern plays in modernity, namely one of subordination, exclusion and eventually erasure.

ENTANGLED ONTOLOGIES

The fundamental body of theory that fuels this book embraces a wide tradition of thought that supersedes an elemental and primal essence of things with a non-essentialised, processual and intense form of being. Accordingly, the text tends to not speak of the nature or the essence of things, beings and actors, but of notions such as ontogenesis or genealogy, for, in a Whiteheadian fashion, the book appreciates that being is its process of becoming. In vein with this philosophical trend, this process of becoming is never isolated, but constitutively entangled with further processes of becoming, or events, deemed by Whitehead the true composites of a relation.[6] Therefore, these entangled ontologies recognise that beings and processes of the world compose one another in relation. In other words, relations precede the relata. The most prominent figures who arguably engendered and pioneered relational and process thinking are, amongst many others, Baruch Spinoza, Gottfried Wilhelm Leibniz and, more recently, Henri Bergson, Alfred North Whitehead and Gilles Deleuze.[7] Aware that the comparative scrutiny of these masters of philosophy would deserve a thoroughly nuanced study, I dare to suggest that, together, they compose a materialist corpus of reflection that, contrary to orthodox Marxist materialism, always undermined an excessively human-centred cosmovision, in which a human separated from the rest of the universe is at the centre of a limitless and linear form of progress.

In contemporary conversations, the aforementioned relational and processual accounts have distinguishably resurged unleashing a renewed interrogation of the human condition and, particularly, its relations with the rest of earthly elements. Arguably, the re-emergence of discussions about entangled ontologies throughout the past two decades should be mostly attributed to the work of three authors and, more specifically, the publication of three books: *Reassembling the Social* (2005) by Bruno Latour, *When Species Meet* (2007) by Donna Haraway and *Meeting the Universe Halfway* (2007) by Karen Barad. Alongside other prominent authors, these intellectual interventions, by and large, have sought to unpack three lines of argumentation. First, Cartesian binaries (subject-object, human-world, mind-matter) as well as Kantian universalising categories, on which modern epistemology is underpinned, have been deemed hubristic, reductionist and insufficient to comprehend reality, which is portrayed as inaccessible by the human, hence the call for looking into non-modern speculative forms of mediating the theatre of the real, for instance, story-telling practices. Second, the human role in the planet is being re-examined in light of a reconsideration of the beyond-the-human agency, which is increasingly presented as a source of ontological erosion of a hitherto conceived of as a master, superior and dominant human over the rest of the world. Third, more and more, the ontology of earthly elements, material and immaterial, is reflected upon as entangled, relational and co-emergent. Thus, the very being stems from a co-constitutive encounter with other beings, which are not thought of as essentialised but continuous processes of becoming. Admittedly, these current cutting-edge conversations, which have not escaped from critical scrutiny,[8] along with the earlier philosophical traditions mentioned earlier, significantly inform the arguments brought forward in this book.

To be sure, the critique of modernity embedded in entangled ontological assumptions should be markedly distinguished from postmodern post-positivist analyses. In fact, contemporary non-Marxist forms of materialism and similar (i.e. new materialism, Object-Oriented Ontology [OOO]) as well as new forms of anti-Kantian realism (i.e. critical realism, speculative realism), both significant sources of inspiration in the present text, openly and vehemently problematise the sociocultural discursive criticism and the whole linguistic or semiotic turn, to a large extent resulting from the works of Jacques Derrida, Michel Foucault and Judith Butler, amongst others. Without disavowing the undeniable remarkable contributions of these authors to critical thinking, their work has also stirred an intellectual dispute.[9] First, while for post-structuralists relations are mostly used as an analytical tool to unravel and contest how certain social (and solely social) structures in a position of power oppress the powerless, in new materialist conversations relations are the *sine qua non* processes through which all matter becomes. As Bergson puts it, matter becomes through processual repetition.[10] The ontogenesis of matter and life cannot be explained without iterative relationality, which is utterly overlooked by the cultural turn. Second, social constructivist frameworks still reproduce the hubris of culture-centred epistemological formulas and lack the capacity to explain how current complex events, including exponential technoscientific progress and pressing ecological challenges, amongst others, continuously reconfigure and blur the material-semiotic boundaries between the human and the non-human. In this sense, as Timothy Morton puts it, 'postmodernism is nothing like what it takes itself to be, and is indeed just another version of the (white, Western, male) historical project'.[11] Informed by these formulations, the following chapters seek to suggest that what has deliberately been divided into the observer/subject/human/mind/culture and the observed/object/non-human/matter/nature ultimately shapes the expression of a same plane, fold or actuality, the composites of which are in ongoing co-constitutive intense negotiations.

Seeking to stretch the boundaries of the validity of entanglements as a mode of thinking peacebuilding landscapes, the book discusses detracting positions on this entangled ontological turn. In brief, three major counterarguments are being brought forward by different contemporary thinkers.[12] On the one hand, from a rather post-structuralist Foucauldian angle, entangled ontologies are accused of overlooking the implications that power relations have over social reality. In this line of critique, new materialist debates are deemed depoliticised and therefore potentially reproductive of the violence of neoliberalism and socio-economic struggles. From a different perspective, authors in tune with philosophical movements such as OOO argue that, in entangled ontological assumptions, relations are overrated. In this vein, these accounts criticise that, contrary to the di-hierarchising and flattening purposes that new materialisms claim to have, they are instead prioritising entanglements over the rest of 'things'. To OOO, 'relations are short-lived objects'.[13] Finally, a third trend of critiques describes the emphasis on ontological relationality as a method of eschewing the very first ontological question, which is, 'what is the being, without being in relation?' This critical account outlines that reducing the existence of beings to an entangled ontogenesis might intensify the normative stress on being and becoming as relation. By attempting to move these insightful narratives forward, entangled peace intends to shun normative and deterministic entangled cosmovisions. It is not the object of this book to suggest that through a specific emancipatory entanglement-sensitive enterprise, the human and the rest of earthly beings will be and become in endless harmony. Rather, in line with Shaviro's position,[14] the text seeks to explore the ultimate metaphysical question, namely how to surpass the overdeterministic and oppressive character of entanglements, thus enabling a radical opened-up future composed of beyond-relational worlds.

PEACE: A SOURCE OF KNOWLEDGE PRODUCTION

Peace and war have nurtured a bottomless source of knowledge production for countless authors across history, from Thucydides to Machiavelli, Tolstoy, Arendt and Deulofeu, amongst many others. Throughout the first half of the twentieth century, notorious scholars such as Pitirim Sorokin, Abraham Maslow and John Burton began to thoroughly examine the causality of war, the phenomenon of peace and the basic human needs from a scientific angle. The 1942 book *A Study of War* by Quincy Wright became a milestone for the coming area of peace research studies. In that context, young researchers inspired by these predecessors as well as by the dominant behavioural trend in social sciences, led by psychologists such as Burrhus Skinner and Charles Fertser, adopted a positivist epistemological approach to unpack the nature of war and peace through quantitative empirical methods.[15] As in further emerging disciplines in the first half of the twentieth century, including political science, sociology and International Relations, a highly normative and prescriptive rationale underlaid the early ethos of peace research, ultimately aimed to shape human behaviour in order to ultimately establish durable peace.

In the late 1960s and the 1970s, Johan Galtung, a Norwegian sociologist, underpinned the theoretical basis of modern peace and conflict studies and prompted the process of institutionalisation of this area of research. Detouring from the positivist approach adopted by peace researchers in the early stage, Galtung received the influence of critical theorists from the Frankfurt School, who conspicuously interrogated the objectivity of the researcher and the deterministic behaviour of human beings under the rational choice scheme. In this vein, further peace researchers warned the epistemic community in their field against excessive confidence on quantitative methods to capture the essence of war and peace.[16] The approach adopted by Galtung, remarkably deviant from scientific positivism, along with his conceptualisation of notions such as structural, cultural and direct violence, negative and positive peace, as well as peacebuilding and the transcendent approach, played a key role in the modernisation of peace and conflict studies.[17]

In the 1980s and 1990s, major violent episodes in countries like Vietnam, Afghanistan, Iraq, Somalia, Rwanda and the former Yugoslavia conquered the attention of mass media, leading a growing number of international organisations, policy makers and academics to strengthen the focus on enhancing the understanding of these events with the ultimate goal of preventing war and establishing lasting peace. After almost thirty years of sustained international peace endeavours, mostly led by the UN, peacebuilding actors have achieved noticeable, and troubling, limited results. Indeed, despite manifest discursive and field efforts towards peacebuilding, a critical number of contexts have not been pacified and, on top of this, violent outbreaks are (re)emerging in different parts of the world.[18]

A vast amount of critical accounts have sought to investigate over the past two decades the blatant failure of international peace efforts. Throughout the early 2000s, two major critical trends centred these intellectual conversations.[19] The first cluster, led by authors such as Roland Paris, never put into question the validity of the conceptual and operational framework behind the international peacebuilding enterprise, which was unambiguously founded on liberal principles and values. Instead, they elaborated on a top-down policy critique, emphasising the need for technical and institutional reforms, that is, statebuilding practices, to overcome the problematic results of liberal peacebuilding missions. The second trend, led by authors of a more theoretically radical background such as Oliver Richmond, questioned the very foundation of this so-called liberal peacebuilding project, hinting at the problematic implications of the behind-the-scenes intentionality to expand a worldwide liberal order through peace engagements. This line of critique placed at the heart of the peacebuilding game the local society of conflict-affected countries, as an attempt to counter and readdress the controversial hierarchical relation between the interveners and the intervened.[20] From these early rather opposed viewpoints, critical peacebuilding literature has grown exponentially. In the following chapters, emerging peacebuilding debates become ground for engagement through the critical lens enabled by the entangled peace configuration.

Endorsing the validity and relevance of this body of critique in advancing the area of critical peace and conflict studies, the book nonetheless intends to detour from the all-encompassing peace-affirming standpoint, from which, regardless of the angle of criticism, in the end, the overwhelming majority of practitioners and scholars seek to contribute to the consolidation of durable peace. As extensively unfolded in the text, there is no such thing as an 'out-there' state of peace waiting to be attained, conquered and mastered by a subject. Hence, the following pages are an attempt to illustrate the vulnerability, fragility and weakness of peace, which hinges on a constitutive encounter between beings and events. In the domain of peace, entangled ontologies call for abandoning human exceptionalist premises and sensitising with a modest position of the human in a broader political ecology of peacebuilding scenarios. Thus, the book draws on recent scholarly incursions in relationality and entangled ontologies as analytical tools to better understand peacebuilding. In brief, these critical peacebuilding accounts emphasise the suitability of focusing on relations, interactions and ex-changes between actors and processes in conflict-affected contexts over partaking entities themselves. Brigg, for example, argues for the potential of this approach to dihierarchise power relations between stakeholders through the internalisation of a flatter ontology.[21] The author emphasises the need to recognise other forms of thinking, doing and knowing as constituencies of our forms of thinking, doing and knowing.

Building on these contributions and on the basis of aforementioned entangled ontological assumptions, the following chapters unpack three major debates within critical peacebuilding literature that are thoroughly examined through the lens of entanglements. First, through critically reflecting upon the limited results of UN peacebuilding efforts in engaging 'the locals' in the peacebuilding enterprise, the text problematises the UN mode of knowing and engaging the host society as an essentialised and objectifiable actor that is epistemologically accessible and, subsequently, capturable, manipulable and engageable. Rather, it is hinted that knowing is a materially entangled process, meaning that the ontologies of the observer/UN and the observed/'locals' are mutually constituted in relation. In the field, the UN and the host society reinvent each other through knotty, continuous and negotiated entwinements, which renders any hierarchical intervening attempt from the UN side, cognitive or material, unfeasible. Second, thinking with the flawed UN performance to achieve system-wide coherence and intra-coordination presumably leading to enhanced peacebuilding outcomes, the text questions the assumption of the linear unfolding of events in conflict-affected scenarios and, by extension, in the broader world. The book attempts to argue that affirming the entangled ontology of actors and processes in these milieus requires the reconfiguration of linear Humean cause-effect relations. Entangled peace speculates over a continuous and non-static conception of space-time framings, which are not seen as void canvases that the human fill, but the expansive outcome of world relations. Thus, the possibility of change is reworked and resituated not on a given Euclidean and fix space-time coordinate but on the generative entanglement. Third, by examining the faulty UN peacebuilding endeavours to achieve efficient inter-actor strategies, it is suggested that the growing complex multiplicity of actors deployed in some conflict-affected contexts compromises the autonomous and purposeful agency of peacebuilding stakeholders. Rather, agency is conceived of as an ongoing changing constituency, thus undermining once again the rigidness, prescriptiveness and linearity of UN goal-oriented strategies. Crucially, entangled peace intends to push current peacebuilding debates on entanglements and relations by arguing that entangled peace does not entail a celebratory, normative and deterministic invocation for a relational world, which reduces all forms of being and becoming to a very particular and exclusionary mode of existence. In this book, the relational fluxes of war-torn scenarios, and by extension of the broader world, are seen as radical openness, underpinned by the clash of multiple possible futures.

UNITED NATIONS PEACEBUILDING DISTORIES

In the late 1980s, UN peace missions started increasingly widening the scope of their mandates by designing a multidimensional political agenda tackling various challenges, including environmental protection, gender equality and human development, as potential sources of conflict.[22] Shortly after taking office in January 1992, the Secretary General (SG) Boutros-Ghali consolidated UN capabilities for peacebuilding through a major internal institutional reform as well as a transformation of programmatic lines. The General Assembly (GA) resolved that this organisational reform would include the creation of the Department of Political Affairs (DPA),[23] which throughout the 1990s became the core body within the UN system aimed at political and peacebuilding post-conflict engagements. Along with this internal institutional reform, the UNSG Boutros-Ghali introduced in the report 'An Agenda for Peace' the concept of post-conflict peacebuilding, defined as the UN commitment to support the transformation of deficient national structures and capabilities, and the strengthening of new democratic institutions to reduce the risk of relapsing into conflict and laying the foundations for sustainable peace.[24] Beyond security-oriented mandates, the UNSG made an emphasis on the need to address the deepest causes of conflict: economic despair, social injustice and political oppression.

Illustrating this ethos, in the early 1990s, the UN operationalised various peacebuilding tasks, including supporting the political transition and free elections in Namibia through the United Nations Transition Assistance Group (UNTAG, 1989–1990), the reform of the judiciary system in El Salvador through the United Nations Observer Mission in El Salvador (ONUSAL, 1991–1995), the protection of human rights during the Cambodian transitional period through the United Nations Transitional Authority in Cambodia (UNTAC, 1991–1993) as well as monitoring an entire electoral process in Mozambique through the United Nations Operation in Mozambique (ONUMOZ, 1992–1994). In that context, and under the UN leadership, the peacebuilding enterprise was agreed upon amongst the international community as a generally accepted response to war-torn societies' demand for conflict resolution and lasting peace. As mentioned earlier, this international policy framework soon became highly associated with the spread of liberal democratic values and the consolidation of Western-mirrored state structures through technical, top-down, intrusive processes in post-conflict societies, seemingly aimed at establishing lasting peace.[25]

Despite the enthusiasm stemmed from the arguable successful results in these early missions, blatant humanitarian catastrophes dampened the UN optimism about the peacebuilding endeavour, including the disastrous implications resulted from the UN withdrawal from Somalia in 1993, the UN outright failure in preventing the Rwandan genocide in 1994, the disastrous role played by the UN in securing heavens in the Bosnian war giving place to the Srebrenica genocide in 1995 and the UN inability to stop violence in the aftermath of the Angolan peace process in 1998. These flawed engagements prompted the retreat and decay of UN peacebuilding missions and stirred severe detracting debates amongst the academia and policy experts, thus undermining the legitimacy of the peacebuilding international policy framework.

Alongside this context of crisis and criticism of the liberal peacebuilding project, the UN carried out an internal process of evaluation, revision and reform, which, most substantially, included the creation in 2005 of the new Peacebuilding Architecture (PBA), composed of the Peacebuilding Commission (PBC) as well as the auxiliary Peacebuilding Support Office (PBSO) and the Peacebuilding Fund (PBF). On the one hand, the PBC was aimed to bring together and include all relevant stakeholders in the peacebuilding process, with a noticeable emphasis on local actors, reified in the principle of 'local ownership'. On the other hand, this advisory body was meant to endeavour towards system-wide coherence and intra-co-ordination in peacebuilding settings.[26] The disputed implications of both strategic dimensions are widely problematised in chapters 1 and 2, respectively. While the efforts towards engaging 'the locals' in the peacebuilding processes expose the ontological limitations of the UN essentialising view of the peacebuilding event, the objective of system-wide coherence for a better peacebuilding leads to questioning the linear unfolding of processes in the war-torn scenario. Over the first decade of existent, the PBC deployed strategic frameworks for engagement in six countries, including Sierra Leone, Burundi, the CAR, Liberia, Guinea and Guinea-Bissau.

Despite all these efforts, the almost thirty-year UN-led liberal peacebuilding project is, at the time of writing, still in profound crisis.[27] Neither the highly intrusive, top-down and technical peacebuilding strategies from the late 1990s and early 2000s nor the allegedly context-sensitive and locally focused engagements from the past decade have succeeded in consolidating functioning liberal democracies, delivering the leadership of the peace process to the locals and consolidating durable peace in war-torn scenarios.[28] At this point of quasi-anxiety, in line with the abandoning of linear and technical problem-solving logics, the UN began to flirt with a gradual acknowledgement of the overwhelming complexity of peacebuilding settings. The 2015 report 'The Challenge of Sustaining Peace', developed by an Advisory Group of Experts (AGE) for the review of the PBA in its tenth anniversary, is illustrative of the manner in how this shift seeks to be operationalised in the particular frame of UN-led post-war engagements. The AGE report ostensibly sensitises with the complexity, fragmentation and intractability of conflicts.[29] Chapter 3 problematises the UN capture of complexity as an exogenous particularity of a given milieu filled with a plethora of peacebuilding actors, the efficient coordination between which is crucial for successful peacebuilding. Instead, the book suggests how the complex multiplicity of situated clashing actors erodes their autonomous and purposeful agential condition.

Far from genuinely recognising the limits of a modern cosmovision and the intrinsic and connate faultiness of the worldwide peacebuilding venture, the UN, it is argued in the text, seeks, first, to blame and delegitimise an allegedly ill-capable host society and, second, to mould it so that it can fit the UN peacebuilding configuration. Inattentive to the entangled ontogenesis of actors and processes in these landscapes, the book suggests that the UN is ultimately erasing alter forms of being and becoming in the theatre of the real. Through the notion of distory, defined in the book as a story that systematically obliterates alter stories, the text illustrates how the UN seeks to expand a very particular and problematic planetary undertaking, rooted in a liberal and totalising order. While stories engender composites of further stories, distories decompose and obliterate such possibility, hence tending to trigger exclusionary and essentialising forms of being and becoming. Distories eradicate worlds that never came into being. Through the peacebuilding distory, the UN seeks to taxonomise the world in a Kantian uniforming mode. Thus, the UN disregard of multiple entwined possible worlds conduces to the obliteration of vernacular stories, situated far beyond the universalising modern cosmovision. By linking the notion of distory with the conversation on entanglements, the book cautions that a fetishised version of an entangled worldview, that is to say, a determination to realise the world as an all-out relational and interconnected unit, might conduce narratives on entanglements to reproduce the same exclusionary logics as other scrutinised distories, for instance, modernity.

Beyond interventionary and moralistic systems of judgement, entangled peace resonates with a Spinozist view on ethics, whose contemporary interpretation has noticeably informed the so-called affirmative ethics. From this angle, 'good' or 'bad' cannot be predefined, as these hinge on the unpredictable outcomes of a primary collapse of multiple possibilities. Thus, the ontology of the world is inextricable from ethicality, and none of the happenings pre-exist the uncertain encounters from which they stem. Grosz defines this process of blending as onto-ethics, which is not so much about how the world should be, but about how the world is, and about affirming events with which one is bound.[30] With this is mind, entangled peace delves into a reconfiguration of a more careful action and responsibility, detouring from normative and deterministic intrusive modes of doing. Thus, the ethics of entangled peace eludes invocations for emancipatory and redeeming moves towards saving seemingly fragile milieus. In fact, the affirmation of the entangled ontogenesis of beings and events reconfigures the world in a withinness, without subjects and separate 'out-there' objects. Thus, external wilful transformatory actions, such as those of the UN peacebuilding enterprise, become senseless, for acknowledging this possibility would reposition the subject in a modern, hubristic, mastery level. Instead, farm from savour claims, entangled peace modestly recognises the infinite world-making forces that assemble all imaginable cosmologies.

BOOK STRUCTURE

With the goal of pushing forward recent scholarly attempts in critical peacebuilding literature to inform international relations theory on the basis of UN peacebuilding performance,[31] the book follows a qualitative reflexive methodology inspired and supported by field observations, interviews and documentary content analysis. The chosen qualitative mode of enquiry is based on an exploratory approach to narratives and practices through which the UN materialises the peacebuilding endeavour. Articulated around the analytical lens of entanglements, the data and observations allow to create a comprehensive picture of the events occurring in the peacebuilding setting and, by extension, in the broader world. Specifically, entangled peace unfolds a worldview through critically examining the UN peacebuilding limited results in the post-war cases of Sierra Leone, Burundi and the CAR, cases that I have substantially investigated over the past seven years. These instances of peacebuilding share similarities to the extent that they have become the main focus of attention of UN peacebuilding strategies since the creation of the PBC in 2005.

The book is organised into five chapters, the assembling of which compose the broad conceptual framework of entangled peace. With a focus on the case of the UN peacebuilding involvement in Sierra Leone, chapter 1 problematises the UN failure in knowing and engaging 'the locals' in peacebuilding undertakings, hinting that knowing is not a unidirectional process in which one knowing subject cognitively accesses an 'out-there' object. Instead, knowing unravels a generative process that reinvents the elements involved in their encounter. Chapter 2 examines the flawed UN peacebuilding engagement to reach a system-wide coherence as conducive stage to successful peacebuilding questions the assumption that events unfold in a sequential and linear cause-effect formulation. Thinking with the UN peacebuilding involvement in Burundi, entangled peace invites to a reworking the notion of causality as well as that of space-time framings beyond a void canvas waiting to be filled out by a subject in a teleological mode. Chapter 3 scrutinises the complex deployment of multiple actors in a peacebuilding scenario and the inability of the UN to orchestrate an efficient inter-actor engagement, as illustrated by the case of the CAR. The chapter attempts to illustrate how the complex entanglements of agencies in the field dispute the autonomous and purposeful character of actors' agential condition. Chapter 4 introduces proliferating debates on entangled ontologies and reassembles the arguments from the previous three discussions to provide a concise definition of entangled peace. Most crucially, this chapter also exposes the limits of a mode of entangled thinking that projects a normative and emancipatory cosmovision by reducing world-making possibilities to the relational ontogenesis of beings and processes. Instead, the book calls for seeing the future as radical openness, where the world becomes the composite of colliding possibilities, entangled and non-entangled. Finally, chapter 5 embarks on a speculative attempt to portray UN peacebuilding as a distory, defined in the book as a story that undoes other stories. Through its interventionary narratives and practices, the UN peacebuilding enterprise totalises a modern and universalising political project, thus preventing immanent stories from thriving. Ultimately, the book invokes an ethicality which is inextricable from the entangled ontogenesis of world events, thus suggesting a mode of responsibility sensitised with the affirmation of the future as the entwinement of indeterminate possibilities. This ethics disables the possibility of acting from an external position *in* the world, as the contours between the subject and the world are blurred. Seeking a purposeful intervention would simply reproduce this modern violent hierarchisation. Rather, entangled peace opens up a worldview that conceives of the world as the by-product of an infinite multiplicity of clashing events.

Chapter 1

Failing to Engage 'the Locals'

Knowing does not come from standing at a distance and representing but rather from *a direct material engagement with the world*. (emphasis in original)

– Barad (2007:49)

The following chapter delves into entanglements and relations as the basis of a knowledge production process to critically capture the UN practices towards knowing and including the local civil society, hereinafter interchangeably used with 'the locals', in the peacebuilding milieu. In the first section, the text reviews how this international organisation has conceptualised the local civil society in peacebuilding strategies, programmes and agendas over the past three decades. The second section examines how Critical Peace and Conflict Studies have engaged with the debate about the inclusion of local civil society in externally assisted peacebuilding contexts, commonly known as the 'local turn' debate, particularly emphasising a growing generation of critique that centres on matter as an active asset to the theatre of the real and, more relevant to the present investigation, on a form of world relations that, in turn, debunk the human from the top of an alleged ontological hierarchy. Different to hierarchal epistemological circuits, where a knowing subject captures the essence of an object waiting to be known, in this section, the process of knowledge production is portrayed as a materially entangled process, in which the involved parts transform one another in relation. With a focus on UN field experiences in the post-conflict case of Sierra Leone seeking to know and engage 'the locals', the third part of the chapter hints at the limits of entanglements as a mode of thinking and seeing peacebuilding scenarios and, by extension, the broader world.[1]

Chapter 1

THE UN CONCEPTUALISATION OF LOCAL CIVIL SOCIETY

Civil society has been an increasingly contested concept since its expansion in the Western world, particularly in the context of the May 1968 student movements, the mobilisations against the Vietnam War in the 1970s and the opposition movements during the 1980s in Eastern and Central European communist regimes. Although it is not the object of this chapter to examine the vast amount of literature approaching the contentious conceptual contours of civil society,[2] in a nutshell, civil society became conceptualised as one more component of the expanding worldwide liberal democratic system. Yet, due to frictions and resistances to the homogeneity of this ideal type of liberal civil society, these scholarly conversations have tended to outline the lack of consensus and ambiguity of such a complex notion. Rather than unpacking this convoluted conceptual debate, the following lines centre on providing an account of the way in which the largest international organisation in the planet, namely the UN, has conceptualised and institutionalised civil society in pursuit of its founding goal of maintaining international peace and security.

A close exploration of the UN mode of capturing, manipulating and embracing local civil societies in peacebuilding contexts, both through the analysis of narratives as well as operationalised missions, might be useful in shedding light on a form of entanglement illustrative of what is defined in chapter 5 as a distory, namely a story that undoes other stories. As Shepherd puts it, 'It matters how UN documents represent civil society's role in peacebuilding and it matters how UN staff think and talk about civil society as a concept, a space and an entity because these discursive structures are the conditions of possibility for peacebuilding practice'.[3] In this vein, with a focus on this international organisation, the following lines review the history of an epistemological process in which an externally objectified actor, namely the local civil society, has deliberately been brought to the forefront of peacebuilding policy schemes. This rather descriptive account on reports, resolutions, reviews and statements is later examined through entanglements and relationality as an analytical framework and, more importantly, the chapter intends to expose the limits of this growing mode of speculating over the ontogenesis of world events.

The civil society was formally introduced in the UN conceptual framework during the World Summit on Social Development in 1995 in the city of Copenhagen, the final report of which recognises that most productive polices and investments are those that empower civil society, and that equality and equity between women and men must be at the centre of economic and social development across the international community. The report follows to state that the international community should promote a favourable political environment, amongst other tasks, by 'reinforcing the capacities of Governments, the private sector and civil society in the countries with economies in transition, with a view to helping them in the process of transforming their economies from centrally planned to market-oriented ones'.[4] Therefore, and crucially to understand the critical debates exposed in the following sections, the celebratory role that local civil societies started playing in the 1990s in the frame of major international organisation such as the UN was inextricable from the expansion of a worldwide liberal project.

The path ushered by Copenhagen was consolidated a decade later in the final report of the Panel of Eminent Persons on UN-Civil Society Relations (2000–2004), known as the Cardoso Report. Despite receiving the criticism from the non-governmental organisation (NGO) community, which claimed an underestimation of the role of civil society in the UN framework, the report stressed the prominent role of the civil society 'to further the global goals of the United Nations, to fight injustice, to enhance human security, to foster a more inclusive and harmonious world order and to amplify Southern voices in global debates'.[5] Beyond this, the UN highlighted in this report that the civil society was pivotal in addressing contemporary challenges to international peace and security, including terrorism, war, ethnic tensions and international crimes, amongst others.

Indeed, since the early 1990s, the UN efforts toward including local civil societies in field programmes have been particularly noticeable in the area of peacebuilding.[6] Already in 1992, UNSG Boutros-Ghali stressed in the report 'An Agenda for Peace' that, as global governance trends progress, peace in its most complete sense should be accomplished with cooperation amongst UN, governments and civil society actors such as NGOs, academic institutions, businesses, the media and the public at large.[7] In the aftermath of the disastrous international peace interventions in the Balkans, the 2000 final report from the Panel on United Nations Operations, also known as the Brahimi report, expressed that 'the Secretary-General has consistently emphasized the need for the United Nations to reach out to civil society and to strengthen relations with non-governmental organizations, academic institutions and the media, who can be useful partners in the promotion of peace and security for all'.[8] By seeking to strengthen this endeavour, former UNSG Ki-Moon also invested a substantial amount of resources in enhancing the inclusion of local civil societies in peacebuilding scenarios. In the 2009 report Peacebuilding in the Immediate Aftermath of Conflict, he stated that civil society actors, including marginalised groups, play a critical role as drivers of post-conflict recovery and development.[9] In the spirit of pushing this narrative forward, and despite acknowledging difficulties in its early stage, the first internal review of the PBC, developed in 2010, outlined that the commission would

benefit from a 'genuine national ownership ensured through capacity-building and greater civil society involvement'.[10]

More recently, the 2015 final report from the High-Level Independent
Panel on Peace Operations (HIPPO) reinforced that UN missions should
seek objective feedback from local and international civil society experts to
improve their impact.[11] In a similar vein, the 2015 report 'The Challenge of
Sustaining Peace', in the context of the 10th anniversary of the PBC, argued
that 'partnering with ... the civil society is essential to making peace sustainable'[12]. These two reports point out the reasons why and how the inclusion of
these civil society actors contributes to peace: first, by bringing civil society
closer to the process, the UN can have a more accurate picture of the local
context, strengthening aspects such as early warning mechanisms; second, the
UN considers that the participation of local women civil society organisations
in post-conflict engagements enhances processes such as conflict mitigation
and prevention, recovery and reconciliation; third, the reports also document
that women and religious leaders can play a positive role in countering the
emergence of violent extremism, particularly amongst youth; fourth, civil
society agents can have a positive influence in eradicating peace-disrupting
challenges such as corruption.

On top of all these discursive and conceptual gestures, as illustrated further,
over the past fifteen years, the UN has most prominently sought to materialise the attempt to engage local civil societies in peacebuilding processes
through the so-called new PBA, particularly its three main components: the
PBC, the PBSO and the PBF.[13] In the frame of the PBC, civil society is conceptualised as a key element for the national (or local) ownership principle,
a term which was popularised in 1996 when the Organization for Economic
Co-operation and Development (OECD) called for the respect of local ownership in development processes.[14] Local ownership, an essential feature of
UN peacebuilding processes, entails that 'it is the citizens of the countries
where peacebuilding is underway, with support from their governments, who
assume the responsibility for laying the foundations of lasting peace'.[15] With
this goal, the UN seeks to build local civil society's capacity as well as its
level of participation in different areas of the post-conflict recovery process,
including supervision of security-oriented reforms, political dialogue, electoral processes, good governance, equitable access to justice, transitional justice mechanisms, promotion of human rights, gender issues, socio-economic
recovery and development.

From a historical perspective, by seeking to broaden legitimacy and
effectiveness in its liberal peacebuilding engagements,[16] the UN endeavour
towards including and prioritising the interests of 'the locals' has gradually
turned the highly top-down and externally led engagements from the late

1990s and early 2000s into seemingly bottom-up, context-sensitive peace-building processes. Shepherd develops a concise critical analysis of this conceptual and operational UN journey. The author observes how local civil societies, in the frame of the UN peacebuilding enterprise, have evolved over time from a passive to an implementing actor: 'The emphasis on 'national ownership' and the construction of the national community as agent of its own renaissance is in keeping with the construction of civil society actors as agents of change'.[17] External peace interventions, the author continues, are those engagements to which local civil society must consent and from which local civil society will benefit.

Unveiling the problematic intimacies of this patronising entwinement, Shepherd sharply interrogates the self-appointed role of 'midwife' by the UN, as expressed in the aforementioned 2010 review of the PBC. The international community, as the author unpacks, 'serves as a midwife, while the nation effectively gives birth to itself.... The "role" of the international community, in this metaphor, is to support, nurture and generally make possible (read: act like a midwife) the "national birthing process", which it can only do if it has the relevant knowledge and expertise. Just as conventional medical discourse strips pregnant women of their agency in the birthing process, in representing the international community as midwife and the national community as a labouring woman, the review document depicts the national community as lacking this knowledge and expertise'.[18] In essence, the fact that the UN bestows itself with the role of a crucial person in the process of the birth of another illustrates two major assumptions behind the UN peacebuilding endeavour. On the one hand, the organisation strengthens an ontological boundary between who is 'the internationals' and who is 'the locals', a binary which is object of examination in the following section. On the other hand, the UN is also revealing how the relation between both components is not neutral or under conditions of equality. Far from this, the international organisation maps out an interaction based on dependency, assistentialism and, therefore, inferiority. As Shepherd sums it up, '"local" knowledge is at once valued (in the process of extraction) and yet subordinated'.[19]

This discourse-methodological approach on the UN conceptualisation of local civil societies is framed and expanded in the following section by the broader 'local turn' debate in critical peacebuilding literature. Beyond revising the well-established critical families within peace and conflict studies, the section also embarks on a discussion about the role of the locals in peacebuilding through a recently emerging generation of critique which intends to surpass the human sphere as the minimum unit of analysis and bring to the front the meaning of matter in world events as well as the implications of human-matter relations.

THE LOCAL TURN AMIDST THE RISE OF MATTER AND ENTANGLEMENTS

Throughout the 1990s, civil society became associated with a social sphere composed of active citizens resisting authoritarian political systems, even precipitating the fall of the Second World and contributing to building liberal democracies in most former soviet countries. In that context, civil society was often theorised as a universalising, liberal and cosmopolitan project and was presented as a *sine qua non* condition for the establishment of a democratic and peaceful world.[20] Some argued that peace processes led by international organisations cannot thrive unless they are able to generate a critical mass of domestic legitimacy.[21] In support of this, studies showed that peace accords which include civil society are at least 50 per cent more likely to endure.[22] As exposed in the previous section, this resulted in a consensus amongst key international actors, such as the UN, over the essential role that local civil society must play in an inclusive mode of peacebuilding.[23] The bulk of peacebuilding literature that bought into the principles of this expansive liberal international peace project found in the conceptual framework of inclusion, particularly the inclusion of the local civil society, the recipe to solve the problems that the peacebuilding enterprise had encountered in several assisted countries. In spite of not escaping scrutiny,[24] the revelation of the inclusion of local civil society in peacebuilding scenarios helped justify the reproduction and perpetuation of a liberal international peace project which, in the late 1990s, due to the disastrous results in countries like Somalia, Bosnia or Rwanda, was close to a state of demise.

Beyond this problem-solving approach, underpinned by this liberal cosmopolitan belief of a global civil society as a constitutive actor of the liberal peacebuilding project, the production of knowledge on the 'local turn' and, more specifically, on the role that 'the locals' play in peacebuilding scenarios has generated over the past decade an enormous amount of a more critical approach that casts doubt upon the conceptual construction and instrumentalisation of 'the locals' as a form of saving and perpetuating the liberal international peacebuilding endeavour, to a large extent led by the UN.[25] Amongst the large bulk of ink spilled over the underlaying problematics of this contentious encounter between the liberal internationals and the non-liberal locals in the peacebuilding milieu, the dominating critical voice is anchored in the post-structuralist Foucauldian tradition. Illustrative of this vein, Chandler argues in a pungent critical analysis that the conceptual production of civil society in the international peacebuilding framework reproduces the foundations of an ontology of difference which previously established the taxonomies of race and culture, successively, as well as their resulting violent implications. In the author's words, 'In the civil society paradigm, the hierarchical views of race and cultural difference are reproduced, but through the focus on the autonomy and rationality of the post-conflict subject rather than through the focus on their alleged lack of rationality or lack of autonomy. This emphasis on the autonomy of the subject of peacebuilding intervention presents external intervention as an act of empowerment or of capacity-building, consciously disavowing colonial discourses of fixed distinctions of superiority'.[26] From this angle, the condition of civil society is only bestowed upon by the external actor when that particular host society behaves 'rightly' and 'civically'. Accordingly, the rationale of the international intervener is underpinned by the ability to assist this host society in the process toward a state of civility. Chandler elucidates that 'the clash of cultures, in the self-understanding of international peacebuilders, is played out in the policy interventions that attempt to transform traditional (non-)civil society into a civic polity in which social and political divisions are submerged, mitigated or disappear'.[27] This book, as exposed in chapter 5, captures this international will to unreflectively impose specific forms of being and becoming on host societies as a distory, which encompasses an actor's intention to violently erase the possibility for other stories to emerge.

From a similar theoretical layout, Richmond has approached the messy entwinement between the international and the local, what he describes with concepts such as post-liberal, hybrid or everyday peace, through the lens of power and knowledge as co-constitutive elements. To this author, external peace actors create a hegemonic discourse that intervened societies struggle to say no to.[28] As he puts it when describing the agency of 'the locals', 'agency is, of course, an Enlightenment concept depending on mutually agreed regulatory frameworks, within which it will be exercised autonomously for the good life, circumscribed and facilitated by institutions.... Local actors have nascent agency, not yet fully formed. These agencies enable policy and institutions to follow interests or norms. It forms the basis for emancipation, and enables mediation or peacekeeping, or local ownership of peacebuilding',[29] thus establishing a strict boundary between a 'good' international and a 'bad' local forms of thinking and doing, often deemed by external actors as the 'uncivil society'[30] or 'less-civil society'.[31] Also from this power relations approach, Paffenholz argues that 'the external' and 'the local' tend to be inappropriately constructed as binary opposites, which oversimplifies the nature of sources of power interacting in the whole peacebuilding spectrum.[32] In short, these critical understandings of the international-local assemblage are based on Foucault's famous theoretical contribution which argues that the relation between power and knowledge is not one of antagonism, but of dependency and co-constitution. 'It is within discourse that power and knowledge are joined together'.[33] Accordingly, from this Foucauldian lens, international actors such as the UN, from a position of power, produce a hegemonic knowledge about local civil society's role in peacebuilding, the implications of which result in an extension of control over these intervened societies.

The limitations of the dominating post-structuralist Foucauldian analyses in the 'local turn' conversation have been increasingly noted in recent critical peacebuilding literature.[34] Lewis outlines three major analytical inconsistencies behind this corpus of theory. First, the categorisation of knowledge as an element entangled with power and discourse on the one hand, particularly in the international sphere, or subordinated on the other hand, when conceptualised in the domain of the locals and therefore a potential source of emancipation, is misleading, as it denies the agency of those locals whose agendas do not pursue an emancipatory project. Second, the emphasis on the international peacebuilding framework as a project led by Western states, international organisations and think tanks has overlooked and curtailed the role of non-Western host states. Failing to acknowledge these as imbricated in an international system based on state sovereignty principle has rendered an important analytical gap in critical peacebuilding literature. Finally, in the author's own words, 'the characterization of liberal peace as a "unitary discourse" discourages recognition of any competing discourses. While Foucault develops a productive framework through which to critique a single dominant discourse, in a highly contested international system a Foucauldian gaze leaves its own blind spots, concealing from view important new dynamics of power, agency and discursive practice in international relations'.[35]

Seeking to break through this impasse of critical peacebuilding literature stagnated in post-structuralist approaches as well as akin culture-based analysis, in the recent times a more and more growing number of scholars in the area of critical peace and conflict studies are exploring a new form of critique in the frame of the so-called new materialist sensitivities, which are inspired by and resonate with continental philosophical debates unpacked later in the book. As a mode of a general introduction, these new voices challenge the centrality of the human as the minimum unit of analysis to understand the world, in turn, reinvigorating the role that non-human matter plays in planetary events.[36] By focusing on natural phenomena, non-human living beings, material and immaterial non-human objects, built infrastructure, technology and so on, these studies seek to overcome the shortcomings of the forty-year dominance of discursive human-centred analysis such as post-structuralism, which has blatantly ignored the properties of things and its effect on the social realm. More important to the present book, this theoretical shift comes alongside a reconsideration of earthly relations, debunking the ontological position of superiority of the human and emphasising the primacy of relations as the very first condition for possibility.[37] World events are thought out to emerge from countless relations in which the human simply becomes one more component of this human and non-human entanglements, thus blurring

the all-encompassing culture-nature analytical boundary on which both modern and post-modern frames of thinking are based.

Without disavowing the contributions of the post-structuralist critique of
the 'local turn', as well as the vast majority of further critical literature within
this debate, these approaches seldomly overcome the reproduction of modern
exclusionary binaries in their process of knowledge production, that is, the
external and the internal, the international and the local or the intervener and
the intervened. For example, from a rather post-colonial approach, Sabaratnam argues that externally led empowerment of local actors reproduces the
Western division between 'the liberal' and a culturally different 'local'.[38]
Danielsson conspicuously engages with this impasse by shedding light and
recurring to the gradual emergence of the new materialist critique, with a
focus on the inclusivity of the locals in peacebuilding. *Grosso modo*, this
author argues that, while acknowledging how the local turn has unveiled
colonial violence as the prime entanglement and the historical condition upon
which the peacebuilding enterprise is founded, the process of knowledge
production on this event should not be grasped through the modern binary
colonisers/internationals-colonised/locals but instead as an embodied, situated and co-constituted phenomenon. Following a Harawayan trend, Danielsson admits that a situated knowledge might 'inform a new type of scholarly
critique better suited to making known, disentangling and critiquing the
contemporary politics and power relations of peacebuilding inclusivity projects'.[39] Contesting recent decolonial contributions,[40] Danielsson first admits
that revising colonial conditions as the ontogenesis of the category of 'local'
in peacebuilding theory and practice might enable an analytical sensitivity
to processes of entwined emergence, which is essential to the critiques presented further. In addition, the author recognises how this decolonial critique
attempts to break power relations into various beyond-the-human configurations thus surpassing conventional binaries, without ruling out that the local
turn is yet one more colonial stance reproduced through the peacebuilding
endeavour. However, Danielsson also observes a fundamental inconsistency
in this type of decolonial mindset: 'Dominant modes of critique think from
rather than about the category of "the local" (and "the international"), and
do not thoroughly problematise this as a relevant epistemic category....
As a result, there is little analytic space to think more open-endedly about
potential intrinsic relations between the "local" and the "international"'.[41]
Provocatively, Danielsson reveals how the decolonial critique, despite its
attempt to overcome modern binaries, still reproduces and reinforces those
local-international cuts from which the vast majority of critical peacebuilding
debates sorrowfully fail to scape.

Following up on her attempt to overcome this theoretical standoff, Danielsson revises the colonial distory by centring the attention during the

process of knowledge production on the material aspects of this violent encounter as well as the beyond-the-human relations from which those historical events result. The author argues how the whole colonial event responds to a co-constituted process in which colonised societies, their knowledges, artefacts as well as the natural environment co-produced the colonial form of being and thinking. In other words, the colonial and colonised cosmovision became intimately entwined in a co-constitutive socio-material arrangement in which actors, environments, objects, power dynamics and countless other beings, human and non-human, material and non-material, collided. As the author puts it, 'The notion of co-constituted knowledge disrupts binary ontologies and epistemologies as it refers to how the European/colonial and the local made each other possible throughout situated, simultaneous, open-ended, and ultimately contingent and transformative processes'.[42] Drawing from Haraway and Barad, Danielson unfolds the practice of knowing as a materially entangled process through which beings mutually compose one another. Importantly, this ontological co-emergent formula involves not only humans but also material and immaterial beyond-the-human beings. From this theoretical standpoint, the author reformulates the international-local relation in the peacebuilding domain. First, the analytical focus shifts from pre-existing actors to multiple clashing constellations of actors and knowledges, and how these emerge relationally in a particular socio-material milieu. Second, this analytical step forward requires in turn a focus on the generative force of the built and natural environment. Following a similar explorative venture, next session draws from faulty UN field experiences in seeking to know and engage 'the locals' in peacebuilding settings. More importantly, the section also exposes the limits of this materially entangled ontological configuration to capture the peacebuilding milieu and the broader world.

THE FAILURE OF KNOWING AND ENGAGING 'THE LOCALS': ENTANGLEMENTS AND ITS LIMITS

As detailed earlier, while over the past two decades the UN has discursively and operationally made a significant effort to engage the host local civil society in peacebuilding missions, the results of this endeavour remain remarkably problematic.[43] Despite all the efforts made by UN peacebuilding officers, policy-makers as well as academics towards centring the peacebuilding process on 'the locals', externally led engagements are increasingly becoming protracted and real self-government remains deferred.[44] Numerous scholars have rethought and criticised why these international policy attempts have had rather limited outcomes in turning externally led peacebuilding processes into bottom-up processes in which field-based local actors adopt a central and meaningful role.[45]

By examining the particular case of the UN peacebuilding engagement in Sierra Leone over the past two decades, civil society organisations have often questioned that the PBC, in its endeavour to comprehensively engage local civil society, fails to grasp a representative sample of this host stakeholder. As stressed in an external report, the urban and ethnic biases are usually presented by civil society representatives as well as by critical voices within the UN as the expression of this inaccurate conceptualisation.[46] For example, the PBF National Steering Committee's selection of two civil society representatives, one from the West African Network for Peacebuilding (WANEP) and another from the Mano River Women's Network for Peace, was highly controversial. Some argued that those chosen were primarily urban-based actors, not representative of the grass-roots level, and that they had been hand-picked by the government. In response, independent civil society members agreed to establish the Civil Society Peacebuilding Engagement Committee, a nineteen-member committee responsible for monitoring and evaluating PBF impact. However, as the same report observes, the methods of this committee of engaging with the PBC remained highly vague and unclear. Beyond Sierra Leone, the case of the CAR also illustrates these limitations. Resonating with the implications of the urban bias, a former officer from the United Nations Multidimensional Integrated Stabilization Mission in the CAR (MINUSCA, in French) commented that, beyond Bangui, external agencies barely exist.[47] In addition to the urban bias, the Burundi case reveals that in Burundi, the Tutsi local community was prioritised over Hutu-led local civil society organisations by the PBA.[48] Therefore, failure to engage partly responds to these urban and ethnic biases which, as argued below, might be associated with a UN-promoted ontological essentialising form of thinking the local civil society.

Resonating with these ontological hindrances, the technical mechanisms that the UN peacebuilding apparatus enabled for the engagement of 'the locals' also resulted problematic. In Sierra Leone there have been numerous initiatives that the PBA has promoted to incorporate civil society further into the process. The first initiative involved a south-south learning process in which Sierra Leonean civil society representatives as well as election officials engaged in structured dialogue about the electoral processes with their Burundian counter-part, aiming to enhance the electoral contexts of 2007 and 2010, respectively.[49] The second initiative involved the creation of a PBF National Steering Committee, where the PBA sought active participation of Sierra Leonean civil society. This committee was established to collectively coordinate a national action plan process and development, as well as the joint progress report on the Government-led Agenda for Change (2008–2012) and the successor Agenda for Prosperity (2017). Moreover, since 2007, the PBA also supported civil society engagement in the reconciliation process, particularly in the work of the Truth and Reconciliation Commission.

Similarly, the cases of Burundi and the CAR also shed light on these inclusive endeavours. In Burundi, the top-two PBA-supported initiatives which served to bring civil society closer to the peacebuilding process were the *Cadre de Dialogue et Concertation*, a platform to institutionalise dialogue mechanisms and further unite the Government and civil society, and the *Justice de Proximité*, an initiative to bring civil society closer to the justice system. In addition, the PBA supported the creation of a Tripartite Steering Committee, a unique platform tasked with addressing the Burundian peacebuilding process, composed of the government, the UN and civil society. The inclusion of civil society in the design of the new Land Code, the *Libre Blanc* and the Defence Review were also critical attempts of this inclusive endeavour. Furthermore, the Partners Coordination Group, established in Burundi in 2007 by the Government and its partners, consisted of a mechanism to institutionalise a framework for dialogue. One of the components of this mechanism was the creation of strategic forums for discussion, which were spaces for debate which included civil society.[50] A PBC review also stressed the impact of a co-promoted 'naming and shaming' campaign by the United Nations Integrated Office in Burundi (BINUB, in French), the civil society and the international community in diverting attention from the public on charges of torture during the elections and afterwards. In the case of the CAR, which was the first country in the PBC agenda to include an 'inclusive approach' as a prime principle, the Strategic Framework for Peacebuilding established that the follow-up and coordination committee would be composed, among other stakeholders, of two civil society representatives.[51] Another PBA-supported initiative in which civil society was widely recognised to be involved was the voluntary partnership agreement, created by the government and the European Union (EU) to deal with issues such as forest law enforcement, governance and trade timber products in the CAR.

Despite these policy inclusive attempts, numerous interviewees shed light on the limited results of this objective towards inclusion. The former chair of the Truth and Reconciliation Commission in Sierra Leone, Bishop Joseph Humper, highlighted how the PBC failed to make itself attractive to and inclusive of locals. In his own words, 'The PBC merely used the locals to receive inputs from the field, as a source of information on the ground level. But they should have involved them in the sense that they are part and parcel of the peace mission. You cannot just arrive and say: "this is the peace commission". It seems one more different body, with its own goals, that come and does things its own way'.[52] This account expresses disappointment with the UN failure to truly consider Sierra Leonean local civil society as a fundamental aspect in the process.

Additionally, a few more commentators echoed this resentment: The head office of Fambul Tok, a Freetown-based NGO, defined the PBC mandate as narrow and not visible, claiming it dealt mostly with state actors, leaving minimal space for others;[53] the Country Director of Search for Common Ground, another Sierra Leonean NGO, highlighted the UN-civil society relationship as still presenting a challenge, as power relations continue to be uneven;[54] the head office of the Freetown-based WANEP expressed that the UN failed to identify and address the complex and diverse nature of local civil society;[55] a former Burundian director of Doctors of the World expressed that although the PBC tried to engage Burundian civil society, people were ultimately disappointed with the UN as they viewed the organisation as bending under pressure from the government; and as an independent consultant at the European Centre for Development Policy Management put it, civil society in the CAR was frustrated due to a lack of influence in decision-making. As she clarifies, 'in that meeting I attended of the PBC, civil society was quite frustrated because they were seen as sort of being co-opted just to be informed about decisions. And to sort of say "Yes, we did inform civil society". They were present in this meeting, to sort of ticking the box'.[56]

In seeking to make sense of these field limitations, the chapter problematises how the UN peacebuilding system conceives of local civil society inclusion as necessarily materialised through embodied, formal, organisational and technical processes, that is, the PBF National Steering Committees, the Truth and Reconciliation Commission, the *Cadre de Dialogue et Concertation*, Partner Coordination Groups and Strategic Frameworks for Peacebuilding, amongst others. When these formal channels of interaction cannot be established, the engagement becomes rather unfeasible. In other words, the lack of technical, organisational and bureaucratic capacity is perceived by the PBA as a hindrance for civil society engagement in the peacebuilding process. Supporting this argument, Graben and Fitz-Gerald argued that the institutionalisation and standardisation of spaces or programmes for engagement contribute to the inclusion of local civil society in the UN-led peacebuilding contexts.[57]

In light of the aforementioned interviewees' bold statements, the technical capacity that the UN-led engagement demands could hardly be met by the war-torn local civil society. On top of this, there is no sign that the PBC ever made a real effort to assist this local civil society in overcoming these technical barriers. For the PBC, local civil society either gets engaged fitting the technical parameters of the UN peacebuilding system or it cannot fit them and remains left out. The UN is therefore restricting the engagement of local civil society in the peacebuilding process to a particular civil society which can fulfil the highly technical requirements included in their method of engagement. Anything that cannot fulfil these premises is not engaged with. For example, Action Aid et al. reported that the PBA-civil society

relationship often deteriorates over time because the PBC announces meetings at very short notice, hindering a wide consultation with civil society, as
they often depend on the timing of projects and therefore they do not have
the institutional capacity to engage in protracted or periodic policy discussions.[58] As Does argues, the UN internal system does not provide sound
formal mechanisms of engagement such as protocols, guidelines or channels
of communication to consult and consolidate a sound relationship with local
peacebuilding actors. Any attempt of engagement based on grasping local
civil society as an objectified actor through a technical and materialised form
of engagement would result as fruitless.[59]

  In all, civil society thus seems perceived by the UN as an isolated stakeholder from the conflict-affected context that can be externally known,
captured and engaged with for the success of the peacebuilding enterprise.
Vogel has critically conceptualised this biased picture of local civil society
by international agencies: 'Peace-oriented civil society describes the type of
civil society that attempts to support an inclusive settlement of a conflict.
International NGOs and donors tend to have "peace-oriented civil society"
in mind when referring to civil society in peacebuilding and conflict resolution. This group includes, as the name suggests, those citizens that actively
engage in resolving the conflict in a multitude of forms; but it spells out
the underlying conjecture of the peace cause that has been implicit in many
assumptions made about "civil society"'.[60] As a result of this, the UN-biased
and narrow approach to grasp civil society results in the exclusion of a large
part of this host stakeholder from the peacebuilding process, including rural
areas, less organised civil society, undermined ethnic groups, ill-equipped
local organisations and so on. Thus, the image of a unique, objectifiable and
homogenous form of civil society seems, at minimum, questionable.

  Seeking to instrumentalise the emergent critique based on entangled ontologies, the UN peacebuilding faulty inclusive strategy could be made sense of
by arguing that the international organisation overlooks the ontological tension between different forms of conceiving of a wide and diverse spectrum
of actors and processes which are in unpredictable relation in these conflict-
affected contexts. Failing to acknowledge the uncertain entanglements
between these actors and processes as constitutive of their very being renders,
first, UN static categorisations ineffectual to capture the complexity of local
civil society, namely to know 'the locals' and, second, UN highly technical
forms of engagement non-viable and unfit to this host local civil society.

  From this new generation of critique, the knowledge production process on
local civil society should sensitise with its material underpinnings and, more
importantly, the outcomes of the co-constitutive relations amongst those. Following authors like Barad, knowledge becomes a performative phenomenon
that calls into question the possibility of ontologically 'out-there' and separate

entities that are waiting for representation, for being known. Detouring from Cartesian epistemology, there is no subject separated from an object awaiting to be cognitively recognised. In her own words, inspired by Bohrian quantum physics, 'knowing is not about seeing from above or outside or even seeing from a prosthetically enhanced human body.... Knowing is not a bounded or closed practice but an ongoing performance of the world'.[61] As it will be further developed in chapter 4, this account on knowledge production is underpinned by the assumption that the human and the object of observation are intra-acted, meaning that their relations pre-exist and are constitutive of their very existence. Therefore, the human and the world are reconfigured through a shared and continuous space-time framing that stems from their materially entangled and dynamic engagement. In this vein, the complex scenario of entangled actors exposed above enables to approach local civil society as a 'collective actor',[62] which results from interconnections and ex-changes with further actors and processes.

Illustrative of this ontological configuration, the current Sierra Leonean minister of Tourism, Memunatu Pratt, was a relevant figure of the Sierra Leonean local civil society by the time the PBC included the country in its agenda in 2007. Particularly, Pratt was the head of the Department of Peace and Conflict Studies at Fourah Bay College, the University of Sierra Leone, and she was also actively involved in various peacebuilding initiatives and entities, including the Freetown-based WANEP. The United Nations Peacebuilding Task Force as well as the United Nations Development Program (UNDP) in Sierra Leone regularly consulted Pratt regarding aspects tightly connected to the peacebuilding process, such as poverty reduction strategies and mass youth unemployment, amongst other issues, which are still nowadays deemed deeply associated with the breakout of the civil war. The Pratt-UN relation became so intimate that she was eventually appointed to the UN-backed Special Court for Sierra Leone from 2007 to 2010. From the entangled ontological angle, the ontogenesis of both Pratt and the UN stems from their co-constitutive relation, which makes it unfeasible to trace a clear ontological cut to distinguish what is the international organisation and what is the local civil society representative.

Contrary to providing static, finite and limited categorisations, the relational sensibility focuses on the spontaneous outcomes of uncertain interactions between things. Therefore, contrary to ontologically uncover the essence of local civil society, relational sensibilities intend to question this taken-for-granted ontological assumption that things can be separately framed in fixed categories. Instead, entangled thinking unveils the process of becoming of local civil society, and of any other actor, as the result of unexpected entwinements with other actors and processes such as the UN, which, likewise, comes to existence relationally. In this regard, the UN peacebuilding apparatus and local civil society are deemed to be mutually constituted in intrinsic association. In other words, ontologically continuous beings and processes come to existence through their relational condition. Haraway elucidates of how relationality is a constitutive part of 'things', thus indicating that beings, human and non-human, compose each other. As detailed in chapter 4, Haraway defines 'com-post' and 'becoming-with' as concepts that prominently illustrate this relational and entangled conditionality. Things become-with, as they give each other existence.[63] Accordingly, the very first assumption in conceptualising local civil society from this entangled ontological view is recognising its non-essentialised character. In turn, the second assumption invokes the non-objectifiable ontogenesis of this actor, thus rendering the effort to capture it through static and fix modern mechanisms of categorisation perpetually fruitless.

In sum, local civil society is presented through a relational lens as a non-essentialised and non-objectifiable collective actor in the whole realm of things, whose very nature stems from processual interactions with other processes and actors. What ultimately sets the conceptualisation of local civil society is not a limited ontological definition, but the countless entangled interactions from which it stems. These intimate co-emergent associations include easy-to-figure-out encounters between policy-makers, UN peacebuilders, governmental officers, non-governmental representatives, fundraisers and local community members as well as less imaginable collisions such as the impact produced by the natural environment, the built infrastructure, the available material resources to unfold their strategies or even the mystical and spiritual narratives operating in their societies. All these ex-changes enable the emergence of local civil society, which becomes the product of entangled negotiations between actors and processes.

Thus, a large part of local civil society does not fit UN embodied conventions precisely because of the earlier-exposed non-essentialised, unobjectifiable and relational condition. Yet the UN, purposely or not, does not pay attention to these alternative forms of knowing and thinking about local civil society. The narrow and static conceptualisation of local civil society as an externally objectifiable being, as well as the highly technical and formal mechanisms used to grasp it and include it in the peacebuilding process, might contribute to explaining the failure of the UN peacebuilding apparatus in engaging with this actor. As a breakthrough in the unmet UN problem-solving logics, this chapter has elaborated on the potential of thinking local civil society on the basis of entanglements, thus invoking the complex, uncertain and vulnerable ontogenesis of this host actor. As it will be extensively exposed in chapter 5, far from acknowledging different forms of knowing and thinking about the local civil society and its broader context, the UN peacebuilding apparatus intends to delegitimise, mould and instrumentalise this local stakeholder so that it can eventually fit the modern liberal parameters of the international organisation. This pattern will be described later in the book as a UN attempt to totalise and expand a liberal, homogenous and universalising political project.

On a cautionary mode, the entangled character of the knowledge production process involving actors and processes should not escape scrutiny. Different to Danielsson, who argues that attention to knowledge as situated and co-constituted offers a conceptual baseline to address and formulate inclusive projects in peacebuilding scenarios,[64] the text intends to eschew celebratory claims on entangled ontologies as an emancipatory mode of thinking and seeing the world. Explaining the UN failure in knowing and engaging the local civil society in the peacebuilding enterprise by simply outlining that actors and process become through co-constitutive relations faces some theoretical and practical challenges. As developed more extensively in chapter 4, the all-encompassing entangled reading of the world, where all things are related, entails a moralistic and normative problematic. As Colebrook notes, the moralism embedded in relationality as the primary ontological state 'privileges becoming and relations over the horror of something that simply is, bearing no relation to anything'.[65] The claim that everything is entangled does not fully overcome the normative and teleological claims of modernity. On the contrary, by loading the being with the relational burden, future possibilities within peacebuilding scenarios as well as in the broader world are reduced to an entangled determinism.

In other words, a problem of positionality might arise in affirming the entangled ontogenesis of all forms of being and becoming in the world. The attempt to dehierachise human-dominated ontological relations by exalting the role of matter and, particularly, how all beings, human and non-human, material and immaterial compose one another in relation, does not seem to overcome the problems of inclusion and exclusion which paradoxically characterise the anthropocentric project of modernity. In the present's book terminology, this all-inclusive projection of relationality becomes one more distory, described in chapter 5, a story that alienates, supresses and obliterates the possibility for alter stories to thrive. Thus, these new materialisms and the intimately associated co-emergence and entanglements intensify difference and constrain the future to a fetishised relationality. 'What might happen if, rather than an expansion of relations for the sake of becoming proximate to the cosmos, one pursued the destruction of relations for the sake of something less than the whole?',[66] provocatively asks Colebrook.

Reflecting back upon the world and peacebuilding in particular, the practices occurring in the theatre of operations should be freed from constraining and deterministic forms of being, as these create expectances in peacebuilders that generate never-ending anxieties when rigid strategic goals are not fulfilled. As developed in chapter 4, the entangled peace approach seeks to surpass this seemingly elitist and universalising relational framework by opening up the future beyond the relational and non-relational binary. Entangled peace draws from Whiteheadian relational formulations not as a constraining element that redefines the world in an enclosed mode, but instead as the infinite atomisation of possibilities in ongoing collision, including the entangled and the non-entangled. This radical openness for the future convolutes all forms of being and becoming beyond imaginary deterministic binaries and modern ontological cuts.

Chapter 2

Problematising System-wide Coherence and Linearity

> We project time into space, we express duration in terms of extensity, and succession thus takes the form of a continuous line or a chain, the parts of which touch without penetrating one another.
>
> – Bergson (2003:101)

Over the past decade, an increasing number of scholars and policy experts have critically questioned the linear unfolding of events in peacebuilding scenarios. To these authors, phenomena in the conflict-affected milieu, as well as in the broader world, do not occur in linear cause-effect relations. Far from this modern conceptualisation of space-time framings rooted in Newtonian mechanics, non-linear peacebuilding accounts suggest that events are the outcomes of the messy and unpredictable entanglements between actors and processes. The following pages engage with this conversation by reflecting upon the implications and the limits of affirming the non-linear causality of peacebuilding developments. With a focus on the UN peacebuilding endeavour towards a system-wide coherent strategy, as illustrated by the case of the UN peacebuilding involvement in Burundi, the chapter first exposes and problematises the expectance that certain inputs under certain conditions lead to certain outcomes in a linear and predictable manner. Specifically, the chapter sheds light on the inconsistencies of expecting that system-wide coherence and a more efficient Headquarters-field relation will lead to a system-wide coherence and, in turn, this will result in better peacebuilding. The second part of the chapter examines critical literature on non-linear understandings of peacebuilding. In short, these accounts elucidate how liberal, top-down peacebuilding from the 1990s and early 2000s was based on Enlightened rationalities which assumed that social events unfold in the same deterministic fashion as the natural world. In response to this, in the recent years, many scholars as well as policy actors have shifted towards frameworks of understanding and action sensitised with a non-linear conception of the war-torn milieu, the entangled ontogenesis of actors and processes within, and with the uncertainty of their relational outcomes. Seeking to push this debate forward, the text problematises how these non-linear peacebuilding accounts still reproduce an emancipatory and normative circuit, as they eventually assume that affirming and dealing with non-linearity is conducive to better peacebuilding. In the last section of the chapter, it is discussed how the UN peacebuilding engagement in Burundi fails to achieve strategic coherence between the New York-based headquarters and the field. As suggested below, beyond normative frameworks, non-linear causality might open up the future by reconfiguring how space is thought out. Resonating with the Whiteheadian concept of 'extensive continuum', space is not a fix, discontinuous and void canvas that awaits to be filled out. Instead, space is reimagined as the extended outcome of the entanglements between actors and processes. Therefore, externalities become 'externalities within', which can potentially free peacebuilders from the anxiety of having to transform a given context from an ostensible outside. Interventive frameworks, understood as a transaction from the outside to the inside, are thus invalidated, and transformation only resides in the entanglements which precede the constitution of actors and processes.

THE UN ENDEAVOUR TOWARDS A SYSTEM-WIDE COHERENCE

The process of mutability that the ethos of international peacebuilding frameworks have undergone over the past three decades, reflected through the 'local turn' debate in the previous chapter, has also unleashed major international efforts towards refining operational coherence and coordination, manifestly perceived as a *sine qua non* condition for the success of lasting peace. Within the plethora of current international theoretical and policy attempts at preserving international security, delivering humanitarian aid and triggering economic development there is a broad consensus that the lack of field coherence and coordination, resulting in waste of resources, duplication of tasks, and stagnated inefficient action, amongst others, hinders the consecution of strategic goals long pursued by major international organisations.[1] Notwithstanding the lack of a conceptual consensus, in the domain of peacebuilding, coherence is often defined as the 'effort to direct the wide range of activities undertaken in the political, development, human rights, humanitarian, rule of law and security dimensions of a peacebuilding system towards common strategic objectives'.[2] With the goal of achieving this institution-wide coherence, peacebuilding actors have designed and put in place a wide range of approaches and tools, including shared agendas, common goals, role- and responsibility-sharing initiatives as well as a shared disposal of human, political, economic and military resources.

Most notoriously, in the past fifteen years, the UN, particularly its peace-building architecture, has dedicated countless amount of time and resources in achieving an effective and coherent system-wide strategy by seeking to enhance coordination between bodies, agencies and various forms of organisational engagement on the ground. Ironically, the former Doctors Without Borders (DWB) country director in the CAR assured during an interview that the UN spends half of its time on coordination.[3] Already in the 1990s, Annan made the first significant attempts in facilitating coherence across the organisation, specifically between UN headquarters guidance and field operationalisation. In a 1997 report aimed at an internal institutional reform with a focus on the enhancement of peace missions, Annan suggested addressing issues such as the relationship between the New York-based headquarters and field missions, improving the effectiveness on the ground level, approaching civil society or emphasising the necessity for merging concepts such as peace, security, development and human rights.[4] In pursuit of these objectives, the 2004 Integrated Mission Plan Process introduced general planning principles and assumptions, including the establishment of integration as the prime principle for complex UN operations in post-conflict scenarios, intended to maximising efficiency and effectiveness of the UN presence on the country level as well as to enhance the coordination between the New York-based headquarters and the field.[5] In 2005, Annan appointed a High-Level Panel on UN System-wide Coherence, leading to structural changes within the Chief Executive Board (CEB), which became an instrument composed of all executive heads of the UN system, thus illustrative of this aim at enhancing internal coordination. Furthermore, he promoted the Triennial Comprehensive Policy framework, consisting of a comprehensive three-year strategic and monitoring plan to reinforce coordination within the UN system. All these efforts converged in Annan's most acknowledged milestone achievement in the area of UN coherence, namely the 2006 'Delivering as One' (DaO) report, which was intended to coordinate humanitarian aid systematically across the entire UN system. The eight DaO pilot countries, including Albania, Cape Verde, Mozambique, Pakistan, Rwanda, Tanzania, Uruguay and Vietnam, experimented with a more robust and determined form of coherence, involving the implementation of the 'Four Ones': one leader, one programme, one budgetary framework and one office.[6]

Thus, along with the shift towards the inclusion of the local civil society in the peacebuilding enterprise described in chapter 1, the UN has also embraced the goal of a system-wide coherence and coordination as essential for successful peacebuilding.[7] In a nutshell, greater coherence amongst different components of the UN has the potential to lead to more effective operations in post-conflict contexts.[8] The UN-hosted 2005 World Summit unambiguously recognised the need for a new institution with capacity to strengthen and, more importantly, operationalise strategic coherence. These discursive efforts towards coherence and coordination across the UN coincided and merged with the design and creation of the new Peacebuilding Architecture, which would become the internal mechanism through which coherence was first attempted to be implemented, particularly when countries such as Sierra Leone and Burundi entered the PBC agenda in 2007.[9] The resolution that established the PBA stressed the necessity for a 'coordinated, coherent and integrated approach to post-conflict peacebuilding … and to advise on and propose integrated strategies for post-conflict peacebuilding',[10] particularly between donor states, the UN headquarters and field missions.[11] Annan's legacy in the area of coherence and coordination endured beyond his mandate. UNSG Ban Ki-Moon expressed in a 2009 report that a system-wide coherence and coordination was critical to peacebuilding processes.[12]

Along with PBC field engagements, one of the most significant operational steps to enhance coherence in the frame of political and peacebuilding post-conflict operations was the implementation of integrated missions, led by the DPA.[13] The UN resolved that 'an integrated mission is based on a common strategic plan and a shared understanding of the priorities and types of program interventions that need to be undertaken at various stages of the recovery process. Through this integrated process, the UN system seeks to maximize its contribution towards countries emerging from conflict by engaging its different capabilities in a coherent and mutually supportive manner'.[14] Thus, integrated missions are designed to integrate peacekeeping and peacebuilding efforts in conflict-affected areas.[15] A former ONUB staff member and current DPA officer mentioned during an interview that he considered it foolish to try to conduct peacebuilding efforts in an unintegrated way due to two reasons. First, because some actions involve dealing with sectors which go beyond the DPA scope, and second, because the DPA operates under the host government's consent and with more limited resources, forcing the UN to collaborate with other agencies in order to achieve success, such as the Department of Peacekeeping Operations (DPKO) or the UNDP.[16] Along these lines, a further UN source states that 'the main purpose of integration is to maximize the individual and collective impact of the UN's response through a strategic partnership between the UN Country Team and the UN mission, concentrating on those activities required to consolidate peace'.[17] With a focus on the UN peacebuilding involvement in the African continent, the 2015 report of the HIPPO stressed that 'to strengthen integration, joint UN assessments, integrated planning and an agreed division of labour should be in place. (…) [and] strategic coherence in the field must be achieved'.[18] The policy document delves into filed missions' management arrangements as key to ensure coherence and avoid duplication of efforts, which should be led by a strong sense of guidance from the UN headquarters. In summary, coordination, integration and coherence, successively, across all UN peacebuilding-oriented organs, from the headquarters to the field missions, should result in more flexible, efficient and successful peacebuilding results.

De Coning, one of the contemporary authors who has most extensively covered the topic of coherence and coordination in peacebuilding theory and policy, particularly in the UN framework, points out that the key operational issue of UN coherence, and its associated mechanisms of coordination and integration, is that it seeks to be system-wide, hence the apparent significant complexity of the process. The author continues to classify this UN system-wide endeavour as facing four major challenges, namely, facilitating its own internal coherence; supporting coherence amongst all host government's agencies; encouraging coherence among all international or external actors; and facilitating coherence between the external and internal actors.[19] As expressed earlier, in order to pursue coherence, UN agencies endeavouring to consolidate peacebuilding have to make use of all available tools of coordination, described as 'the process that ensures that an individual peacebuilding agent is connected to the larger peacebuilding system of which it is a part, and without which is has no meaning'.[20] In the words of the HIPPO report, 'coordination mechanisms should facilitate strategic coherence between the various organizations' presence and operations in-country'.[21] De Coning identifies that while coherence is the aim, coordination encompasses the whole set of technical mechanisms though which coherence is achieved. At this point, the author makes a conspicuous observation that intimately resonates with the critical engagement unfolded in the following pages, in turn, stirred by a problematic assumption underlaying the topic of coherence and coordination in the peacebuilding milieu. In brief, while coherence and coordination are portrayed as tightly interlinked from the UN perspective, 'one should not assume a linear or causal relationship, as the one does not necessarily lead to the other'.[22]

Emulating the scientific revelation of an alleged determinism and linear unfolding of phenomena in the natural world, the social domain, particularly its transformatory practical endeavours as those of the UN, overwhelmingly embraces the assumption for which certain inputs under certain conditions result in certain outcomes. As extensively covered in the following section, critical peacebuilding literature has long questioned that events in conflict-affected scenarios unfold in a pre-determined, predictable and cause-and-effect linear path. Far from this, non-linear peacebuilding accounts stress that actors and processes in the war-torn milieu collide in a rather uncontrollable mode, as illustrated below by reflecting upon real case scenarios such as the noticeable limited results of the UN peacebuilding efforts in achieving system-wide coherence in Burundi. Most importantly, the chapter invokes the notion of entangled peace to problematise how these so-called non-linear peacebuilding interpretations still reproduce the deterministic emancipatory language of top-down, linear peace attempts. By the end of the chapter, the text poses an invitation to stretch even further the implications of seeing the world differently from its unquestioned and long-assumed linear progression in a cause-effect quasi-teleological fashion, that is, by speculating about a reformulation of space more than just pre-fix and given canvases that world beings and events fill out.

PROBLEMATISING LINEAR PEACEBUILDING

Over the past decade 'the local turn' in critical peacebuilding literature has become closely associated with the affirmation of non-linear peacebuilding, namely a form of seeing and implementing peace strategically responsive and sensitised with the unpredictability of outcomes in peacebuilding scenarios.[23] As introduced earlier in the book, the first wave of peacebuilding theory and practice, prompted by the outbreak of major violent conflicts in the aftermath of the Cold War, was underpinned by an eagerness to remove dysfunctional political systems and impose a state apparatus adaptable to the peaceful liberal international order,[24] as, for instance, the UN-North Atlantic Treaty Organization (NATO) involvement in the Balkans illustrated. In light of the blatant limited results of this international peace enterprise, some critics began to openly question the highly intrusive, linear and top-down essence of these interventions.[25] The almost unison response to these often referred to as statebuilding practices was an all-encompassing refocus on the role that local civil societies should play on the path towards peacebuilding. The expansion of this bottom-up approach centred on empowering host populations to adopt a meaningful leading role in the peacebuilding project took a strong hold both in literature as well as in policy frameworks throughout the 2000s.[26] More importantly to the present discussion, the shift towards 'the locals' resonated and reinforced the emergence peacebuilding conversations articulated around the notion of non-linear causality. The resistances to the liberal, top-down and linear form of externally imposing peacebuilding hinted that lasting peace should instead stem from the multiplicity of entangled micro-relations at the field level among 'invisible' or 'hidden' local agencies, which often operate in an unpredictable, undetermined and non-linear mode.[27]

Moving this conversation forward, Chandler reads the rise of non-linear peacebuilding as a process-based approach aimed at ensuring the societal reproduction of those relations and practices at a level where conflicts are managed pacifically. In the author's words, 'The local production and repro-duction of difference through micro-practices, spaces and relationships is at the heart of non-linear understandings and the 'embedded' understanding of the subject'.[28] Here Chandler criticises how previous linear peacebuilding frameworks, which were highly intrusive, linear and top-down, were guided by the assumption that rational subjects from conflict-affected societies were awaiting to be freed by the external intervening actor. 'The non-linear subject can no longer be 'freed' by peacebuilding interventions, as if the "blockages" somehow existed outside the subject and its relations and understandings'.[29] He continues by elucidating how non-linear peacebuilding represents a shift away from liberal rationality and a theoretical and practical move towards a sensitivity with deeper and entwined social practices that eventually com-pose the overall peacebuilding outcome. Pushing this argument further, it seems that critical peacebuilding debates on non-linearity were rooted in a contestation over Enlightened rational frameworks and their blind faith in deterministic science and life-guiding reason. More specifically, the critique was directed to the modern expectation that social events in the world occur in a linear, progressive and quasi-teleological fashion, which was founded on the Newtonian contentious assertion that space expand in the world linearly. It is precisely this unquestioned approach to spatial framings what is critically reflected upon in the following pages.

Formulations on non-linearity did not only capture the attention of critical peacebuilding theory, but in addition, major international organisations such as the UN[30] and the EU[31] bought into this approach, seemingly best suited to deal with the increasing complexity and interconnectedness of challenges in conflict-affected scenarios as well as in the context of broader crises. The 2015 UN report introducing the sustaining peace approach is a clear example of this shift. In it, an advisory group of experts acknowledges the primacy of deploying mandates under a locally focused model and recommends to merge in a coherent format the previous linear distinction between preven-tion, action during conflict and post-conflict intervention.[32] In brief, world's leading institutions admitted that, rather than resorting to external interven-tion, contemporary challenges, especially in most vulnerable environments, should be best faced by strong, full-equipped and resilient internal societies.[33] As a matter of fact, non-linear theorising and its various forms of operation-alisation arose alongside the narrative of resilience, an akin form of seeing the world which similarly uncovered and exposed the limits of linear interventive practices.[34] In the domain of peacebuilding, resilience came to be defined as 'the internal capacity of societies to cope with crises, with the emphasis on the development of self-organization and internal capacities and capabilities rather than the external provision of aid, resources or policy solutions'.[35]

Although soon critical authors accused international organisations of misappropriating the concept of resilience as a method to extend societal control over fragile scenarios,[36] international peacebuilding policy frameworks have continued to absorb sensitivities over non-linearity and resilience as guiding principles for the deployment of strategies, programmes and field missions.

Returning to the topic of interest in the present chapter, recent peacebuilding literature has interrogated the contentious link between the emergence of non-linear and resilient discourses, and the efforts by international organisation towards promoting mechanisms aimed at enhancing system-wide coherence and coordination in the peacebuilding milieu. Juncos problematises how international organisations such as the EU and the UN have developed a peacebuilding strategic turn towards an integrated approach as a mechanism to surpass linearity and the more and more evident growing complexity of contemporary conflict-affected processes.[37] To this author, non-linearity and resilience become proxies for coherence to those actors whose external action has been long-accused of being overtly uncoordinated, which admittedly reduces resilience to a goal-oriented strategy,[38] away from the non-linear, micro-political and processed based approach presented earlier. In other words, the consecution of a system-wide coherence through measures aimed at strengthening field coordination and integrated strategies is contemplated by international peacebuilding actors as an essential step towards becoming resilient and overcoming the inefficiency of intrusive, top-down and linear peacebuilding processes.

The phenomenon of integrated missions has been vastly discussed throughout its conceptual and operational evolution.[39] The rationale behind this emerging form of peace missions assumes that peacebuilding only makes sense as part of a larger system of related programmes.[40] The UN peacebuilding engagement in Burundi, along with Sierra Leone the first country to be place on the PBC agenda in 2007, illustrates this case. Throughout the decade from 2004 to 2014, the most significant endeavour of UN peace operations deployed in Burundi, including the United Nations Operations in Burundi (ONUB, in French), the BINUB and the United Nations Office in Burundi (BNUB, in French), was in pursuit for a system-wide coherence.[41] The mandates of these missions emphasised the need to enhance, on one hand, field coordination between deployed UN peace actors and, on the other hand, the relation between the New York-based headquarters and the field. In 2003, the African Union (AU) deployed the first peacekeeping mission in the country, the African Union Mission in Burundi (AMIB), which some consider as one of the biggest success of all AU performances.[42] The signature of the peace agreement between the transitional government and the National Council for the Defense of Democracy – Forces for the Defense of Democracy (CNDD-FDD, in French) was followed by the transferring of the peacekeeping responsibility from the AU to the UN, which established its first UN peacekeeping mission in Burundi in June 2004, the DPKO-led ONUB, whose main achievement was the disarming and demobilisation of about 21,700 fighters at the end of its mandate.[43] Following the National Forces of Liberation's (FNL, in French) ceasefire agreement in December 2006, ONUB was replaced by the BINUB.

The establishment of BINUB in 2007 marks a breaking point regarding the UN peacebuilding efforts in Burundi towards an integrated strategy. The Security Council (SC) requested the mission to ensure 'coherence and coordination of the UN agencies in Burundi, under the leadership of the Executive Representative of the Secretary-General (ERSG)'.[44] Effectively, the transition from the DPKO-led ONUB to BINUB, which would initially be deployed by the DPKO and later led by the DPA, was specifically aimed at implementing a multidimensional, integrated and coordinated mandate tackling a wide range of areas, including security and governance.[45] In pursuit for field coordination, BINUB's head took on responsibility for four additional roles, including ERSG, Resident Coordinator, Humanitarian Coordinator, and head of the UN Information Centre.[46] The UNSC resolution that established BNUB in 2010, the subsequent integrated mission in Burundi prompted by an increasing deterioration of the security situation,[47] similarly underlined 'the importance of establishing a fully integrated office with effective coordination of strategy and programs among the UN agencies, funds and programs in Burundi, and emphasizes the need for the UN system to support and cooperate fully with BNUB'.[48]

Despite all the aforementioned discursive and operational efforts, UN results in achieving a system-wide coherence and coordination in Burundi were significantly limited.[49] The first major internal evaluation process that the PBC underwent in 2010, mostly focused on the performance in Sierra Leone and Burundi, acknowledged that the PBC failed to fulfil the coordination and coherence goal by highlighting the inability of the PBSO to take leadership and distribute peacebuilding efforts across departments.[50] The second major UN assessment report, coinciding with the tenth anniversary of the PBC, despite recognised efforts, such as the establishment of the CEB, the Integration Steering Committee and the DaO initiative, identified that fragmentation and a lack of clarity in distribution of responsibilities within the UN peacebuilding system persists. The report cites issues of miscommunication between different levels and a lack of a culture of coordination from the top as serious obstacles to system-wide coherence. The assessment concludes that fragmentation within headquarters mirrors arguments in the field, stating that 'the mindset of UN leaders and staff on the ground too frequently still reproduces the same tectonic divide seen at the level of the intergovernmental organs, and at the level of the UN system globally'.[51] Reinforcing the evidence of this non-fulfilled goal of coherence and coordination, further early PBC engagements experienced similar results. Concerning the Sierra Leonean case, a former advisor to the United Kingdom (UK) government on the Security Sector Reform (SSR) process expressed in an interview that UN coordination is characteristically 'terrible'.[52] Similarly, the executive director of the Freetown-based Center for Accountability and Rule of Law described UN coordination as a major problem.[53] In the same context, the head of WANEP, also based in Freetown, described UN coordination as problematic, confusing and opaque. He added that efforts to avoid duplication and competition are scarce.[54] In the case of the CAR, a former MINUSCA officer, one more attempt at a multidimensional integrated mission, acknowledged that UN coordination in the peacebuilding domain remains a 'nightmare'.[55]

The faultiness of the UN peacebuilding endeavour towards a system-wide coherence puts into question the managerial inclination of the international organisation and its regulatory mechanisms, based on the assumption that certain inputs under certain circumstances should predictably result in certain outcomes, in this particular case, more successful peacebuilding. Notwithstanding the UN conviction that coordination leads to coherence and coherence to better peacebuilding, a formulation that resonates with cause-effect linear framings, the complex and non-linear essence of war-torn scenarios means that coherence can never be fully attained.[56] Paradoxically, one of the remedies that the UN designs and executes to presumably overcome field complexity and rigid, top-down and linear peacebuilding, namely system-wide coherence, is underpinned by the Enlightened rationale for which events in the social domain unfold in a linear and predictable manner, so that one can manipulate certain inputs to determine an expected outcome. Shedding light on this argument, Zanotti suggests that 'ambiguity is a central dimension in the situations of conflict that peace operations attempt to govern through technocratic and calculating rationalities'.[57] To this author, the attempt at holistic and integrated peace strategies intensifies regulatory aspirations for international organisations, who sorrowfully realise that, in real case scenarios, 'relations of causality and the effects of the interaction of an increasing number of variables are difficult to predict'.[58] Therefore, the limits of coherence-oriented mechanisms such as coordination, integration and highly technocratic planning illustrate how the outcomes of peacebuilding scenarios stem from unpredictable and entangled micro-political processes amongst a wide range of actors and processes at the ground level. Once again, it seems that the UN fails to codify the peacebuilding milieu through prescriptions and standardised instructions.[59]

In sum, non-linear peacebuilding literature refuses the approach that conceives of conflict-affected scenarios as contexts filled with problems waiting for solutions to be solved. The authors referred to in this section are more inclined to embrace the peacebuilding enterprise as an open-ended and even goal-free event, the outcomes of which respond to undetermined collisions between a vast amount of ongoingly changing actors and processes. This has serious implications for UN peacebuilders in the form of, for example, how they develop 'lessons learned' programmes as a guidance for future action. Hence, advocates for the non-linear essence of the peacebuilding milieu tend to invoke a relational and process-based approach, arguably better suited to deal with unexpected outcomes, setbacks or continuously transforming patterns. Seeking to move this conversation forward, next section questions that most non-linear peacebuilding accounts exposed earlier unnoticeably reproduce a similar normative and deterministic circuit to that of the UN. To be precise, the capture, accommodation and adoption of non-linear forms of seeing the world and being in it is perceived as the breakthrough towards a more meaningful fashion of peacebuilding. Thus, these peacebuilding-affirming theoretical and practical non-linear settings are reduced to just one more emancipatory claim embedded in the same normative and deterministic parameters as those of liberal linear rationalities. The following section speculates over the implications of conceiving of the world as a messy experience where events do not occur in a long-assumed Newtonian linear fashion. More specifically, the text hints at a reformulation of spatial framings that renders meaningless any attempt to exert an action from 'out-there' into a pre-fix Cartesian coordinate, thus undermining the self-appointed hubristic decisive human role not only in peacebuilding scenarios, but also in the broader world.

PEACEBUILDING AND SPECULATIVE SPATIAL FRAMINGS

As developed in chapter 4, in the entangled peace account cause-effect linearity does not become a hurdle that needs to be coped with or surpassed in order to achieve better peacebuilding. Instead, the reformulation of causality, which has been extensively covered in the discipline of International Relations,[60] uncovers an invitation to speculate over, first, the implications of the assembled composition of actors in the peacebuilding milieu and, second, how a non-linear lens to spatial framings might open up the future beyond normative, deterministic and teleological forms of being and becoming in the world.

Seeking to make sense of the unmet objective of system-wide coherence in the case of UN peacebuilding, this section hints that this organisational enterprise illustrates a problematic UN self-perception of its own assembled configuration. To the UN, the more fluid and greasing the relations between its internal parts, the more efficient and fruitful its problem-solving. Thus the UN fails to recognise the inexistence of rigid boundaries between one part, for example, a department or an agency, and the whole. Far from this, both the messy intra-organisation entanglements as well as the exogenous encounters with non-UN actors make it fruitless to ontologically distinguish between the parts and the whole. As Deleuze and Guattari note, one cannot 'say anything about the intra-assemblage without already being on the path to other assemblages'.[61] The authors continue to make a suggestive analysis, by which the components of an assemblage become components of new assemblages. Crucially, 'an assemblage is precisely this increase in the dimensions of a multiplicity that necessarily changes in nature as it expands its connections'.[62] Distinctively, as they suggest, the stories one perceives are not based on the subject matter of those stories, but instead on the processes of becoming from one story to another. Different to the fix and static ontological categorisations through which the UN thinks its parts and its wholeness, Deleuze and Guattari emphasise the continuous forces, relations and ex-changes through which assemblages pass from one to another in an indeterminate fashion.[63] Building on this Deleuzian analysis of assemblages, Delanda exposes that Making the properties of a whole depend on the interactions between its parts ensures that these properties are not taken to be *either necessary or transcendent*. When the properties of a given whole are taken as a brute fact, and listed as the unexplained characteristics that the whole must possess in order to be an entity of a given kind, the list of necessary properties swiftly becomes an *essence*. Essences belong to a different plane of being from the entities whose identity they define, a transcendent plane overflying that which the entities populate. But if the properties are view as *produced* by interactions between components, and their existence and endurance explained by the continuity of those interactions, then the properties are *contingent*: if the interactions cease to take place the emergent properties cease to exist.[64]

From this account, assemblages are composed of semiotic-material flows: the materialised elements one perceives in UN missions, including the geographical accidents, the people, the built environment and ground missions, become assembled through immaterial dynamic forces, which are contingent properties of the assemblage. In Delanda's line of reasoning, the UN cannot simply expect that a better coordination of its parts will result in system-wide coherence, as these parts have no autonomy per se, but they are contingent: they are produced through their interactions with other UN components. This framing requires a reconfiguration of the associations between the UN, its components and strategies, and the world. Instrumentalising Deleuze and Guattari's ontological dissection of a book as an assemblage, 'there is no longer a tripartite division between a field of reality (the world) and a field of representation (the book [organisational coherence]) and a field of subjectivity (the author [the UN]). Rather, an assemblage establishes connections between certain multiplicities drawn from each of these orders'.[65] This understanding of assemblages renders linear causality, according to which assembled parts naturally form a whole, rather reconceptualised.

Within Western epistemes, there are two major traditions of thought as per the conceptualisation of causality. On the one hand, the modern, enlightened and Eurocentric tradition, pioneered by thinkers such as Descartes, Newton, Hume and Kant, assumes that causality is an explanatory phenomenon that can only be accessed through human experience.[66] To these authors, cosmology is underpinned by an all-encompassing divide: the subject/mind/human and the object/matter/world. Barad critically reflects upon this dichotomic rationality, for which causality is either deterministic (objects simply do their things) and the human has little to do about it, or there is absolute freedom, meaning that humans have an interventionist role that can affect things.[67] On the other hand, challenging this modern understanding of causation, other thinkers such as Leibniz and Whitehead invoke a sort of God intervention, creativity, eternity and even self-causation. In this tradition, the existence of the human is independent to causal explanations. In contemporary thought, the non-anthropocentric ontogenesis of causality from this second tradition has been secularised, thus rendering causality always materially mediated and localised.[68] Causation is therefore compositional, meaning that any relation between separate things produces (causes) a new composite object.[69] Although events are caused by what precedes it, no cause is ever in a position to define how it will cause.[70] To Morton, 'objects entangle one another in crisscrossing mesh of spacetime fluctuations',[71] thus questioning the unchallenged linearity of causal relations. From this perspective, no being can determine with full certainty how it will matter for other beings. These accounts reflect that causality does not respond to linear Newtonian mechanics.[72]

Returning to the case of the UN peacebuilding endeavours towards a system-wide coherence in the Burundian context, some episodes clearly illustrate that the unexpectedness of reality disarticulates any possibility for events to unfold in a predictable cause-effect linear path, thus resonating with a materially localised and relational form of perceiving causality. For example, in 2010, Nkuruziza's expelled Youssef Mahmoud, BINUB's ERSG, from the country. Later, BNUB allegedly leaked how the CNDD-FDD took steps to arm and train its youth,[73] which precipitated the expulsion in 2014 of Paul Debbie, BNUB's security chief. Both unforeseen episodes severely hindered UN's progressive and linear strategy towards organisational coherence and, ultimately, successful peacebuilding. Furthermore, the relations between the UN and other stakeholders such as the local civil society might also be unexpectedly trumped by UN attitudes deemed hostile or disrespectful by the local population. A commentator in an interview criticises the UN presence in Bujumbura for being too visible, with UN officers insensitively displaying wealth, creating distrust and dislike amongst locals.[74] One further instance that reveals the inconsistencies of expecting a linear unfolding of cause-effect relations captures the intra-organisational conflicts of interests as well as leadership[75] and personality traits,[76] often resulting in competition and turf battles. As Delanda points out, 'in some cases the decisions made by individual human beings are highly constrained by their position and role in a hierarchical organization and are, to that extent, geared toward meeting the goals of that organization. In other cases, however, what matters is not the planned results of decision making, but the unintended collective consequences of human decisions'.[77] As early PBC assessments express, unexpected turf battles rooted in a conflict of interests represented a widely recognised operational inability to the PBC in its mandate to deploy a coordinated peacebuilding action, particularly in Burundi.[78]

Importantly, these accidental conflictual encounters do not only unexpectedly trump the linear becoming of actors and events on the ground but, on top of this, they recompose the entangled ontogenesis of colliding actors, who happen to become through co-constitutive relations. Barad, in a Whiteheadian fashion, invokes a reworking of the notion of causality, which cannot be explained as specific relations between isolated objects, as one cause-thing resulting in an effect-thing separately. Rather, bodies materialise as particular patterns of the world as a result of the specific cuts and reconfigurations that are enacted. Cause and effect emerge through intra-action, namely they are mutually constituted at the point of their entanglement. The author acknowledges that creativeness and liveliness reformulate the traditional notions of causality in an ongoing reconfiguring of both the real and the impossible. 'The future is radically open at every turn, and this open sense of futurity does not depend on the clash of collision of cultural demands'.[79] Along this line, Delanda notes that 'our world is governed not only by nonlinear dynamics, which makes detailed prediction and control impossible, but also by nonlinear combinatorics, which implies that the number of possible mixtures of meshwork and hierarchy, of command and market, of centralization and decentralization, are immense and that we simply cannot predict what the emergent properties of these myriad combinations will be'.[80] By pushing forward this creative exercise of imagining a non-linear world, the following lines intend to elaborate on how the limits of the attempt at coherence of the UN Burundian adventure might resonate with a speculative reconceptualisation of spatial framings.

The PBC's Strategic Framework for Peacebuilding in Burundi established the so-called Partners Coordination Group as one of the three components of the Monitoring and Tracking Mechanism, aimed at dialogue, coordination and monitoring for the Poverty Reduction Strategy paper and the Strategic Framework itself. The Partners Coordination Group is composed of three structures, the sectoral clusters (base), the Strategic Forum of Partners Coordination Group (second level) and the Political Forum of the Partners Coordination Group (third level). This Political Forum serves as counterpart to the PBC Burundi configuration in New York, therefore aimed, among other tasks, at enhancing coherence between the field and headquarters. Despite these operational efforts, evidence illustrates the limited results of the PBC to enhance system-wide coherence by improving New York-field relations.[81] As Rugumamu explains, 'Some key members of the PBC ... rarely attended scheduled PBC meetings. Worse still, their respective representatives who participate actively in the field, in New York and via their capitals, have not always engaged with a single, coherent voice but instead have taken contradictory positions in different venues. Equally disturbing, some PBC members from developing countries who are neither donors nor represented in the field have always missed the opportunity to meaningfully and objectively add their views'.[82] The author problematises videoconferencing as a failed technical arrangement to enhance coordination and communication between the headquarters and field missions, from where video calls were perceived as cold and ineffective compared to physical and face to face meetings.

To most peacebuilding policy experts, these limited results in achieving headquarters-field coordination can be explained by noting ill-equipped institutional capacity, including a lack of guides or protocols, the sometimes excessively hierarchical relationship and the lack of channels of communication between the two levels.[83] In line with the earlier-introduced notions of non-linear causality, this section intends to shed light on the ambiguity and inexactness of thinking spatial framings as pre-fix and rigidly separated, as illustrated by the compartmentalised UN peacebuilding action in between the New York-based headquarters and the field. With the goal of exploring the potential implications of affirming the non-linearity of the entangled ontology of actors and processes in peacebuilding settings, a reconsideration of the spatial conditions in which these relations materialise is invoked. To do so, the text elaborates on current debates that question the relationality of the world as unfolding in static and fixed categories of space.[84] As Barad elucidates, 'The indeterminacy of space, time, and matter at the core of quantum field theory [as opposed to Newtonian linear mechanics] troubles the scalar distinction between the world of subatomic particles and that of colonialism, war, nuclear physics research, and environmental destruction'.[85] By surpassing Husserlian phenomenologist readings of linear projection, the following standpoint essentially questions how modern geometry and temporality hubristically separated the human from its context, from the world.[86]

Inspired by a Whiteheadian account, it is problematised how peacebuilding accounts presume space as a fixed regime in which interactions and ex-changes between actors develop. Whitehead engages with how Bergson illustrates this point: 'the human intellect spatializes the universe; it tends to ignore the fluency and to analyse the world in terms of static categorisations'.[87] The Newtonian/Euclidian conception of space, namely the milieu

in which causal dynamic processes unfold, misadjusts Whitehead's idea of
the 'place' of intra-actions. Whitehead criticises classic materialism from the
eighteenth and nineteenth centuries for believing that 'what is real in nature
is matter, in time and in space and with inertia'.[88] Differently, he defines
space as 'the outcome of relations between different attributes of matter'.[89]
Developing this idea further, for the philosopher, there is no fixed context,
no space, but instead there is an 'extensive continuum'.[90] Whitehead defines
the 'extensive continuum' as a relational complex in which all actual entities as well as potential objectifications, namely previous to their existence,
find their niche. The most fundamental characteristic of this 'extensive continuum' is the relatedness of the things that make up the world. The relations
between actualities form a continuous datum, also real, which is an extensive
continuum derived from the actual world. Explicitly invoking the recently
discovered quantum understanding of space-time, Whitehead contends that
this extensive continuum is the whole world and is past, present and future. It
is not a fact prior to the world, it is the first determination of order arising out
of the general character of the world, that is, real (and relational) potential-
ity. Therefore, the continuum is present in each actual entity, and each actual
entity pervades the continuum.

Without disavowing the aforementioned accounts on non-linear peacebuilding, it is differently suggested that what is at stake is the possibility to
reimagine and reframe the ostensible existence of a given 'out-there' space in
which peacebuilding supposedly unfolds. Whitehead's extensive continuum
reflects the absence of any fixed frame in which exchanges develop. There is
no world as a static vacuum, a container, that humans and non-humans fill and
live. Instead, space-time framings should be thought as manifold and part of
the universe, not ontologically outside of it.[91] Harman, who admittedly shows
resistance to the relational composition of the world, also suggests that 'space
is the network of relations and non-relations between objects'.[92] What one
thinks of the world is defined here as the composition of exchanges that one
does not subjectively perceive because our agentic condition is not in play,
as more extensively developed in chapter 3. Unframing entangled ontologies
is a way of arguing that the Newtonian idea of space, Whitehead's 'extensive
continuum', is not fixed, but performative. Therefore, the essence and conditions of this 'extensive continuum'/world are a reflection of the emergences
of relations between 'actual entities'. Changes in the extensive continuum
are thus changes in the relations. Barad reflects upon this by elucidating how
'landscapes are not stages, containers, or mere environments for human and
nonhuman actors. Landscape is not merely visually akin to a body; it is the
skin of the earth. Land is not property or territory; it is a time-being marked
by its own wounds and vitality, a layered material geo-neuro-biography of
bones and bodies, ashes and earth, where death and life meet'.[93] Space-time

positionality does not reveal an inert given coordinate, but an encounter, a collision, a negotiation, the outcome of which projects what most perceive as a static canvas, but what it is instead seen in this text as the expression of the very entanglement, therefore ever-transforming.

Seeking to illuminate in a more comprehensive manner all these onto-logical reconfigurations which presume that space-time framings do not unfold in a linear, progressive and teleological manner but instead abide by continuous, simultaneous and 'weird' scales of space, Kirby instrumen-talises quantum sensitivities to argue that 'nothing' pre-exists the relation-ality that is the scene of ontological genesis as enfolding, becoming. In her account, relationality is associated with a limit that separates human exceptionalism from substantive reality, a limit that 'has prevented us from appreciating that our corporeal realities and their productive iterations *are* material reinventions'.[94] This author reformulates part-whole relations by affirming that the unit does not pre-exist the system. Instead, the 'unit is "thrown up" or "authored" by the system'.[95] Similar to Barad's definition of 'externality within', Kirby's notions of scales that inform a situated form of relationality a radically transformed, surpassing Euclidean foundations. To this author, a quantum geometry does not involve a given outside that the human can access, as humanness is actually articulated in an entangled form within its *relata*. Thus, the human cannot be bound to a separate 'out-there' if one assumes that this ostensible 'externality' and the human are actually a co-constitutive generative unfolding.[96] In sum, linear connectivi-ties in apparently different systems as well as the integrity of these system are profoundly disrupted and universally dispersed.[97] Quantum sensitivities towards relationality enable to comprehend that 'what binds all of us is a sense that the way the world works isn't at all straightforward'.[98] Through the concept of 'uncanny alliance', Kirby hints at the inextricable position-ality of the initial and final conditions of all events, thus portraying the quantum space-time framing in which relations occur.[99] In vein with previ-ous accounts, this quantum condensation also presupposes the blending of ideality and materiality, which collapse in a manner unreachable by modern rational logic and classic physical laws.[100]

Zanotti, who has playfully theorised along these lines in the area of criti-cal peace and conflict studies and broader International Relations, unravels a picture of an 'onto-epistemological horizon that opens possibilities for reconceptualizing the way we can engage with the interdependent world of which we are a part',[101] thus elaborating on Barad's idea that reality is not an externality, endowed with properties we may discover from an outside, but instead an 'externality within'. It is suggested here that imagining the possibility to unframe relations in this fashion has radical implications to capture the 'externality within' of the milieu in which actors such as the UN peacebuilding seek to make an impact. In light of the earlier, neither the New York-based UN headquarters nor Burundi-based field missions are located in spatially separated and fix theatres of operations. Instead, actors and processes collapsing in the same event unfetter an 'extensive continuum', problematically perceived by modern epistemes as outside actors' ontogenesis. Resonating with Whiteheadian concepts of concrescence and actualisation, both agents and social structures are potentialities rather than actualities, and when they become real they do so in a co-emergent situated form.[102] Unlike transformative and emancipatory interventions which ultimately seek for changes responding to 'out-there' objectified externalities in a given static frame, for example, a peacebuilding milieu, the 'extensive continuum' concept opens up the possibility of reconfiguring the spatial framings beyond normative endeavours. The possibility of an outside from where an action originates such as attempting at a system-wide coherence becomes unfeasible, as it is the precise momentum of the action, the encounter, the relation, that from which a continuous notion of space appears. This reconceptualisation of space has the potential to reconsider how UN peacebuilders perform in the field, abandoning the anxious horizon of having to meet a goal like coordination and to transform a given context, and instead sensitising with their own form of being and becoming as entangled, and therefore vulnerable, to the rest of actors and processes in the conflict-affected scenario, which becomes the ever-changing extension of these relations.

In sum, different to critical accounts exposed in the previous section, the non-linearity of peacebuilding processes, meaning the messy micro-political relations that occur at the ground level, is not perceived in the entangled peace account as a challenge that needs to be sensitised with, coped with or even overcome in order to achieve and consolidate a more successful peacebuilding. Assuming this form of doing, in which non-linear peacebuilding approaches lead to 'better' ways of developing peacebuilding, ultimately reproduces normative and emancipatory frameworks in a similar way to linear, top-down peacebuilding. Rather, this section has hinted that the realisation of non-linear causal paths might open up the future by offering the possibility to speculate over different forms of seeing the world. Particularly, it has been suggested that the entangled condition of actors and processes and the non-linear unfolding of their relations might be an invitation to reimagine spatial framings beyond the modern Newtonian assumption, for which space is a linear, 'out-there', given canvas that beings and processes fill out. Instead, space is reconfigured as the outcome and expansion of the co-constitutive relations between actors, thus turning externalities into 'externalities within' and therefore invalidating the rationale behind peacebuilding interventive frameworks, where an actor can externally intrude into a context for transformatory purposes.

Chapter 3

Rethinking Agency through Complexity

Complexity thinking transcends the division between determinism and free will, in particular because it sees material worlds as unpredictable.

– (Law and Urry, 2004:402)

In addition to the concern with recentring the peacebuilding enterprise on 'the locals' as well as the endeavour towards a system-wide coherence as prime conditions for the success of peacebuilding engagements, this chapter unpacks the efforts and the implications of the UN goal to overcome the challenge of delivering peacebuilding amidst a plethora of actors with dissimilar political rationalities. In other words, UN peacebuilding objectives do not occur in isolation, but amongst a multiplicity of actors and processes that constantly interact, negotiate and collide with the UN. This quasi-chaotic amalgamation of actors is illustrated in the first section of the chapter through the paradigmatic case of the CAR, which over the past two decades has strikingly hosted up to fourteen peace missions, most of them led or authorised by the UN. Seeking to scrutinise the effects of these inter-actor messy entanglements on the conflict-affected scenario, and particularly on the ontogenesis of actors within, the second section draws on complexity theory as a helpful analytical framework to grasp the interconnectedness of events in the peacebuilding milieu. On the one hand, complexity is conceived of as an analytical tool enabling a more comprehensive understanding of the behaviour of beings (actors) in this remarkably busy war-affected landscape. On the other hand, complexity is also conceptualised as a performative contextual quality stemmed from the non-linear, unpredictable and entangled interactions between beings in any materialised event. The third section unpacks how complexity and the co-constitutive material entwinements from which it results unnoticeably render agency as a vulnerable, continuously reinvented and therefore non-purposeful form of being, seeing and doing in peacebuilding settings.[1]

THE UN IN A CONVOLUTED ASSEMBLAGE
OF EXTERNAL PEACE MISSIONS

The UN peacebuilding field endeavour barely occurs in isolation, but amidst an array of multiple actors and processes that enter in constant negotiation with each other. In fact, wary of the strategic challenges that this increasingly complex set-up poses to the UN telos in conflict-affected scenarios, over the past fifteen years, the organisation has resolved relevant measures determined to grease operational relations amongst further peace actors. The 2005 World Summit Outcome, which prompted the creation of the new UN Peacebuilding Architecture, states that 'the main purpose of the Peacebuilding Commission is to bring together all relevant actors to marshal resources and to advise on and propose integrated strategies for post-conflict peacebuilding and recovery'.[2] The document continues to stress the necessity for the UN to consult and cooperate with regional and sub-regional organisations with the ultimate goal of preventing armed conflict and consolidating peace. In countries like Sierra Leone, Burundi and the CAR, all early cases of attention of the new Peacebuilding Architecture, these discursive performances towards efficient inter-actor relations were attempted to be operationalised through the task of the PBC and the auxiliary PBSO. Even more explicitly and determinately, the 2015 report of the HIPPO endorsed the reliance on cooperation frameworks with domestic, regional and global organisations in order to successfully pursue the international peace agenda. In brief, the report acknowledges that regional and sub-regional actors 'are becoming more prominent features in the global peace and security landscape … and bring longstanding relationships, depth of understanding and determination, and often a willingness to respond…. Navigating the regional dimensions of conflict and collaboration with regional partners will be an essential aspect of planning and deploying all UN peace operations in the future'.[3] Along the lines of the new Peacebuilding Architecture approach, the UN presents itself here too as an actor with a dual paternalistic mission. On the one hand, the organisation envisions its own operational leading role in the future of global peace, and on the other hand, it deems itself as condition for possibility of broader inter-actor partnerships in the shape of enabler and facilitator. Most importantly, this enabling role is self-bestowed upon not from a position of neutrality or impartiality, but from one in which the

UN becomes a 'standard-nearer', thus upholding certain values that enact intrusive hierarchies and a position of superiority over the rest of actors and processes.

The UN objective to cooperate with a multiplicity of actors in the conflict-affected arena has been extensively covered in contemporary peacebuilding literature.[4] The vast majority of these engagements observe inter-actor relations as a complex hurdle that requires skilful strategic management to collectively meet the purpose of lasting peace. De Coning emphasis how in the present networked global era, several international actors, regional organisations as well as domestic actors, both country-wide and local, play an essential role in the large political project of peacebuilding, the success of which hinges on these actors' combined and cumulative result. In the author's words, 'UN regional offices, special political missions and peacekeeping operations ... need to have the capacity to support the effort necessary to coordinate, track and take stock of this larger political project. The complexity of maintaining overall strategic political coherence among such a large and diverse group of self-governing actors should not be underestimated. Nor can it be avoided as it seems to be the organizing feature of global governance in the twenty-first century'.[5] De Coning continues to exhort that the outcome of the UN peacebuilding enterprise will not be judged in the future on the organisation's own achievements, but on its capacity to effectively contribute to a broader national and international shared effort towards the consolidation of lasting peace. Similar to what has been discussed in the previous chapter about the inclusion of 'the locals' in peacebuilding processes or the UN goal of system-wide coherence, both the organisation itself and a substantial amount of literature envision unproblematic and cooperative relations between the UN and the rest of the actors as a *sine qua non* condition for the possibility of durable peace. From a different approach, this chapter examines what the mere fact of being related entails for the unquestioned agential condition of actors in the field. The chapter suggests that the growing complexity of war-torn scenarios, to a large extent resulted from the deployment of numerous peace missions in the same space-time coordinate, leads to an erosion of the long-assumed purposeful, autonomous and even teleological mode of agency of the wide range of involved actors, whose form of being, becoming and doing in the peacebuilding setting remains ongoingly transformed due to its entangled ontogenesis.

With the goal of illustrating the complex embroilment of actors and processes that the UN often encounters itself in the peacebuilding milieu, further, the text elaborates on the configuration of the CAR case, particularly on the deployment of an unprecedented number of international and regional efforts aimed at enforcing, keeping and building peace.[6] The CAR has widely and insistently been depicted by scholars and policy experts as one of the most complex instances of the African continent,[7] often without nuancing the onto-logical boundaries of this notion of complexity and its theoretical and practical implications. This rather ethereal complexity is often discursively sustained on disastrous macro and micro socioeconomic indicators, a conspicuous pro-tracted political instability, markedly high indicators of direct violence as well as the dysfunctionality of basic liberal democratic mechanisms, tools and pro-cesses, among others. In other words, as in most African states, these external concerns about the complexity of the country are unambiguously bound to the biased and rather contentious hermeneutic operators of liberalism, which are utterly detached from the genealogy of pre-Colonial CAR history.[8]

In peacebuilding literature, the CAR is considered a particular case study due to the unexampled amount of international and regional actors that have intervened in the country over the past twenty-five years. More specifically, since the crisis of 1996, which included three military mutinies, the CAR has hosted the astounding number of fourteen peace missions aimed to mitigate the effects of conflict, set political stability and consolidate peace (see table 3.1). These peace operations, led by the UN, the EU, the AU, the Central African Economic and Monetary Community (CEMAC) and/or the Economic Community of Central African States (ECCAS), have had a deter-minant impact on the evolution of the violent struggles as well as the eventual signature of the Comprehensive Peace Agreement (CPA).

The African response to the high levels of political instability in the CAR materialised in the establishment of the Inter-African Observation Missions of the Bangui Accords (MISAB, in French) in 1997 aimed to restore peace and security in the country. MISAB was deployed at President Patassé's request with the support from Burkina Faso, Chad, Gabon, Mali, Senegal and Togo. Its main tasks were to disarm the former rebels, civilian militias and all unlawfully armed individuals. In August 1997, the UNSC officialised MISAB as a UN-authorised force.[9] Shortly after, in April 1998, the DPKO deployed the United Nations Mission in the Central African Republic (MIN-URCA, in French), the main purpose of which was to 'assist in maintaining and enhancing security and stability in Bangui and the vicinity; supervise, control storage and monitor the disposition of weapons retrieved in disarma-ment exercise; assist in capacity-building of national police; provide advice and technical support for legislative elections'.[10] The MINURCA, which had absorbed MISAB, was replaced by the UN Peace-Building Support Office in the Central African Republic (BONUCA, in French), authorised in Decem-ber 1999 by the UNSC and deployed in February 2000 by the DPA. The BONUCA was tasked with 'supporting the Government of the CAR's efforts to consolidate peace and national reconciliation, strengthening democratic institutions and facilitating the mobilization of international political support

Table 3.1   Peace missions deployed in the Central African Republic (CAR), 1997–2014

Name	Duration	Agency	Scope
Inter-African Mission to Monitor the Bangui Accords (MISAB)	February 1997– April 1998	Regional (Burkina Faso, Chad, Gabon, Mali, Senegal and Togo) UN-authorised	CAR
United Nations Mission in the Central African Republic (MINURCA)	April 1998– February 2000	International (UN)	CAR
United Nations Peacebuilding Support Office in the Central African Republic (BONUCA)	February 2000– January 2010	International (UN)	CAR
Force Multinational de la Communauté Économique et Monétaire de l'Afrique Centrale (FOMUC)	October 2002– July 2008	Regional (CEMAC)	CAR
United Nations Mission in the Central African Republic (MINURCAT)	January 2008– December 2010	International (UN)	Regional (CAR/Chad)
European Union Force in the Republic of Chad and the Central African Republic (EUFOR TCHAD/RCA)	January 2008– March 2009	Regional (EU) UN-authorised	Regional (CAR/Chad)
Mission for the Consolidation of Peace in Central African Republic (MICOPAX)	July 2008– December 2013	Regional (ECCAS)	CAR
Peacebuilding Commission	June 2008 (still on)	International (UN)	CAR
United Nations Integrated Peacebuilding Support Office in the Central African Republic (BINUCA)	January 2010– April 2014	International (UN)	CAR
United Nations Regional Office for Central Africa (UNOCA)	Marc 2011 (still on)	International (UN)	Regional (ECCAS)
International Support Mission to the Central African Republic (MISCA)	December 2013– April 2014	Regional (AU)	CAR
'Operation Sangaris'	December 2013– April 2014	France	CAR
European Union Force in the Central African Republic (EUFOR RCA)	February 2014 (still on)	Regional (EU) UN-authorised	CAR
United Nations Multidimensional Integrated Stabilization Mission in the Central African Republic (MINUSCA)	April 2014 (still on)	International (UN)	CAR

Source: Author's own.

and resources for national reconstruction and economic recovery'.[11] Although the transition was developed without major drawbacks, scepticism within experts arose before the discernible ongoing contextual instability. As the former DWB director in the CAR put it during an interview, Maybe it was too early to leave the country, just after the peacebuilding mission, in the sense that, in that time, and the first attempt of coup by Bozizé was in 2001 already, there was an underestimation of the potential instability in the country. I don't think that BONUCA during its first years would have really worked on some peacebuilding objectives. Patassé was really worried about staying in power and really worried about the intentions from Bozizé. And there was a big defiance of regional forces from Chad, from Congo, from Libya, France … that ended up in the 2003… but I think honestly, it was too early to take out the peacekeeping part. And in this sense BONUCA was somehow left alone in the beginning.[12]

The security situation notoriously deteriorated again in 2002,[13] triggering this time a regional response. In October 2002, the CEMAC deployed the Multinational Force of Central Africa (FOMUC, in French), which was composed of around 400 troops and aimed to support political stability and reconstructing the *Forces Armées Centrafricaines*. Due to their wide and multidimensional scopes, the BONUCA and the FOMUC became the largest peacebuilding actors in the CAR. Shortly after the approval of the 2005 constitution under the newly constituted Bozizé's government, and a timid attempt to direct the country towards functional democracy, in 2008, the ECCAS established the Mission for the Consolidation of Peace in Central African Republic (MICOPAX), which co-existed with the FOMUC until replacing it in July 2008. The MICOPAX, composed of over 2,500 military and police officers, included staff from Cameroon, the Republic of Congo, Gabon, Guinea Equatorial and Chad. Primarily aimed at the protection of civilians in significantly violent areas such as Bossanga, in 2009, the MICOPAX witnessed the renewal of activities of armed groups, which accused Bozizé of not implementing the agreements reached with the rebels.[14] Throughout the first half of 2008, the three missions, BONUCA, FOMUC and MCOPAX, intended to ex-change collaborative efforts in pursuit of peace.

In June 2008, the CAR became the fourth country after Burundi, Sierra Leone and Guinea to be placed on the PBC agenda, which illustrates the firm determination the UN had to implement a peacebuilding approach in the Central African case. One of the primary tasks the PBC carried out was to transform the BONUCA into a fully peacebuilding-oriented mission, the UN Integrated Peacebuilding Office in the Central African Republic (BINUCA, in French). Deployed in January 2010, the BINUCA aimed to support national and local efforts to consolidate peace, enhance governance and complete the Disarmament Demobilisation and Reintegration (DDR) process. The security deterioration in the CAR, as a result of increasing inter-religious tensions, prompted the UNSC to authorise the AU-led International Support Mission to the Central African Republic (MISCA, in French) in December 2013, while also replacing the MICOPAX. Promoted by the AU's Peace and Security Council and supported by a robust French unilateral military deployment, known as the 'Operation Sangaris',[15] the MISCA was mandated to contribute to the protection of civilians, the restoration of security and state authority, political stability, the creation of conditions conducive to the provision of humanitarian assistance, the DDR process as well as the SSR, all conducted in close collaboration with transitional authorities and BINUCA.

Beyond Chapter VIII of the UN Charter, enabling and promoting regional arrangements, over the past fifteen years, the UN and the AU have designed and institutionalised several frameworks of cooperation, including the Regional Consultative Mechanism, aimed at a fluent communication between the AU and other agencies like the UN in peace and security matters; the Joint Task-Force on Peace and Security, established to enhance strategic cooperation between the two organisations; and the UN Liaison Office to the AU, aimed to further strengthen their relations in various societal domains, especially on peace and security issues. With over 80,000 personnel, including UN- and AU-led peace missions, Africa has become the top contributing continent to the global peace enterprise.[16] In spite of this seemingly growing institutional intimacy, the essence of the UN-AU partnership has been often problematised. The UN syndrome of superiority, the persistent lack of complementarity and misconceptions on the division of labour and responsibilities turn out to be embedded hurdles in UN-AU relations.[17] As the case of the CAR illustrates, UN partnership with regional organisation such as the AU 'coexist in a loosely defined manner that requires voluntary coordination and causes both tension and competition'.[18] Importantly, this institutionalised negotiated experience has reshaped not only the narratives and practices of peacebuilding in the frame of both international organisations, but also how further actors pursue peace efforts in the African continent.

With the goal of reinforcing the MISCA and providing support to African-led efforts towards containing the CAR conflict, in February 2014, the UN authorised the establishment of the European Union Force in the Central African Republic (EUFOR RCA). The EUFOR RCA became responsible for providing temporary support in order to achieve a safe and secure environment in Bangui, contributing to international efforts to protect most at-risk populations. This, in effect, marked the beginning of a new chapter in EU-UN cooperation in crisis management.[19] As a response to the limited results of these hitherto operational efforts, particularly to a prolonged spate of inter-communal fighting between Muslim and Christian militias[20] as well as to the struggle in the north between the pastoralists and farmers,[21] in 2014, the

UNSC enlarged its presence by establishing the MINUSCA, which absorbed the BINUCA, the MISCA and the French 'Operation Sangaris'. Still active to date, MINUSCA is a peacekeeping operation aimed to protect civilians, support the implementation of the transition process, facilitate humanitarian assistance, protect UN personnel, promote human rights, support the national and international justice and support the DDR and SSR processes.

On top of the wide array of domestic struggles, the Central African border with the Chad has also undergone major tensions and violent episodes, principally because of the hostility of south-eastern Chadian population against the arrival of both Central African refugees escaping from the war in the CAR and Sudanese refugees escaping from the humanitarian crisis in Darfur. As the security situation gradually worsened in this area, two peace missions were deployed in 2008. On the one hand, the UN established the United Nations Mission in the Central African Republic and Chad (MINURCAT, in French) and, on the other, the UN authorised the establishment of the European Union Force in the Republic of Chad and the Central African Republic (EUFOR TCHAD/RCA) for a period of one year, both primarily mandated to deal with security issues and the protection of civilians in the border area, as well as to guarantee human rights, the provision of humanitarian assistance and the prevalence of the rule of law. After a year of its deployment, in 2009, the EUFOR TCHAD/RCA transferred responsibilities to the MINURCAT, whose responsibilities were eventually assumed by Chadian security and justice bodies in December 2010. Fearing a further deterioration of stability in this bordering area leading to a major regional crisis, the UN launched in March 2011 the United Nations Regional Office for Central Africa (UNOCA), which included the ten members of the ECCAS. Amongst other goals, the UNOCA was mandated to strengthen regional conflict prevention mechanisms, cooperate with ECCAS and other stakeholders in the promotion of peace and security in the broader Central African sub-region, strengthen the DPA's capacity to advise the UNSG on different matters, enhance linkages in the sub-region to promote an integrated sub-regional approach and facilitating coordination and information ex-change, and report to the headquarters on developments of sub-regional significance.

Notwithstanding such an astonishing number of operational attempts, the current situation in the CAR remains strikingly convoluted and plagued by violent conflict,[22] which illustrates the inability of this complex multiplicity of actors, particularly of the UN, to deliver lasting peace. Informed by theories and practices of adaptation to complex scenarios, a large part of critical accounts in peacebuilding literature resonates again with Foucauldian power relations analyses and governmentality. In a nutshell, these suggest that UN interventive practices, far from seeking to consolidate peacebuilding, remain framed within an unchanged will to extend control over the conditions that led up to the messiness of war-torn societies.[23] With the goal to push this conversation forward, the following sections stretch complexity theory to reflect upon the implications of the unpredictable and chaotic entanglements between peace actors and processes in the peacebuilding setting. More specifically, the text problematises how these critical peacebuilding debates take for granted agency as a purposeful, autonomous and intentional condition of actors. Instead, it is suggested that a complexity-sensitive analysis of conflict-affected scenarios questions viewing actors as teleologically acting to ultimately pursue a goal. From this assumption, the following lines hint that actors reconfigure themselves constrained by their spontaneous interactions with others, for the forms of agency that are at play, both react to and enable the ontological complexity that is embedded in their relations. Hence, as described in the following section, complexity is performative to the extent that, in these interactions with other agents and the environment, actors unexpectedly and unintentionally reproduce and contribute to the very complexity they observe. To be sure, prejudging peacebuilders such as the UN as purposeful agents seeking to manage, instrumentalise and control complexity from the outside may in fact contribute to a form of categorisation that would, on the one hand, place actors and processes in the peacebuilding context into distinct groupings and, on the other, also assign hierarchies that may come to reinforce linear assumptions about power and resistance. Not only are such categories not always manifested in the same material manner across all post-conflict milieus but, arguably, the uncritical acceptance of these categories could also presume that the undoing of such power relations might simply be a matter of reversing top-down approaches and replacing them with bottom-up ones.

COMPLEXITY IN PEACEBUILDING DISCOURSES AND PRACTICES

The busy amalgamation of peacebuilding missions in the CAR has turned the country into a complex theatre of operations involving numerous actors and processes in ongoing unpredictable exchange. The notion of complexity is particularly relevant to recent assessments of peacebuilding theory and practice, both because it enables the outlining of those epistemological and ontological conditions that come to determine the reality of the post-conflict milieu, and because it unravels peacebuilders' challenges by unpacking the limitations of linear planning for peacebuilding engagement. Critical engagements from peacebuilding conversations with the concept of complexity are, to a large extent, informed by complexity theory debates. Whilst some are only loosely informed by such theories,[24] others contribute actively to theory building for peacebuilding along complexity theory lines,[25] or rely on peacebuilding empirics to contribute to new conceptualisations of complexity theory itself.[26] Whilst there is no singular theory of complexity but rather an assemblage of different approaches to complex systems, the perspectives engaged with here share a common interest in using the unpredictable nature of the outcomes of social processes as a starting point for continuous processes of experimentation and re-adjustment.[27]

Adapted from the natural sciences, complexity theory is one of several approaches that systematically addresses what a more organic engagement with the socio-political processes one identifies as post-conflict reconstruction and recovery may look like.[28] In this sense, complexity is defined not only as an analytical tool that enables us to 'investigate emergent, dynamic and self-organizing systems that interact in ways that heavily influence the probabilities of later events',[29] but also as contextual quality rooted in the chaotic entwinement of actors and processes. Complexity is tightly linked to the emergence and immanence of those non-linear effects that cannot be reduced to individual components or micro-dynamics,[30] and which have been offered as explanatory factors to understand phenomena which interfere with liberal peacebuilding agendas, such as resistance by local actors. Therefore, complexity accounts for the uncertain interactions between the components of a system which eventually develop into system-wide patterns.[31] At its core, this strand of complexity theory applied to human communities reflects a fundamental scepticism of universality, generalisability and predictability; yet on the other hand, it is also suspicious of the abstractification typical of certain post-modernist approaches which focus primarily on the role of linguistic constructions.[32]

Inspired by these postulates, the concept of complexity is used in several ways by critical peacebuilding scholars. Some, for example, use it to point to the limitations of linear process-tracing typical of peacebuilders' diagnostic approach to conflict resolution.[33] De Coning, for instance, uses the concept of complexity to point to a shift in how peacebuilding processes are seen, from something that is 'programmatic' to something that is 'essentially political'.[34] Here, the study of complex relational systems can shed light on how social systems respond to a variety of inputs, from the pressures of societal unrest, to the involvement of external actors.[35] Others rely on the concept of complexity to outline the resources available to agents involved in re-building societies after war. As Schwartz and Nichols point out, regenerated societies do not 'reinvent the wheel', and analysis of the creation of complex societies sheds light on processes which ensure the survival of pre-existing institutions that bleed into what these authors call 'second-generation states'.[36] Whilst one of the characteristics of complex systems is, arguably, the innate unpredictability of processes that makes it impossible for actors to identify general principles on the basis of which to affect the system, it is also this unpredictability that can help to shed light on processes of 'experimentation and feedback'[37] which give rise to adaptive qualities one often associates with the endurance of certain social or political orders. In other words, whilst many critics of peace-building consider 'unintended consequences' as the outcome of the processes of peacebuilding, of the encounter between international and local, and of the endogenous processes of re-conciliation after war, complexity is hereby used to push the envelope by reflecting on what these unintended consequences can tell us about the complex processes that birthed them.

Beyond these accounts, the importance of recognising complexity for peacebuilding is particularly embedded within the wider critique of the liberal peace. Though this has been largely examined elsewhere,[38] and though cri-tiques substantially differ in focus and methodology, the underlying concern running across these perspectives relates to the necessity to acknowledge the impossibility of reducing the complex socio-political dynamics of post-conflict milieus to a generic 'local'.[39] This, critics suggest, is what has con-tributed to the numerous failures of peacebuilding. Complexity then becomes a tool for critiquing simplistic peacebuilding praxis as well as to conceptually outline what makes top-down peacebuilding unsuitable for its own given aims of restoring peace to war-torn societies. As a whole, the bid to reflect on the complexity of societies emerging from conflict is one that is consistent with the wider attempt to engage more directly with the subjects of peace-building and, more specifically, in so doing, to 'facilitate a more realistic (i.e. closer to the reality of how the social world works) and open approach to analysis and action for change'.[40]

Complexity can therefore be deployed as an explanatory tool to cri-tique liberal peacebuilding, one which does not rely on linear reasoning to sustain its analysis of social reality, and one which also does not reduce interactions to human components. Rather, it examines the context as a self-organising whole that encapsulates actors' interactions as they evolve through contact with the environment within which they are situated and from which they emerge.[41] In sum, the focus on complexity in the context of the analysis of peacebuilding is, at its core, used to describe and engage with those 'real', messy and fluid, local processes,[42] without relying on abstraction, or on linear case and effect logics.[43] In this sense, the con-cept contributes to the debate of a more ontologically significant state of interconnected emergence, which has become recently acknowledged in the social sciences,[44] and which has brought about the end of linear peace-building as we knew it (not only the top-down, but also the locally-focused bottom-up). If the limits of liberal peacebuilding have become painfully clear to scholars engaging with its theoretical logic, the embracing of the rhetoric of complexity has also become evident at policy level. Follow-ingly, this section turns to examining how UN peacebuilding engagements seem to be gradually operationalising complexity-sensitive strategies in conflict-affected societies.

In line with the abandoning of linear causality and modern problem-solving logics at the theory level described in chapter 2, at the policy level, the UN seems to be gradually acknowledging the unreachability of social processes and developing practices increasingly more sensitive with the complexity of relations between a wide range of actors in intervened societies.[45] In the current context of multidimensional missions, the UN System Chief Executive Board for Coordination recently stated that coherence amongst actors in the UN system in the areas of peace, security, human rights and development represents a milestone in the process towards the 2030 Agenda, and is aimed at achieving effective responses to emerging complex situations, ensuring durable peace.[46] Notably, despite over two decades of UN peacebuilding efforts, results continue to be questioned.[47] As extensively covered in chapter 2, it is suggested that the implications of the limited results in achieving peacebuilding goals in the face of complexity go substantially beyond the issue of organisational efficacy. These problematic implications are in fact directly relevant to understanding the manner in which peacebuilding actors such as the UN have shifted towards acting on the basis of a complexity-sensitive strategy[48] and the effect this has had on our understanding of the agency of peacebuilding actors. Crucially, the UN peacebuilding apparatus seems to be gradually internalising new operational frameworks to meet this complexity, vagueness, uncertainty and non-linearity of developments in conflict-affected societies. The report 'The Challenge of Sustaining Peace', developed by an AGE for the 2015 review of the PBA in its 10th anniversary, is illustrative of the manner in how this shift has been conceptualised as well as operationalised in the face of the growing complexity of conflicts: 'After two decades of steady decline, major civil conflicts are once more on the rise. Worse, those conflicts have become more complex, increasingly fragmented and intractable.... A broader, comprehensive approach of 'sustaining peace' is called for, all along the arc leading from conflict prevention (on which, in particular, the UN system needs to place much greater emphasis), through peacemaking and peacekeeping, and on to post-conflict recovery and reconstruction'.[49]

In an analysis of this report, De Coning argues that the UN sustaining peace approach is based on three concepts: holism, that is, the idea that a system cannot be understood by its component parts alone but rather by its whole; non-linearity, the fact that causal patterns of interactions in a given context are non-linear; and self-organisation, the ability of a system to organise, regulate and maintain itself.[50] Holism reflects the lack of isolation of beings in conflict-affected processes and the relevance to sensitise with over-arching messy interactions. The AGE report reads: 'Improving UN performance in sustaining peace is truly a systemic challenge, one that goes far beyond the limited scope of the entities created in 2005 that have been labelled the "Peacebuilding Architecture"'.[51] As a result, the UN would not tackle war-torn contexts through separate departments, but rather through an organisation-wide strategy towards sustainable peace. A closer examination of UN involvement in the CAR exemplifies this trend. In April 2014, the DPKO deployed MINUSCA, established due to worsening security conditions in the country. This mission absorbed not only the DPA-led BINUCA but also non-UN engagements such as the AU-led MISCA and the French 'Operation Sangaris'. The UNSC established MINUSCA as a multidimensional peacekeeping operation aimed at protecting civilians, supporting the implementation of the transition process, facilitating humanitarian assistance, protecting UN personnel, promoting human rights, supporting the national and international justice and supporting the DDR and SSR processes.[52] Therefore, MINUSCA appears to be merging multiple peacebuilding dimensions in one single pole of operations, thus illustrating a form of system-wide, holistic engagement. Resonating with these accounts, a former MINUSCA officer stated during an interview that the integration of missions facilitates the operationalisation of a synergistic strategy that seeks to encompass political as well as security challenges.[53] Juncos elaborates on the UN 'integrated mission' concept by arguing that this type of missions has also shaped the understanding of comprehensive security in the frame of other international organisation such as the EU and the NATO, which increasingly seek to achieve coherence between a wide range of actors in diverse domains such as humanitarianism, development, security, migration issues or counter-terrorism.[54]

Additionally, the UN's current approach also seems to reify the trend identified by De Coning as 'non-linear temporality'.[55] This can be seen in the attempt to abandon the strategy of assigning singular temporal phases to individual departments.[56] Sustaining peace seems to open up the possibility for an ongoing systemic and non-linear engagement with neither strict objectives nor deadlines. In practice, as UNSG Guterres has pointed out on different occasions, the sustaining peace approach unveils the possibility of major organisational reforms such as the possibility to merge the DPKO, traditionally associated with the mitigation of ongoing violence, and the DPA, mostly in charge of conflict prevention and post-conflict missions.[57] Thus, sustaining peace seems to emerge from questioning of the linear problem-solving approach as the right way to establish durable peace, which is problematised in the following section as it overlooks the critical implications of growing complexity on the agency of peacebuilding actors.

In sum, alongside critical theoretical debates, the adoption of complexity-sensitive field programmes appears to be gradually settling down in UN policy frameworks. Nonetheless, declaring a progressive tendency away from linear peacebuilding and the shift towards complexity may not be sufficient to understand the implications for future developments in peace theory and practice. The next section examines how complexity in peacebuilding scenarios, conceptualised as the outcome of entangled relations between actors and processes, can enable a deeper questioning of the autonomy and purposefulness of external actors' agential condition.

PEACEBUILDING AGENCY IN ENTANGLED COMPLEXITY

In vein with the aforementioned context, complexity-sensitive analysis enables an engagement with the plethora of ways in which actors do not always necessarily pursue goals in a linear form, but often compromise, fold to, or co-opt elements of the other actors they unpredictably interact and relate with. Here, complexity helps us to see agents engaged in peacebuilding, such as the UN, as embroiled in uncertain, non-linear and entangled patterns of relations with other actors in a resulting increasingly complex scenario, the boundaries of which are constantly shifting and eluding categorisation. As a result of this, these peacebuilding actors appear to be less autonomous and purposeful agents with a telos and a goal to be reached, as they are captured by constant and unfixed practices of non-determined transformation, reinvention and adaptation.

In order to unveil a more conspicuous understanding of the transformation of agency as a result of this complexity in peacebuilding settings, it seems critical to reflect on the relational and entangled ontogenesis of actors in the peacebuilding milieu. As described earlier, complexity as a performative contextual quality of a given process stems from the uncertain and entwined interactions between actors and events. Here, relationality can be helpful to illustrate not only the genesis of complexity but also how the agential condition of actors is ultimately interrogated and compromised. As developed in the following chapter, scholars have increasingly elucidated relations between beings and events as constitutive parts of themselves, meaning that relations precede the very existence of these beings and events.[58] Relationality provides a deeper understanding of the nesting of social processes, of the co-emergence and co-constitution of all elements in any given context, suggesting that actors, environments and social processes are all fundamental components of one another and that, as a result of this, the process of becoming of all beings is always tightly linked to their entangled relational condition.

This insight speaks to the transformative and boundary-blurring effect of a focus on processes rather than individual actors themselves. Increasingly, as widely exposed in the next chapter, critical scholars of peacebuilding have illustrated the suitability of relationality as an analytical tool to enhance understandings of the nature and dynamics of post-war contexts.[59] Brigg, for instance, defines relationality in peacebuilding settings as giving greater importance to relations over entities by attending to the effects of interactions and exchanges.[60] Similarly, Martin De Almagro reads that a relational account is taken to mean a focus on the 'dynamic and ever-changing relationship amongst agents …, who acquire meaning through and are constituted by their transactions, connections and relations with other actors'.[61] In other words, in these perspectives, the focus is placed on the outcomes of non-linear transactions and entanglements between actors and processes to reach a more comprehensive understanding of the complexity of contemporary social phenomena, in which entanglements produce sharp and obvious unintended consequences, such as the 'local resistance' that critics of liberal peacebuilding have pointed out.[62]

Nevertheless, it can also be suggested that relationality's focus on undermining 'fixed endpoints, strategies and linear interventionary rationalities towards open-ended processes, non-linearity and adaptive tactics'[63] can also open up space for questioning the nature of the implementers' agency alongside that of the recipients of peacebuilding, nowadays widely accounted for. As Loode suggests, it has become increasingly clear that acknowledging complexity means accepting that complex relations cannot be instrumentally modified to suit a pre-established goal, as 'even sophisticated peace and conflict impact assessment cannot guarantee that particular programs and projects will improve the situation'.[64] This insight thus enables a deeper questioning of notions of autonomy and linear purposefulness of agents in any social and political context.[65] Drawing on this understanding of relationality, it is suggested that the growing unpatterned entanglements of beings in situated realities render actors unconceivable of as solely purposeful agents acting autonomously in their pursuit of goals in a linear and teleological way.

To be sure, the question of agency in peacebuilding settings has not gone unaddressed. Although most critical peacebuilding literature associated with the 'local turn' has primarily focused on articulating frameworks for interrogating the resistant (often hidden or marginalised) agency of local actors,[66] others have also sought to engage with the dynamics of the relationship between local and international, with particular emphasis on aspects related to colonial power asymmetries characterising the encounters.[67] Yet despite casting light on the tangible and material manifestations of power imbalances in post-conflict settings, this reconceptualisation of agency still do not shed their reliance on governmentality-affected teleological narratives, nor do they entirely abandon categorisations and boundaries, which are employed to trace the contours of rationalities of social control and exploitation. For instance, Jabri defines the concept of 'hybrid agency', defined in terms of an international civil service at large that functions to service the peacebuilding agenda and that blurs distinctions between the local and the international, and that is driven by a policing rationality the imperative of which is the government of populations and spaces. To this author, this form of agency speaks to a wider network enabling 'practices that view their target as populations to be governed'.[68] Whilst dispelling facile dichotomies between local and international, Jabri's conceptualisation of agency continues to ground the latter in the imperative, governmentalising and policing element that characterises and delineates the actors seen as part of the peacebuilding architecture. This approach embraces international and local discourses and practices and is qualified by its desire to enable further governance and constrain other forms of agency in the process, which are the expression of wider forms of contested politics. Without disavowing these critiques, this section attempts to move this conversation forward by hinting at the seemingly unnoticed effect that increasing entangled interactions between actors have in peacebuilding settings.

With the UN in mind, an adaptive form of agency can be understood as one which does not necessarily concern itself only with pursuing liberal goals, but one which is also fundamentally affected by its own relational nature. Crucially, this does not mean that actors do not possess normative goals, agendas or resources in a manner which is often unevenly distributed. Rather, their purposeful strategic goals are immanently and constantly trumped by an iterative complexity, rooted in uncertain relations, to the point of making the goals themselves vague, ever evolving and, very often, unreachable. Illustrative of how entangled ontologies render a fading agential capacity, when MINUSCA was deployed in the CAR, the African military and policy personnel who had been employed by the AU to serve at MISCA were simply re-hatted and became UN peacekeepers overnight.[69] This is indicative of the vulnerability of agency to ongoing entwinements, negotiations and collisions among a wide spectrum of actors, which erodes the autonomous condition of the agential trait. As Zanotti expresses, 'UN technical regulating and planning rationalities are deployed in situations of conflict where rules, plans, mandates and roles are continuously negotiated with diverging and competing rules, principles, mandates and contingent necessities'.[70] The author suggests that this form of seeing peacebuilding scenarios questions oversimplifications of the complexities of the interactions between political rationalities embedded in the plethora of agents. Host local actors, for example, represent a form of agency stemmed from the interaction between ideal aspirations and contingent possibilities in the messy milieu of all agencies' expectancies.[71] Agency becomes co-constituted in the circuit of a continuous relation, thus entering an uncharted territory with radical implications for future ethico-political disruptions.

Importantly, it is here emphasised that surpassing questions of representation very much common in social critique,[72] the complexity-sensitive analysis that renders actors' agency as continuously transformed is underpinned by the realisation of material entanglements as co-constitutive of the very same agency of these actors. As Law and Urry suggest, 'complexity-sensitive rationalities question the boundaries separating determinism and free will, as martial worlds are deemed unpredictable'.[73] Several contemporary authors have elaborated on the genealogy of the 'actor' and on the reconfiguration of the agency-will scheme beyond cultural criticism, emphasising the material constrains, human and non-human, that affect this equation. Drawing on a non-linear, quantum rationale to expound agency as the result of beyond-the-human semiotic-material entanglements, Zanotti hints that 'as entangled subjects, we may be able to induce change while not being able to over-determine it'.[74] Building on Barad's concept of 'externality within', developed in the previous chapter, Zanotti continues to suggest that quantum projections of entangled space-time horizons might open the possibility to reconceptualise the arguably independent world of which we seem to be separately part of. 'Agents are a part of phenomena within which they operate ontological cuts that "close" a range of possibilities. What "is" comes into existence as an effect of these ontological cuts'.[75] The author reinforces this observation by highlighting Wendt's statement: 'Agents are themselves emergent from interaction'.[76] All these assumptions, in sum, question the stories of the world as read through a human exceptionalist lens. When ontologies are di-hierarchised and the beyond-the-human is conceived of as potentially playing a critical agential role in the world, all that humans are left with is indeterminacy. Thus, Zanotti insists that 'humans cannot over-determine outcomes, but can take part in processes of mattering by navigating intra-agential cuts differently'.[77] Once endorsed that that world is entangled, non-linear, uncapturable, continuously reinvented, the creative possibilities for political agency are underpinned by the ontogenesis of material practices between actors and events.

The ethical implications of this radical assumption on non-deterministic forms of agency are highly sensitive and require careful unfolding and reasoning, as attempted in chapter 5. Latour's notion of distributed agency suggests that the actor 'is not the source of action but the moving target of a vast array of entities swarming toward it'.[78] The author continues to argue, 'The very word actor directs our attention to a complete dislocation of the action, warning us that it is not a coherent, controlled, well-rounded, and clean-edged affair.... Action is borrowed, distributed, suggested, influenced, dominated, betrayed, translated'. The actor thus seems to represent 'the major source of uncertainty about the origin of action'.[79] On a cautionary mode, Barad poses a thought-provoking question: 'Does this mean that humans have no responsibility for the outcomes of specific practices? … Does that mean that human subjects are merely pawns in the game of life, victims of the same practices that produce the phenomena being investigated? Are we not back to square one, to the Enlightenment ideal of the detached observer, the modest witness, who intervenes as needed, either wilfully or in accordance with some master plan, and when all is said and done stands back and watches what temporarily emerges?'[80] The author elucidates how, contrarily, it is precisely the modern liberal conception of the human subject the one that centres responsibility and accountability fully and deterministically on a wilful subject that has to be consequent of its actions. To this author, responsibility does not exclusively fall under the human domain. And although humans have a crucial, even constitutive role to play, the genealogy of this role remains nowadays uncertain.

To be clear, this account of agency in complex conditions is not aimed at providing a power-blind account of relational processes on the ground, nor at bridging the local-international dichotomy in order to improve practice, as is arguably the case for De Coning's 'adaptive peacebuilding'.[81] Instead, it seeks to lay emphasis on the effects of ungraspable interactions, which blur the boundaries between actors and their rationalities. At the same time, being cognisant of the material aspect of these entanglements is meaningful in contributing to an understanding of how the structures of power wherein peacebuilding takes place are shaped, along with the behaviour pattern of actors themselves. As such, complexity itself, through relationality, becomes a way to engage with performative agency, aimed to blur the ontological boundaries (rather than the descriptive ones) that are used to engage with actors and to offer a wider understanding of the menu of constitutive interactions available to them. In this regard, inter- and intra-actor relations can then be regarded as open-ended processes, constantly evolving on the basis of their mounting entanglements. In other words, this approach to complexity can enable re-engaging with the agency of actors as deriving from the iterative processes seen beyond the phenomena that actors of peacebuilding are reacting against, trying to manipulate, or trying to find some leverage to emancipate themselves from (as if these existed outside themselves). This is an essential element of enabling an analytical reflection on the effects of complexity that surpasses the recipients of peacebuilding alone. Whilst it is beyond the scope of this book to outline the practical implications of complexity, it is important to note that the contribution of such an approach would lie particularly in its potential to offer a more relational scenario in which agents constitute each other under unpredictable and emergent ex-changes.

In sum, the conceptual implications of re-engaging with the implementers of peacebuilding through a reading of complexity are clear. By deploying the concept of complexity beyond its common association with either the agency of resisting local actors, or as manipulated by intentional neo-liberal governmental power, complexity tells a rich story of actors affected by and affecting the very interdependencies they enact and experience. Whilst the previous sections have elaborated on how complexity has affected peacebuilding theories and practices, this section has moved this debate forward by arguing that complexity can open up space for contesting these narratives and enable the discussion to move towards a re-engagement with all agents in order to understand how complex scenarios affect and are enacted alike by implementers and recipients in interaction. Indeed, it can ultimately be argued that this also has major policy-oriented implications for actors such as the UN, currently seeking to focus on designing alternative practices and beliefs, more recently conceptualised by some scholars in the context of indigenous communities.[82] If complexity allows us to acknowledge the limits of knowing and affecting the world through purposeful action, this can usher in a position of epistemological uncertainty which ultimately disarms those actors who may have dogmatic and even manipulative tendencies.

The chapter has illustrated how hitherto efforts to reflect on the concept of complexity in peacebuilding have been limited in enabling a reflection on what this concept can tell us about the agency of peacebuilding actors in post-conflict scenarios. What is suggested is to look at the growing entanglement of interactions between beings (actors), to provide a nuanced reconceptualisation of the barely questioned purposefulness and autonomy of agency in these processes. More specifically, acknowledging uncertain and messy relations between actors as co-constitutive of their very essence binds agency with this relational condition. Therefore, these actors cannot be imagined as purposeful entities that can autonomously and teleologically pursue linear goals. This insight enables us to frame spontaneous relations between actors as potential triggers for international organisations' attempts to change their approach to engaging with the social realities of conflict affected territories. As these actors come to realise the extent to which their co-constitutive entanglements with other actors assert the impossibility of autonomous cause-effect linear action, this realisation, in turn, also affirms the non-reachability of early peace-affirming agendas and projects. The example of the agency of UN peacebuilders in the CAR, which is far from being purely intentional and teleological, is only a fragment of wider networks of actors and processes, reflecting a form of adaptiveness, identified here as relational in nature. Focussing on adaptiveness through a relational logic can be efficient in enabling analyses of peacebuilding policies in a wider sense, from those initially intentionally designed, to those of a purely reactive, immanent and contingent nature. A complexity-sensitive analysis that focuses specifically on entangled agency enables us to take centre stage without being prejudiced by the nature of the actor in question, albeit without foregoing issues of power-imbalances. This approach thus captures complexity as a frame in which actors and processes are constrained by their non-linear, relational and co-constitutive condition. In so doing, complexity-sensitive thinking has the potential to unpack the agential weakness of entangled actors, both peacebuilders and recipients alike, which seem surpassed only by the vagueness and unpredictability of developments in social realities.

Chapter 4

Entangled Peace and Its Limits

A world without relationality is a possibility for multiple worlds.

— Colebrook (2019:189)

Preceding chapters have delved into relevant contemporary peacebuilding debates through critically reflecting upon UN peacebuilding field instances under the assumption that beings and processes in the war-torn milieu, as well as in the broader world, come to be through a co-constitutive relation. The book has firstly engaged with the UN attempt to know, capture and engage 'the locals' in conflict-affected scenarios so as to achieve a better peacebuilding outcome. The limited results of the international organisation in this domain have exposed the misconception that the process of knowing involves an external subject that ventures to the encounter of an object waiting to be known. Instead, the process of knowing has been portrayed as materially entangled, meaning that the very being of actors continuously reinvents through their cognitive and experiential collision. Therefore, 'the locals' cannot be known as an 'out-there' objectified reality that the UN can include in the peacebuilding enterprise through a technical and materialised from of engagement. Second, this research has discussed the UN goal of attaining system-wide coherence as a conducive step to successful peacebuilding. The faultiness of observed UN peacebuilding missions seeking to achieve this strategic objective has been accounted for by suggesting that these interventive processes, framed in a broader set of events, do not unfold in a Newtonian, linear and progressive fashion. Drawing from philosophical insights that speculate over non-linear space-time framings, the second chapter has hinted that the unpredictable outcomes of the entwinements between actors and processes in these contexts invite to a reconfiguration of the notion of causality as well as the long-assumed linear and teleological unfolding of space-time framings in the world. Third, the text has examined debates on the agency of actors in the international peacebuilding project. By observing how UN peacebuilding practices problematically develop amidst a complex multiplicity of actors, who are in constant clash and negotiation with the UN, the book draws on complexity theoretical sensitivities to suggest that the entangled ontogenesis of actors and processes renders the agential condition of actors non-purposeful and vulnerable to their relational form of becoming.

Elaborating on the previous findings, the following chapter intends to push forward debates on peacebuilding as a relational event. Through the notion of entangled peace, which is underpinned by but not constrained to the entangled ontogenesis of actors and processes in the peacebuilding scenario, the text intends to interrogate and problematise some of the aspirations of critical debates immersed in the implications that the entwined condition of actors and processes has for peacebuilding theory and practice. As extensively expanded in the following lines, entangled peace is an invitation to think the entangled ontogenesis of actors and processes in the war-torn landscape beyond entanglement fetishism, founded on the deterministic assumption that, in the world, all things are either relational or are not at all. In doing so, entangled peace revolves around two main speculations. On the one hand, the entangled condition of actors and processes, reasoned through and observed in UN peacebuilding engagements, refrains from celebratory and transforma-tory claims, which could lead to normative and interventive arrangements aimed at shaping world relations. Rather, entanglements are projected as a burden of the being, as a dragging and exhausting condition, as an oppressive mechanism that renders beings and their form of becoming within the oppres-sive contours of determinism. In this sense, the future is not envisioned as an emancipatory configuration where lasting relations are enabled and enacted, but instead as a speculative framing where beings and processes have the possibility to break free from the entangled load.[1] To this end, resistances to entanglements are deemed worth of critical scrutiny and illustrative of a more accurate reformulation of the conceptual and material contours of the world.

On the other hand, entangled peace also problematises the hermeneutic effort by critical peacebuilding scholars in dissecting and interpreting what entangled ontology entails. Drawing from continental philosophy, most cur-rent accounts on entanglements think these as a genealogical trait of the being and invoke that relationality is an all-encompassing and universalis-ing equilibrium. In other words, all things are relational. Entangled peace embarks on the reading of the same philosophical trend from a different angle. For example, Whitehead argues that 'actual entities'[2], a concept that one could replace with beings or things, are not simply composed through relating to other actual entities, but beyond that they are atomically divis-ible *ad infinitum*. In the entangled peace account, the infinite atomisation of possibilities that eventually collide in a generative mode, namely unchaining further possibilities, is not indicative of a future restricted to an element of relationality. On the contrary, Whitehead atomises the encounter of all future events, including the entangled and the non-entangled. Otherwise, relational ontologies would be underpinned by the same exclusionary and elitist logics that a hypothetic utter non-relational world would be founded on. Seeking to shed light on this assertion, entangled peace, informed by debates and practices on the interactions between actors and processes in the peacebuilding milieu, intends to reimagine the world beyond the deterministic feature of fetishised relational accounts. The concept of entangled peace attempts to surpass relational supremacy[3] and embrace the indeterminate possibility for multiple worlds.

The chapter revises first a genealogy of entangled ontologies by engaging with classic and contemporary philosophers who have pioneered theoretical accounts on the relational ontogenesis of the being. Informed and inspired by these accounts, the second section recomposes and systematises previous critical observations from chapters 1, 2 and 3 to assemble the notion of entangled peace. More specifically, this part discusses scholarly debates and UN peacebuilding practices on the inclusion of 'the locals', the goal of coherence as conducive to more successful peacebuilding and the reconfiguration that agency goes through in the complex milieu of a multiplicity of deployed peacebuilding actors. The third section scrutinises some of the underlaying assumptions on the entangled ontological condition of beings in the peacebuilding scenario as well as in the broader world. Crucially, the notion of entangled peace in this final part of the chapter seeks to demystify entanglement fetishism by exposing the limits of relationality, which seems to unnoticeably operate in most debates as a deterministic burden that problematically reduces the events of the future to a relational form of being and becoming.

A GENEALOGY OF ENTANGLED ONTOLOGIES

The over-arching assumption underlaying the definition of entangled peace, informed by the critical scrutiny of UN problematic results in contemporary war-torn societies exposed in preceding chapters, acknowledges the entangled ontogenesis of actors and process involved in the peacebuilding enterprise. This ontological assumption, for which relations and interactions between humans and the non-human, both material and immaterial, are constitutive parts of themselves, originates in Western continental philosophy from the early twentieth century,[4] which openly questioned the Cartesian subject-object divide. Heidegger, pioneering the break from orthodox Husserlian phenomenology, which still surmised that the existence of the human being was a pre-condition for the existence of perceived worldly phenomena, eluci- dated the implications of questioning this dualist ontology. To Heidegger, the human subject is no longer a *sine qua non* condition for the existence of the beyond-the-human being. He became one of the first philosophers to theorise the possibility of the existence of things-in-itself (*da-sein*, German for 'there- being') regardless of the existence of human beings.[5] Most eloquently, the process philosophy or the philosophy of organism of Whitehead is the source that inspires and underpins to the largest extent the foundations of entangled peace. Elaborating on the critique of Cartesian subject-object dualism as well as the idealism of the Kantian and Hegelian mind-matter binary, this philoso- pher states that these modern accounts failed to explain the world as it is. To Whitehead, Newtonian and Cartesian empirical categories are not statements of the obvious, but tentative formulations of ultimate generalisations, which are rooted in speculative and imaginative statements that aim to explain the world.[6] Contemporary thinkers involved in intellectual movements such as critical realism, speculative realism and OOO, amongst others, have also dis- cussed the incapacity of modern Humean empiricism to access 'things', real- ity.[7] Famously, for Kant, the world emerges from the subject; for Whitehead, the subject emerges from the world.[8]

In Whitehead's cosmology, 'actual entities' are the nuclear 'things' that compose the world. In an explicit contestation to the Aristotelian 'primary substance', which argues that there is an ultimate substance which is perma- nent, these actual entities are atomic and infinitely divisible. By unravelling the origin of these 'actual entities', Whitehead expresses that they 'satisfy Spinoza's notion of substance: they are *causa sui*'.[9] In other words, all actual entities share the quality of self-causation. The ontological principle is that an 'actual entity' is a composite (term later used by Haraway), meaning that 'every actual entity in the universe is constituent of any other actual entity'.[10] He continues: 'Beings are constituted by their becoming and the nature of every being is a potential for every becoming'.[11] Therefore, in Whitehead, 'things' are not an eventual artificial essentialised state. Instead, things are their process of becoming, what he also calls events. These events are there- fore in continuous composition with other events, which are the true relata of relations.[12] In sum, in Whitehead's process philosophy, as in further con- temporary accounts outlined below, the continuous relations between things are constitutive of their very ontogenesis, and therefore they precede the very being.[13]

Endorsing these philosophical underpinnings, Deleuze, mostly inspired by the work of Spinoza, Leibniz, Whitehead and Bergson, builds his own corpus of theory around parallel conceptual frameworks, including assemblages, co-emergence and immanence.[14] In his comprehensive analysis of Spinozist philosophy, Deleuze associates the essence of every being with the relations 'it enters into composition with other things in existence'.[15] Therefore, things are always composed and decomposed in other things. Deleuze comments: 'An individual is thus always composed of an infinity of extensive parts, insofar as they pertain to a singular essence of mode, under a characteristic relation. These parts are not themselves individuals; there is no essence of each one, they are defined solely by their exterior determinism, and they always exist as infinities; but they always constitute an existing individual to the extent that an infinity of them enters into this or that relation characterizing this or that essence of mode; they constitute the infinitely varied modal material of existence'.[16] Unpacking this relational materialist ontology further, Deleuze argues through Spinoza that a body exists in two simultaneous ways. First, the body, regardless of its 'physical' size, is composed of an infinite number of particles and it is precisely the motions and rests between these particles what defines the individual ontogenesis of the body. Second, at the same time, the body affects other bodies and is simultaneously affected by other bodies. This quality of ex-changes and interactions is also a constitutive element of the individual being.[17] Ultimately, the world is a composite of individual particles that stem from the links at different speeds and slownesses between metabolisms, perceptions, actions and reactions.[18]

In pursuit of parallel philosophical considerations, Deleuze expounds, through Leibniz and, to a lesser extent, Whitehead, how relations are the basis for materiality, or what Leibniz refers to as monads: 'relations surge up in a region that … involves the possibility of creation.… The whole and the parts are not (and similitude) are not already related, but the original formula of a derived infinity, a sort of intelligible matter for every possible relation: thus the primary terms, without relations themselves, *acquire relations* by becoming the requisites or the definers of the derived, in other words, the shapers of this material'.[19] Resonating with Whiteheadian process philosophy, Deleuze insists that relations are themselves types of events, which, in turn, enter in relation with further events giving themselves a concrete existence in a continuous space-time framing.[20] Leibniz uses the notion of 'compossibility' (and 'incompossibility') in order to refer to the over-arching relationality between all possible worlds. More specifically, the incompossible defines the very prime, original and irreducible relation, whose genealogy is unknown to the human.[21] At this juncture, Deleuze attempts to make a distinction between Leibniz's monism and Whitehead's relationalism: 'For Leibniz, bifurcations and divergences of series are genuine borders between incompossible worlds, such that the monads that exist wholly include the compossible world that moves into existence. For Whitehead, on the contrary, bifurcations, divergences, incompossibilities, and discord belong to the same motely world *that can no longer be included in expressive units*, but only made or undone according to prehensive [creative] units and variable configurations or changing captures' (emphasis in original).[22] By critically engaging with these marginally distinct cosmovisions, Deleuze also argues for a world enabled and enacted by captures instead of closures,[23] which emphasise the creative angle of relationality as a metaphysical form of unleashing actuality and materiality.

Throughout his extensive productive academic venture, Deleuze, at times accompanied by his friend and colleague Guattari, exposes how every becoming in the world co-exists and co-emerges.[24] These French philosophers use a terminology that will later be adapted by contemporary authors like Latour, Haraway or Barad, for whom the process of worlding is founded on relational becomings: 'becoming-everybody/everything, making the world a becoming, is to world, to make a world or worlds, in other words, to find one's proximities and zones of indiscernibility'.[25] In Deleuze, the assemblages through which things become, transcend materiality (the strata), as they are composed both of semiotic systems, such as regimes of signs, and pragmatic systems, involving actions and passions. This semiotic-material conceptualisation of assemblages is conceived of on the basis of ontological reciprocity, meaning that both the semiotic and the pragmatic systems are co-constitutive of each other. To Deleuze and Guattari, this is the very prime division of every assemblage: 'it is simultaneously and inseparably a machinic assemblage and an assemblage of enunciation'.[26] Beyond material strata, certain expressions in the relational and assembled world shed light on incorporeal transformations that are also constitutive properties of bodies. By introducing the concept of the plane of immanence, the two philosophers emphasise the interconnected ontogenesis of assemblages.[27] 'There is a pure plane of immanence, univocality, composition, upon which everything is given, upon which unformed elements and materials dance that are distinguished from one another only by their speed and that enter into this or that individuated assemblage depending on their connections, their relations of movement'.[28] Thus, the plane of immanence stresses the composite genealogy of things in the world that come into existence in movement and association through various forms of energy. Like Spinoza, Deleuze reconfigures the particle-assemblage relation by accentuating the conception of the world as founded on the idea of a single fixed plane of immanence, which involves simultaneously absolute immobility and absolute movement. The plane 'is traversed by nonformal elements of relative speed that enter this or that individuated assemblage depending on their degrees of speed and slowness'.[29] In sum, this description hints at the infinite number of bits of tangible and impalpable matter that matters itself by entering into miscellaneous connections.

Over the past two decades, contemporary authors have extensively unfolded the grounds of relational ontologies building on the previous philosophical interventions.[30] In Latour, assemblages are never essentialised, but ongoingly remade, reworked, in transformation; therefore, they are performative, namely enacted through performance.[31] To this philosopher of science, who should be credited to a large extent for the recuperation of relationality thinking in the social sciences, earthly ontological relations are non-hierarchical, and relations between beings, humans and non-human, are processual co-constituencies, meaning that these relations precede the being, thus speaking to Whiteheadian philosophy. Following an analogous logic, Mol also discusses through the term 'ontological politics' the constitutive interactions between practices of 'the real'. 'Reality does not precede the mundane practices in which we interact with it, but is rather shaped within these practices'.[32] Therefore, this author's idea of politics underlines its generative and active relational mode, its co-shaping forces as well as its resulting open and contested character. Resonating with Whitehead's 'extensive continuum', developed in chapter 2, in Mol 'what is "other" is also within'.[33] Reproducing the self-mattering quality of reality, the author elucidates how alternative realities do not simply co-exist, but beyond this, they are found inside one another. Haraway, also crucial for the reconfiguration of material di-hierarchised entanglements in contemporary thought, argues that 'the body is always in-the-making; it is always a vital entanglement of heterogeneous scales, times, and kinds of beings webbed into fleshly presence, always a becoming, always constituted in relating'.[34] She figures that all beings in the planet strive to build attachments and to tie knots that bind the human with the beyond-the-human, which also resonates once again with the critique of Cartesian hubristic human subject-object separation. In her extensive body of theory, Haraway has insistently advocated for worldly encounters that surpass the essentialised form of the individual as well as the collective by demanding alternative practices of entangled reckoning.[35] To this author, things do not become in the world, but 'become-with', insisting, in a Deleuzian fashion, that 'ontologically heterogeneous partners become who and what they are in relational material-semiotic worlding'.[36] She contends that humans are not in a post-human stage, but in a com-post stage, in which critters, human and non-human, compose but also decompose each other, as in a Spinozist relational ontology.[37] As Barad contemplates in the arguably Whitehead-inspired notion of intra-action, relations are not mere forces through which beings and processes relate, but moreover they are constitutive elements of the very same beings and processes. To this author, as in Deleuze, this relationality involves semiotic-material components, as it is the entanglement between meaning and matter what eventually composes the real.[38] The following section draws on all these accounts, which affirm the co-emergent connectivity of beings and processes in the world, to systematise and assemble the critical reflections on peacebuilding debates and practices unpacked in previous chapters. Entangled peace constitutes the conceptual framework that encompasses these entangled sensitivities as a mode of seeing and thinking peacebuilding landscapes as well as the broader world. Beyond this, as elucidated in the final section, entangled peace pushes the debates on entangled ontologies forward by problematising some of the unquestioned assumptions behind the growing trend of affirming the relational condition of beings, which reduces the future to a deterministic and unescapable form of relationality.

ASSEMBLING ENTANGLED PEACE

Along the lines of the aforementioned endeavour towards surpassing cosmologies rooted in the supremacy of the human amidst the plethora of earthly beings and processes, over the past decade, a substantial amount of literature within International Relations, and to the interest of this book also within Critical Peace and Conflict Studies, have inquired into forms of thinking and seeing the theatre of the real that compromise long assumed and uncontested anthropocentric worldviews. This amalgamation of contributions has produced two major theoretical and practical outcomes. On the one hand, under the umbrella of what has become known as new materialism, among other similar theoretical configurations, some authors are rediscovering and exalting the agential role of the non-human in shaping events of the world, which overcomes the inert character ever attributed to matter and, in turn, erodes the primacy of the human as the starring actor in the planet.[39] For example, in a conspicuous analysis of the implications of revitalising the role that critical infrastructure plays in the context of protection and securitisation, Aradau suggests that security infrastructure is not opposed to or independent from people, but it is instead materialised in Barad's intra-actions between humans and non-humans, materialities and immaterialities. Seeking to surpass the arguable faultiness of the linguistic and social constructivist turn, this author engages with the crucial role of matter for theories and practices of security construction.[40] In a similar fashion, by carefully inspecting biographies, letters and further pieces from soldiers in three different conflicts, the First World War, the African conflict within the Second World War and Vietnam, Gregory elucidates how Enlightenment boundaries between culture and nature were persistently eroded in the context of war. While the military, through explosive violence, turned virgin landscapes in wrecked cartographies, forces of inhuman nature such as the rain, the cold, the sun, the mud and the mosquitoes yielded a dreadful militarised nature. As the author comments, what modernity contemptuously described as inert and raw matter, in the battlefield became deadly matter, thus determining the mode of becoming of the human in the warfare.[41] In this vein, with the Palestinian-Israeli case study in mind, Weizman argues through the concept 'politics in matter' that the built environment, the massive infrastructural systems and the environmental conditions, of a human or non-human origin, are not just the background of conflict. Rather, they constitute a fundamentally political space that enables and enacts processes of repression and domination.[42]

On the other hand, and intimately related to this first line of argumentation, other scholars are looking into the genealogy as well as the implications of the relations between the human and the rest of beings in its environment. In these accounts, relations are conceptualised as the rubric that precede the being. In other words, beings are mutually co-constituted through materialised entanglements, which render the human form of being vulnerable to and entwined with the non-human.[43] The notion of entangled peace is an attempt to stretch the theoretical and practical implications of this conversation on relationality and ultimately expose the limits of a fetishised and deterministic view on entanglements. In critical peacebuilding debates, some authors have emphasised the revelatory character of a focus on relations, interactions and ex-changes between actors and processes in conflict-affected contexts. Brigg, whose effort to introduce the relational turn in the peacebuilding debate is notorious, comments that 'historically, social analyses have drawn upon classical Newtonian understandings of the world, relying upon industrial and mechanical metaphors to develop linear, cause-and-effect understandings of social processes, including for influencing and programming social change. These understandings are increasingly complemented and challenged by ideas of complexity, networks, self-organising systems, and emergence- ideas that emphasise fluidity, focus on local-level interaction among agents within systems, and recognise that small inputs to a system can have disproportionately large effects and vice versa'.[44] By and large, the relational perspective in peacebuilding centres on the unpredictable negotiations between actors and processes in war-torn scenarios and, particularly, on what the outcomes of these encounters will be.

Brigg argues that these scholarly developments embrace a flatter ontology in which hierarchy is less important than openness and change.[45] In the extension of this flatter ontology, humans lose their privileged status as surveyors of the world, thus accentuating the critique towards the hierarchised human subject-object divide and even hinting at the relevance of the agency of non-human objects. The author asserts that relationality as an analytical tool entails giving greater conceptual importance to relations over entities by attending to the effects of interactions and ex-changes.[46] Like Whitehead, he stresses that relations bring entities and things into being. Accordingly, in light of this account, the prime position of a peacebuilder in a relational approach is the acknowledgement of the absence of authority and capacity of the individual to know the world over the recipient of peacebuilding, as that knowledge will be the product of ex-changes and interactions. Brigg therefore emphasises the need to recognise other forms of thinking, doing and knowing as constituencies of our forms of thinking, doing and knowing. Concerning the operationalisation of this relational sensibility in peacebuilding contexts, Brigg displays a sense of ambivalence. While acknowledging the potential of this approach to 'dehierarchise' power relations between stakeholders through the internalisation of a flatter ontology, he also warns about the risks of being sensitive and receptive to the unintended effects of non-human driven interactions, giving up the possibility of guiding the construction of peace and opening up space for domination by the powerful in a chaotic context.

Building up on all the aforementioned debates on entangled ontologies, entangled peace seeks to provide a useful tool to reimagine and speculate over generative and creative possibilities for actors to be and become in the war-affected milieu. Different to goal-oriented narratives revealing a path to successful peace, the following account embraces the incapacity to plan or predict the direction, ex-changes and outcomes of entanglements.[47] In entangled peace, the relational ontogenesis of actors and processes involves major implications both for how peace is thought of as well as for the practices of actors in the peacebuilding scenario. The following lines re-assemble the conceptual framework of entangled peace around the three major arguments unfolded in the previous chapters, where the problematic results of UN peacebuilding endeavours have been critically scrutinised through the entanglement lens.

The first major argument, stemmed from the analysis of the limited outcomes of the UN in knowing and engaging 'the locals' in the peacebuilding setting, suggests that entangled peace conceives of knowledge production as a materially entangled process between the observer/UN and the observed/'the locals'. Whiteheadian process philosophy, in which things are not things, but their processes of becoming things, speaks to the ontological assumptions unfolded in chapter 1, for which beings/actors cannot be thought of as isolated, essentialised and static. These actors are actually constituted by their entanglements with other actors. Informed by this account, entangled peace hints that the UN fault in knowing and engaging 'the locals' unveils a failure to think peacebuilding actors and processes as co-constituted by their encounter, which, in turn, leads to the undoing of hierarchical ontological cuts that distinguish between knowing subjects and known objects.[48] For example, as illustrated in the case of Sierra Leone, the UN seeks to include the local civil society in the peacebuilding enterprise as if this civil society was an externally graspable, capturable and manipulable objectified actor. From the entangled peace approach, neither the UN nor the local civil society are essentialised beings, but instead they reinvent one another in constant relation, as exemplified through the case of Memunattu Pratt, a relevant figure of the Sierra Leonean civil society by the time the PBC landed in the country in 2007. Pratt, with ties to a local university and a Freetown-based peace-building NGO, became so intimate with the UN presence in the country's peacebuilding efforts that was eventually appointed to the UN-backed Special Court for Sierra Leone, while still active in the local social civil society sphere. To be sure, this instance is illustrative of the manner in how actors do not have clear ontological cuts, but they are ongoingly transformed by their relational condition. In turn, hierarchies between actors are diminished, as their very form of becoming is co-emergent. In practical terms, this account renders useless the UN efforts to engage local civil society in a materialised form of inclusiveness. Instead, entangled peace invokes a sense of modesty in which actors recognise their interconnected, flat and non-hierarchical ontology and learn to live with the unexpected outcomes that emerge from their relational encounters.[49]

This ontological limitation, for which the UN cannot access and know the real as an 'out-there' objectified thing, is reinforced by apparent evidence of the UN limited results in knowing and including local civil society in the peacebuilding endeavour in Sierra Leone, as highlighted in reports,[50] interviews with experts and field observations. On the one hand, different critical accounts have stressed the flaws underlaying the UN failure in capturing an essentialised version of local civil society, such as the problematic PBF's National Steering Committee election of two civil society representatives, one from the WANEP and another from the Mano River Women's Network for Peace. This resulted controversial as many field practitioners argued that the chosen two were primarily urban-based actors, not representative of the grass-roots level, and that they had been hand-picked by the government. Overlooking the complex entangled genealogy of such an ungraspable and indefinable concept such as local civil society naturally results in troubling outcomes, including ethnic and urban biases, which were also reflected in the cases of Burundi and the CAR.[51] This performance illustrates how the UN intends to know the local civil society as an 'out-there' isolated and objectifiable actor that can be engaged from an ostensible outside.

On the other hand, commentators have also problematised the materialised form of engagement in the peacebuilding machinery that the UN seeks to pursue in host societies.[52] For example, the south-south learning process consisted of Sierra Leonean civil society representatives and election officials engaging in structured dialogue about the electoral processes with their Burundian counter-parts, thus aiming to enhance the electoral contexts of 2007 and 2010, respectively.[53] Beyond this initiative, UN peacebuilding experiences in Sierra Leone include further examples that reflect how the inclusion of local civil society is designed and executed on the basis of a materialised form of engagement, including the creation of the PBF National Steering Committee and the Truth and Reconciliation Commission, where local civil society was expected to play a significant role. Despite these efforts, several field actors reported during interviews the UN failure in engaging local civil society.[54] As the former commissioner of the Truth and Reconciliation Commission regretted, 'the PBC merely used the locals to receive inputs from the field, as a source of information on the ground level. But they should have involved them in the sense that they are part and parcel of the peace mission'.[55] This highly technical and materialised form of engagement pursued by the UN stresses the ontological limitations for which the organisation thinks local civil society as an objectifiable and manipulable object that can be externally engaged in an embodied peacebuilding process.

This form of knowing of the UN involves a hierarchical separation between the 'knower' (the UN) and the 'known' (the local civil society), which, in turn, is based on the Cartesian separation between subject and object. Resonating with Barad's account, entangled peace seeks to reframe the foundation of the modern epistemology underpinned by a hubristic version of a mighty human being that knows the world. Instead, and in line with authors previously referred to within critical peace and conflict studies, I seek to argue that 'the knower cannot be assumed to be a self-contained rational human subject. Rather, subjects (like objects) are differentially constituted by intra-actions'.[56] Danielsson, in an attempt to examine the problematics of the process of knowledge production in peacebuilding, argues that reframing knowledge as the practices through which beings are reified enables the possibility to shift from pre-existing actors, such as the local and the external, to a multiplicity of clashing constellations of actors and cognitive processes.[57] The concept of intra-action in Baradian philosophy, as introduced in chapter 1, reflects the Whiteheadian assumption for which relations precede beings. 'Relations do not follow *relata*, but the other way around',[58] meaning that entanglements are the constitutive elements of beings, which are never static or essentialised, but always on continuous processual mutual reinvention. She continues: 'Knowing is a distributed practice that includes the larger material arrangement. To the extent that humans participate in scientific or other practices of knowing, they do so as part of the larger material configuration of the world and its ongoing open-ended articulation'.[59] And on top of this, when UN peacebuilders intend to think, know and engage WANEP representatives in the peacebuilding process, this process of knowing cannot be disentangled from the connections that these 'locals' have with the immaterial practices that configure their form of living, including the mysticism of the 'bush', black magic and secret societies. All these interconnected material and immaterial elements conform the relata through which these 'locals' become actual, in Whiteheadian terms. Thus, the UN, in its attempt for cognitively capturing them, is becoming one more element in this semiotic-material circuit.

Eventually, these 'locals' and the UN are intra-acted, meaning that their processual ontogenesis is relationally co-emergent. In the field, the UN and the WANEP and its circles reinvent one another. This assumption debunks any possibility for a dualist, Cartesian and hierarchical process of knowledge production. As Barad puts it, 'Knowing is not a play of ideas within the mind of a Cartesian subject that stands outside the physical world the subject seeks to know. (...) Knowing is a physical practice of engagement'.[60]

The second major argument, prompted by the faulty UN endeavour towards a system-wide coherence as a conducive stage to successful peacebuilding, reveals that entangled peace invites to a reconfiguration of causality beyond modern linear space-time framings. As developed in chapter 2, in the assumption of the entangled genealogy of beings and processes, linear cause-effect relations are reconfigured. The following discussion intends to elucidate the potential of relationality to enhance the understanding of non-linear developments of actors and processes in peacebuilding settings. Reflecting upon the UN limited results to meet a strategic system-wide coherence in order to increase the efficiency of peacebuilding endeavours in Burundi, the text problematises the expectations of events in the world to unfold in tune with a Humean cause-effect linearity. Resonating with contemporary accounts that undermine the underlaying linear causality of space-time framings, entangled peace invokes a continuous and non-static conception of space in which events do not follow a linear progress, but instead they are unleashed by the entangle condition of actors and processes. Drawing on quantum physics, Barad notes in her agential realist account that classic notions of causation presume that events unfold sequentially. Rather, she suggests that causal structures are enacted through intra-actions, which do not only transmit a vector of influence, but, beyond this, they are co-constitutive of a reformulated notion of cause. 'Intra-actions effect what's real and what's possible, as some things come to matter and others are excluded, as possibilities are opened up and others are foreclosed. And intra-actions effect the rich typology of connective causal relations that are iteratively performed and reconfigured'.[61] In Barad's account on causality, which does not come without its detractors,[62] the emergence of events surpasses Newtonian space-time linearity. By instrumentalising quantum postulates, this author hints that events and things are not situated in a specific space-time coordinate. Instead, 'space, time and matter are iteratively produced and performed'.[63] In all, the notion of intra-action, by reframing the traditional concept of causality, opens up a reworked notion of possibility and change.

Several analysed sources on the UN peacebuilding missions in Burundi, including reports and interviews, illustrate the problematic of pursuing strategies as if reality unfolded in a linear manner. These accounts shed light on how unexpected events reconfigure the real and trump the pre-designed linear UN strategy. For example, the unforeseen expulsion of BINUB's ERSG by the Nkuruziza government in 2010, the dismissal of BNUB's security chief in 2014, the reported tensions on the ground between UN peacebuilders and local actors,[64] the intra-organisation turf battles as a result of conflicts of interest and leadership,[65] amongst other issues, expose the unfeasibility of operationalising linear strategies that follow a sequential programme. Most importantly to the entangled peace approach, these accidental encounters do not only hinder the UN goal of coherence on the ground, but on top of this, these unexpected entanglements between actors and processes recompose the co-emergent onto-genesis of these same actors and processes, including the UN, its internal bodies, regional actors, the host government as well as other local actors. Chandler argues that non-linear peacebuilding sensitivities represent a shift away from liberal rationalities towards a sensitivity with deeper and entwined social practices that eventually compose the overall peacebuilding outcome.[66] In light of this, causality is reconfigured as the outcome of a relational condition which renders the creativity of the future beyond determinist forms of causality.

In vein with this reimagination of space-time framings, entangled peace also points to a non-fix conceptualisation of space in order to accommodate more nuanced forms of understanding field developments in peacebuilding scenarios. the text problematises the UN peacebuilding endeavour in Burundi to enhance New York-based headquarters relationship with the country team as contemplating space as a void canvas that actors and processes fill with their performance. Reflecting upon the UN limited results on this strategic endeavour,[67] the book critically engages with the controversial policy response to these limitations, which presumes that the problem resides in ill-equipped institutional capacity and lack of protocols, amongst others. Instead, the entangled peace approach, inspired by the Whiteheadian notion of 'extensive continuum', unravels that space is the outcome of the entwinements between actors. Whitehead argues that the relatedness of the things makes up what we perceive as the spatialised world.[68] Therefore, space is not the background in which things exist or where peacebuilding happens, but it is actually potentially embedded in every being. Other contemporary accounts have also elucidated the concept of space as the network between relations and non-relations between objects.[69] This reconfiguration of space might have profound implications for the performance of actors in war-affected scenarios. Instead of seeking to deploy transformative missions, entangled peace suggests that this non-linear and continuous formulation of space opens up the possibility for peacebuilding practices beyond the normative and prescriptive rationale of emancipatory engagements constrained to the purposed of saving communities from a delimited spatial context. Imagining non-linear space-time framings allows for a focus on the negotiated and colliding encounters between actors and processes, from which the projected image of space emerges.

The third major argument underpinning entangled peace questions the autonomous and purposeful agency of peacebuilding actors amongst the complex plethora of deployed stakeholders in conflict-affected scenarios. In brief, entangled peace suggests that the growing messy interconnectedness of beings and processes in the theatre of the real erodes the agential condition of actors in the peacebuilding domain.[70] With the UN peacebuilding efforts in the CAR in mind, the deployment of a multiplicity of varied peace actors has illustrated how the quasi-chaotic field entanglements between them undermines their agency as a purposeful and autonomous feature. Instead, agency is revealed as an ongoingly changing constituency which does not necessarily concerns itself with pursuing linear goals, but which is also fundamentally affected by its own entangled ontogenesis. Importantly, this means that, although the UN has their own normative goals and programmatic agendas, their results are constantly hindered by an iterative complexity stemmed from unpredictable entanglements. In light of this, UN goals become in practice vague, even unreachable. Drawing on complexity theory accounts, the peacebuilding scenario is presented as an assemblage of messy, fluid and unpredictable processes. As an analytical framework, complexity entails a sense of contingent openness and multiple futures, unpredictable outcomes in space-time as well as non-linear changes in relationships between living beings and objects. Thus, complexity-sensitive thinking unveils an emergent, dynamic and self-organising entanglement of systems that influences the development of later events. In sum, non-linear effects cannot be reduced to their individual components, as they are shaped by inter-component, uncertain relations.[71] Complexity thus seeks to push forward an already ongoing conversation about ontologically interconnected emergence.[72]

In the case of the CAR, UN peacebuilding efforts to overcome field complexity, illustrated by an unprecedented number of deployed peacebuilding actors, were mostly materialised through the promotion of a holistic and multidimensional approach aiming to improve inter-actor relations in the peacebuilding setting. The establishment of MINUSCA in 2014, which sought to merge country-wide peace efforts in one single pole of operations, is a clear example of this tendency. As Juncos suggests, this form of integrated missions ultimately seek to overcome field complexity by achieving coherence amongst UN agencies and departments but also with external actors.[73] The UN sustaining peace approach, which has been significant in the UN framework to manage the situation in the CAR, resonates with the endeavour to accept and internalise that compartmentalised field divisions, such as preventive strategies (before the conflict), peace enforcement (during the conflict), peacekeeping (when violence is over) and peacebuilding (long-term lasting peace), are unfit to the vagueness and complexity of developments in war-torn scenarios.[74] Notwithstanding these efforts, various accounts, including reports and interviews, have outlined the limited results of the UN in managing complexity in the CAR.[75] This faulty form of peacebuilding presumes that lasting peace results from the ability to manage a complex network of interdependencies which include local, governmental, regional and international actors.

Resonating with complexity accounts but at the same time pushing it further, entangled peace argues that the complex entanglement of actors and processes in conflict-affected settings ultimately affects the autonomous, free and purposeful agency of these actors. In a thorough analysis of stakeholders' agency in peacebuilding, Zanotti argues that agency 'is not the quest for a pristine freedom by a subject that is ontologically independent from, and inevitably crushed by, power. Instead political agency is the result of one's position within social relations. It is constituted within a series of uneven, agonic, situated responses to contingent conditions that in turn it transforms'.[76] Through observing the role played by NGOs in peacebuilding scenarios, this author suggests that agency is based on a 'continuous negotiation between ideal aspirations and contingent possibilities',[77] involving a wide range of actors such as international donors, regional actors as well as local stakeholders. Resonating with Barad's account, Zanotti also hints at a reconfiguration of the space that actors occupy, which is not a fix and static void. Instead, it becomes ambiguous and transformed by the task actors carry out in ongoing and entangled negotiating practices.

Thus, entangled peace through the reading of complexity enables a reformulation of agency beyond the existence of an essentialised actor that can purposefully intervene in an outside world. Through the example of the UN in the CAR in its endeavour towards overcoming complexity to achieve durable peace, it is argued that the entangled ontogenesis of actors and processes, which accentuates complexity, allows for a recognition of the limits not only of knowing but also of performing in the world. More specifically, the entangled peace account undermines action as the result of a linear and purposeful original force. Rather, action is rendered unpredictable and ever associated with the entwined character of actors and events in the conflict-affected milieu, thus debunking the intentions of actors, such as the UN, which have a dogmatic and interventive ethos. In sum, the example of the agency of UN peacebuilding in the CAR is only an instance of a wider array of networks that reflect the non-essentialised character of agency. The way in which entangled peace instrumentalises the complexity lens enables an analysis of peacebuilding theory and practice by centring stage without prejudging the agential trait of a given actor, albeit without foregoing and ignoring power-imbalances. In so doing, complexity-sensitive thinking has the potential to unpack the agential vulnerability of all actors involved in the peacebuilding event, which seem surpassed only by the vagueness and unpredictability of entwined developments in social realities.

ENTANGLED PEACE AND THE LIMITS OF A RELATIONAL WORLD

Resonating with aforementioned entangled ontologies, peace itself is hereby reformulated as a process constituted by its entanglements with further processes. In other words, peace is not an isolated and essentialised phenomenon, rather it is a composite of a broader milieu or, in Whiteheadian terms, of an 'extensive continuum'. In this present planet-wide order, which some have referred to as the Anthropocene, for the manner in which human action debunks geological forces,[78] challenges are unusually interrelated, thereby problematising rigid categorical boundaries and compartmentalised levels of analyses such as state-centrism. From the stagnation of war in particular regions to climate-related menaces, massive refugee waves, the rise of xenophobic movements, the protraction of endemic poverty in particular countries, the reproduction of patriarchal violence, the unknown implications of neuroscientific progress, the exponential advance in artificial intelligence, the Revolution in Military Affairs and the expansion of tele-war, amongst other challenges, dealing with the interrelatedness of these issues increasingly entail abandoning traditional forms of governance and prioritising constant re-adaptation and experimentation.[79]

Recent cross-disciplinary developments in the humanities are inquiring into the position of the human in the world and, more fundamentally, its relations with the rest of the real.[80] These conversations speculate over creative and durable forms of being entwined with other beings, human and non-human, in the age of a conceivable doomsday. The affirmation of the messiness, interconnectedness and complexity of the Anthropocene age has reinforced the aforementioned accounts on entangled ontologies. Over the past ten years, a vast number of scholars have recognised the mutually constitutive ontogenesis of worldly human and non-human entanglements, thus undermining the Eurocentric hierarchical relation on which human beings have based their understanding of progress: humans have always conceived of the world as if it was theirs, positioning themselves at the top of the hierarchy of life.[81] This form of progress, profoundly rooted in the Western liberal tradition, has been reduced to disturbance-based ecologies, consisting of the using up not only of natural resources but also non-human living species to extinguishing levels. The similar struggle for survival that humans, non-humans and objects unexpectedly face in the Anthropocene has stirred a growing number of scholars to question the dominant ontological position of the human being in the world. Elucidating the concept of the natural contract, Serres depicts the world as the result of an inextricable assembly between the peoples and their environment, their context. The author suggests that, regardless of the violence that has hitherto characterised human-world relations, the natural contract offers a reason for peace and transcendence that surpasses human-centrism.[82] 'We must indeed place things in the center and us at the periphery'.[83]

In an attempt to unpack this omnipresent interrelatedness, Bennet describes globalisation as the realisation of the world as a space of associated events, which are 'intimately interconnected and highly conflictual'.[84] This author utilises the concept of assemblage to capture this knotty amplification of world processes: 'Assemblages are ad hoc groupings of diverse elements, of vibrant materials of all sorts. Assemblages are living, throbbing confederations that are able to function despite the persistent presence of energies that confound them from within'.[85] Bennet hints at the effects generated by assemblages as emergent properties that might unleash creativity beyond the simple sum of the vital force of each materiality within the whole. Along similar lines, by critically elaborating on James Lovelock and Lynn Margulis definition of Gaia, namely the complex composition of all earthly elements in a lively, autopoietic and coherent wholeness, Stengers argues that the concept of Gaia portrays an assemblage of relations presuming two implications. On the one hand, Stengers stresses the facet of Gaia on which we depend, usually identified with an 'out-there' given, stable and fix context, and which is the result of the co-emergence and co-evolution of the entangled stories of earthly elements, from the human to microorganisms. On the other hand, Gaia, beyond a mere addition of processes, is also recognised as a 'being', 'it is not just endowed with a history but with its own regime of activity and sensitivity, resulting from the manner in which the processes that constitute it are coupled with one another in multiple and entangled manners, the variation of one having multiple repercussions that affect the others'.[86] Thus, interrogating the notion of Gaia is ultimately appealing to an arguably autopoietic system that holds together, and the becomings of its constitutive parts might indeed result in unexpected outcomes that can critically affect the whole.

Inspired by and resonating with these accounts, the affirmation of an entangled ontology of peace comes alongside the collapse of human exceptionalist foundations. The entangled peace approach acknowledges that peacebuilding is a process whose genealogy is co-emergent with other processes, unveiling, amongst other aspects, the vulnerability of the human in the face of the current worldwide challenges of the Anthropocene, with which the project of peace is intimately related. Nonetheless, without disavowing the plethora of narratives on entangled ontologies, this text also intends to spread a word of caution about some problematic implications of what the book refers to as entanglement fetishism, namely the blind worship of relationality as the very prime condition for possibility. Illustrative of this fetishised trend of relational thinking, Kurki even suggests thinking relations without things, thus rendering the very existence of the theatre of the real subjected to the relational condition of the universe. In her own words, 'relations are every-where in that "everything" is made of multiple relations and every "thing" in relations is situated in them specifically. Relations of various kinds "shoot through" "things" and "levels" we imagine to fix them'.[87] In response to this noticeable proliferation of entanglement literature, practices and sensitivi-ties, contemporary accounts have problematised entangled ontologies from various angles. Recent academic trends such as OOO and Speculative Real-ism question the ontology of relations as being intrinsically constitutive of entities. Openly criticising Whitehead, Latour and Barad, to Harman, these accounts escape the consequences of full-blown relationism trying to unsuc-cessfully balance everything.[88] From this perspective, processual entangle-ments do not belong to the relata; instead, they belong to the relation, which is defined as a short-lived object.[89] 'Relata are individuals, however transient, with an innate consistency. These individuals have a certain durability that is by no means permanent'.[90] As Harman clearly exposes, whatever meets these criteria is an object. Harman also argues that relational accounts like ANT reduce actors to their mutual effects on one another. These approaches 'reject the notion that compound entities are new things-in-themselves rather than just transient relational events'.[91] To this author, the world is not the composi-tion of beings and events in mutually constitutive interaction. Rather, objects in the world are 'autonomous and enter in relation only in special cases'.[92] The contribution stemming from these anti-relational postulates sustains that accidental encounters in the world have the potential to create new objects independent from a relation between two or more objects.[93]

Within the area of critical peace and conflict studies, Bargués observes a growing appreciation 'of how entanglements of human and nonhuman popu-lations, which were previously hidden or neglected sources of agency, have creative potential'.[94] To this author, critique surpasses the inner contradictions and the limits of a given order and settles the recognition of complex worldly 'assemblages and feedback loops as enabling forces'.[95] In a cautionary note, the author warns that by assenting and affirming the entangled world as it is, these accounts might risk 'reproducing neoliberal logics of precariousness and socio-economic inequality'.[96] In this vein, a close examination of the ontology of difference as an analytical framework to conceptually capture peacebuilding events conduces Joseph to hint that co-emergent, di-hierar-chised, flat ontologies risk overlooking power relations and thus reproduc-ing troubling social orders. He continues to argue that social structures are constantly absent in relational ontological arguments. To him, relationality is important but not without an analysis of the social and material relations that contribute to the production of (ontological) differences.[97]

Pushing these critical accounts, entangled peace seeks to expose the limits of the supremacy of entanglements as a condition for possibility. Appreciative of the value of entangled ontologies and without disavowing their philosophical and political underpinnings, it is suggested that relations are problematically inscribed in a celebratory and emancipatory narrative and practical enterprise, after the attainment of which actors in liveable relations are going to endure in harmony until the end of times. In entangled peace, entwinements are not intended to be depicted from this arguably normative perspective. Instead, relations are simply read as ineluctable and inexorable. As Shaviro suggests, the human fundamental condition 'is one of ubiquitous and inescapable connections. We are continually beset by relations, smothered and suffocated by them'.[98] Entangled peace conceives of entanglements in tune with Shaviro's description of relations as 'oppressive'. Inspired by Whitehead's search for adventure and peace, this author asserts that the ultimate metaphysical question is how to escape these deterministic and overdetermined relations, thus 'finding space that is open for decision'.[99] In the peacebuilding milieu, this oppressive relational burden often becomes an insuperable hurdle to those actors and processes resisting the UN totalising project, as extensively exposed in the following chapter. Therefore, I seek to emphasise the possibility for unleashing and actualising a generative force and a creativity in the world surpassing celebratory revelations of entanglement fetishism.

Moreover, in the journey towards problematising the determinism of linear causality, which seems allegedly overcome by entangled ontological foundations, the entangled peace approach invokes a modest word of caution. Along the lines of Colebrook's reluctance to the supremacy of relations, the overestimation of entanglements conceals an embedded moralism rooted in theological assumptions, which privileges relational forms of becoming over the possibility for ontological solitude, where the being bears on relation to anything. To this author, invoking the entangled genealogy of beings and processes in the world is a form of avoiding the very prime ontological question, namely what is the 'being', without being in relation? In her own words, 'relations are rendered fully immanent in theories of emergence, where there is no foundation to the world – no Absolute, no humanity – other than an ongoing complexity arising from relations among less complex terms'.[100] Colebrook warns that by reducing the existence of beings to an entangled ontogenesis intensifies the normative stress on life, being and becoming as relation. Thus, to this author, imagining a world without relationality enables the possibility for multiple worlds, hence surpassing normative claims.[101] Anything beyond this scheme seems to be ontologically exclusive.[102] In conclusion, the revelation of the immanent ontological interconnectedness of the world as an analytical frame that surpasses the human-centred teleological form of being in the planet seems compromised. Assuming that relations configure an all-encompassing commonality actually reproduces a similar exclusionary, deterministic and elitist logic to that of linear, progressive and totalising ventures of modernity, as illustrated by the UN peacebuilding telos.

Far from the celebratory and deterministic character of a large part of literature inclined to an unquestioned fashion of entanglement fetishism, the notion of entangled peace sees conflict-affected scenarios as the point of encounter of a multiplicity of world-making possibilities, including the relational and the non-relational. Although aware of the lack of conciseness of this claim, any other affirmation would fall once again under modern normative and deterministic modes of seeing, thinking and living in the theatre of the real. Whilst entangled peace recognises the value of sensitising with the relational ontogenesis of actors and processes in the peacebuilding arena, it also admits that entangled ontologies do not seem to overcome the problems of exclusion characteristic of the anthropocentric project of modernity. As developed in the following chapter, this entanglement fetishism might materialise in yet one more distory, namely a story that obliterates the possibility for dissenting alter stories to thrive. Entangled peace intends to eschew this intensification of universalising differences, which have been made explicit in the UN peacebuilding misadventures in the several observed post-conflict cases. The text invokes instead an alternative reading of relationality. To be precise, entangled peace, drawing on the Whiteheadian affirmation of the infinitely atomised divisibility of future possibilities,[103] does not evoke a reductionist conception of a relational peacebuilding setting and, by extension, a relational world. On the contrary, the book hints at a radical openness of the future, where the realm of experience is composed of multiple colliding and generative worlds, where the collapse of the entangled and the non-entangled becomes the prime condition for possibility. The following chapter, through introducing the UN totalising peacebuilding distory, engages with these rather provocative affirmative ethico-political disruptions by projecting the clash of indeterminate events as a speculative configuration of an uncelebrated and non-deterministic world.

Chapter 5

Peacebuilding distories and the Ethical Quandary

[Ethics] is about facing what we cannot control and living -or dying- in the process of willing what we cannot control, willing the event without ressentiment, affirming the events with which one is bound.

– (Grosz, 2017:153)

Entangled ontologies have been presented as a suitable formula to capture the messiness of entwined developments amongst actors and processes in peacebuilding settings as well as of the interconnected complexity of world challenges more generally. Notwithstanding the limits of positionality of a deterministic mode of thinking an entangled form of becoming, in recognising the relational ontogenesis of beings and events in a war-torn milieu, entangled peace seeks to reinforce efforts towards the erosion of the hierarchical Cartesian (human) subject-object binary on which the modern, anthropocentric and liberal form of human progress has been founded. Acknowledging the entangled condition of human beings makes them weak, vulnerable, dependent on other things which, likewise, are ongoingly in mutually constitutive relation with other things. Thus, entangled peace invites to a sense of modesty and opens up the possibility to turn conflict-affected scenarios into instances of generative forces and creativity, where entangled forms of being, thinking and living are enabled beyond the violence of modern, exclusionary and universalising configurations.

By critically reflecting upon the limited UN peacebuilding outcomes in knowing and including 'the locals', achieving a system-wide coherence and overcoming the complex interaction between a multiplicity of actors in the war-torn milieu, previous chapters have unravelled several implications informed by entangled ontologies, including the unattainability of an epistemological formula through which the UN can know the 'locals' as an 'out-there' isolated, objectified and essentialised collective actor. Instead, the process of knowing has been described as materially entangled and mutually constitutive between the artificially created 'knower' and the 'known'. In addition, entangled peace has revealed the flaws and contradictions of expecting events in the world to unfold in a sequential cause-effect linearity. Through the entangled ontologies assumptions, the articulations between cause and action as well as space-time framings are profoundly reconfigured. Finally, entangled peace has expounded how the growing knotty complexity of conflict-affected scenarios, which stems from the embedded entangled genealogy of actors and processes in them, questions the hitherto taken for granted notion of the autonomous and purposeful agency of participants in the peacebuilding enterprise.

As a corollary from all the aforementioned contexts, the following chapter attempts to unveil potential ethico-political disruptions in tune with entangled peace and its limits. First, the text unveils the implications of the UN disregard of the entangled ontology of actors and processes in the contexts where peacebuilding missions are operationalised. Rather than self-reflecting upon the limited results of its strategic goals and genuinely exploring new forms of thinking, seeing and doing, the UN 'blames' the host society and seeks to transform it so that it can fit UN peacebuilding parameters, which is introduced below as a totalising endeavour. It is suggested that totalising UN peacebuilding practices impose distories, namely stories that have prevented alter stories in host societies from thriving. Second, the chapter exposes practices of storytelling as a political disruption aimed to disseminate a form of thinking the world as a complex interconnected ecology. Thus, storytelling interventions present themselves as potential enablers of durable entanglements. Finally, the chapter hints that certain invocations for ontological formulas projected from storytelling methodologies reproduce deterministic forms of being and becoming in the world. Resonating with the limits of entangled ontologies discussed in the previous chapter, entangled peace draws from Spinozist ethics, and their affirmative character rediscovered in contemporary readings, to speculate over how ontology and ethics are inextricable, meaning that ethics should not comprise rationalities on how the world should be, but on how the world is, including all forces, movements and negotiations that compose the cosmos as a multiplicity of possible worlds.

UN PEACEBUILDING DISTORIES

Throughout chapters 1, 2 and 3, the book has sought to illustrate different problematics underlying UN peacebuilding endeavours which, it is suggested, can be made sense of by revealing the lack of sensitivity of the organisation

with the entangled ontogenesis of actors and processes in the war-torn scenario. Neither the UN peacebuilding efforts towards knowing and including 'the locals', nor the UN goal of achieving a system-wide coherence in
peacebuilding settings, nor the management of the complex array of actors
in the conflict-affected scenario have had optimistic results. Beyond these
reflexive considerations, underpinned by documentary data, interviews and
field observations, a further element prevails across these debates, namely the
UN assumption that the host society is somehow the explanatory factor for
these failures. As developed in the following lines, to the UN, in most occasions, the host society is ill-prepared, unable or unwilling to accommodate
the peacebuilding mission, thus becoming a hurdle for the overall success of
the peacebuilding process.

The discredit, weakness, division and poor organisation of local society in
post-conflict contexts has been repeatedly used by the UN as justification for
its limited results. As the 2015 AGE report states, 'Civil society has a critical
role to play. But in societies emerging from conflict, civil society is rarely
well organised in its capacity to articulate demands. Indeed, it too may be
divided, diverse and fragile. And it will likely be dominated by elites, either
from within diasporas or from within the country, who are generally more
"fluent" in the discourse of international development and diplomacy'.[1] On
different occasions, UN peacebuilding officers, including a former PBSO
officer on the one hand, and a former DPA chief for the CAR on the other,
stressed that civil society is often so highly politicised[2] and weak[3] that, first,
it is a difficult actor to work with and, second, it makes it difficult for the UN
to approach it. While the same PBSO officer for the CAR adds that whenever
a civil society-based organisation is strong enough to engage with the UN,
they are often too close to the government and, therefore, too politicised,[4]
the former DPA chief for the CAR continues, 'civil society in CAR is very
difficult to work with, they are very weak ... because they don't have the
capacity, because they don't know what it is to be civil society, they lack the
culture of being an organised civil society.... They haven't reached that level
of maturity yet, so there is a lot that needs to be done in terms of capacity
building of civil society'.[5]

To the UN, these apparently vernacular flaws make it more likely for
local peacebuilding actors to be manipulated by local elites. Beyond that, the
ill-prepared character of host societies prevents them from exhibiting impartiality, independence and representing itself when engaging in post-conflict
processes. As an expert on Burundi commented, one of the key reasons for
this lack of impartiality is that civil society was motivated by remuneration.[6]
In a report from 2011, the PBC notified that civil society representatives had
expressed dissatisfaction with their priorities not being considered when the
UN was deliberating and designing PBF's projects in the CAR. Nonetheless,

these complaints were addressed by the UN by highlighting that the civil society was not organised and lacked capacity to unite their complaints into one united voice.[7] To the eyes of the PBC, a hierarchical and exclusive dichotomy then arises: the 'good' and the 'bad' civil society.[8] It seems that, for the UN, there is a sort of civil society that has inherent elements which prevent it from being part of the UN peacebuilding system. This limited engagement in peacebuilding settings is conceived of as 'their' failure ('their' weakness, 'their' politicisation etc.) but never through a self-reflection on the perceptual ontological limits constrained by the narrow and static conceptualisation and formal and materialised form of engagement offered to host societies. Thus, the UN peacebuilding apparatus seeks to delegitimise and mould the local civil society so that it can eventually be 'fixed' and can accommodate numerous programmes, including the supervision of security-oriented reforms, political dialogue, democratic electoral processes, good governance, equitable access to justice, transitional justice mechanisms, promotion of human rights, gender issues, socio-economic recovery and development, amongst others. As Vogel asserts, 'International support steers civil society discourses and fosters the adoption of global agendas, thus making civil society part of a transnational governance process rather than a counter-voice to it'.[9] The normative and liberal democratic character of these projects and agendas unambiguously reveals a willingness to perpetuate a modern, liberal and capitalist story in conflict-affected societies absolutely on the margins of non-modern forms of living.

Inattentive to the entangled condition of beings and processes and unreflective of the ontological limitations of the modern cosmovision to explore new forms of thinking about peacebuilding realities, once the host society has been delegitimised and blamed, the UN seeks to mould and instrumentalise this host society until it becomes totalised in the UN modern parameters.[10] By ignoring the potential of thinking about the peacebuilding context as a set of relations and ex-changes that compose beings and process in a self-organised system, the UN peacebuilding apparatus is accordingly annulling alter forms of knowing, imagining and creating. Totalising is thus a process associated with the capacity of an actor to produce a homogenised episteme and supress different forms of being and becoming. Drawing on Feyerabend's criticism towards totalising and controlling discourses, Wark defines totality as the result of a top-down causality, countering the bottom-up collaborative understanding of the (human) being in the Anthropocene, which refuses the affirmation of linear and modern causal processes as a valid formula of understanding earthly encounters.[11] This totalising behaviour of the UN peacebuilding setting towards local society in these war-torn countries resonates with Morton's assumption that 'modernity banks on certain forms of ontology and epistemology to secure its coordinates'.[12] The UN peacebuilding apparatus intends to totalise the complexity of the host society so that it fits the global agenda and becomes engaged in a liberal, linear and modern episteme.

Scott famously introduced the notion of 'high modernity' as the face of Enlightenment aimed at the erasure of pre- and non-modern modes of being, thinking and becoming in the planet. To this author, modernity behaves as a homogenising rationality that reduces and simplifies the cartographies of places and their forms of knowledge production so as to turn these vernacular stories in governable, controllable and mouldable beings.[13] Analogously, the UN seems to be an inherently exclusionary apparatus/wholeness that has formal requirements for foreigners to be included in the system. Like Scott, different authors have elaborated on modern homogeneous systems that base their existence on the absorption of external parts that will have to adapt to the parameters of the whole in order to be engaged. As Haraway puts it, the parts are caught by the 'seductions of the organic wholeness through a final appropriation of all the powers of the parts into a higher unity'.[14] Similarly, the UN peacebuilding apparatus seeks to absorb and add up in the entirety of its homogenised nature any incoming element from the outside. Far from rethinking this ontological limitation, seeking different forms of seeing these contexts and reconsidering the expectations from interventions in their engagement with local actors, international interveners tend to reinforce their top-down approach from below rather than encouraging local alternatives.[15]

Pushing the discussion on totalising and erasing processes further, the text here draws attention to the implications behind the imposition of externally-led modern orders, systems and settlements and, particularly, on the way these stories are being told and projected by the all-encompassing and exclusionary cosmology. All stories need to happen or be imagined before being told. On top of that, it is suggested that there is a different kind of story, what is defined in this book as a distory, namely a story that undoes other stories. Distories erase the possibility for other stories to become. Distories prevent other stories from thriving. Distories delegitimise, confront and annulate other stories. In this sense, this book is about possible worlds of the past which never came into being. It tells the UN distory to consolidate lasting peace in war-torn societies whilst systematically ignoring, suppressing and preventing endemic stories from enduring. These semiotic-material peacebuilding distories are eventually portrayed in this chapter as the telos through which the UN secures its own modern distory, thus preventing alter stories from blossoming, manifesting and lasting. Through a detailed account of UN peacebuilding missions deployed over the past fifteen years in the post-conflict landscapes, the text has intended to unveil how the UN designs, operationalises and monitors political strategies that clash and obviate the idiosyncrasy of these host societies. it is suggested that the rationale lurking behind this interventionist framework responds to the burden of securing the expansion of modern distories.

Illustrative of the notion of distory with the UN as starring role is, albeit in the domain of science fiction, the case of the UNOMA (United Nations Office for Martian Affairs) in the context of the colonisation of Mars, as masterly narrated by Kim Stanley Robinson in his masterpiece 'The Mars Trilogy'.[16] The purpose of using science-fiction to illustrate what a distory entails is far from unintentional. As discussed in chapter 4, things in the universe are ontologically inaccessible and thus reality is always unreachable through the means of human logic.[17] 'Reality cannot be wholly presented *in-itself*, be it through language, images, or algorithms, and so what we are presented with is always already fictional'.[18] Therefore, one might assert that any attempt by humans to know the world is always founded on a composition of fictions. Even science, as Whitehead expresses, is a mere, though sophisticated, approximation to reality, an 'imaginative generalisation'.[19] Robinson instrumentalises the enabling creativity of science-fiction to critically narrate a UN totalising distory. Confronted with the possibility to unleash a new form of being and becoming for the human in Mars, UNOMA resolves and is determined to terraform the recently colonised planet. The violence exerted by UNOMA officers against those resisting and contesting the terraforming project and vindicating that Mars should be let become its own way, is analogue to the inattention, disregard and even eradication of vernacular local stories triggered by UN peacebuilding ventures in conflict-affected scenarios. In other words, UN peacebuilding distories trigger the death of other stories. The UN protocols, peace agendas, programmatic strategies and their operationalisation in the field, which are, as exposed earlier, fundamentally rooted in the liberal regime of thought, nurture the expansion of deathwork, in Preciado's words, 'necropeace'.[20] UN-led necropeace practices have obliterated the stories of those who could not keep up with the pace of the totalising wholeness, the stories of the little ones, the stories of the deviated, in sum, the stories of those elements, human and non-human, material and immaterial, whose modes of being and becoming in the planet were never articulated around the modern phantasies of universalising epistemologies, colonising expansion, limitless progress, extractive economic regimes and disturbance-based ecologies.

Envisioning the peacebuilding milieu as the outcome of countless unpredictable entanglements between actors and process ultimately entails a micropolitical disruption with potential to resist and erode the totalising wholeness of peacebuilding distories. As Deleuze and Guattari express, 'There is no history but of the majority, or of minorities as defined in relation to the majority'.[21] The majority, from which the wholeness is projected, is taken as the referential point to make and tell the distory. These authors critically engage with the idea of history as a materially situated wholeness, contingent on a fix space-time framing, and that excludes anything falling off this territorialised scheme. 'Nomads have no history'.[22] History is always the history of the whole, illustrated at times through the figure of the state and its appropriation of the war machine to secure narrative dominance of the all-encompassing wholeness.[23] Instead, to Deleuze and Guattari, 'Every becoming is a block of coexistence'.[24] They insist that 'the nomad exists only in becoming, and in interaction; the same goes for the primitive. All history does is to translate a coexistence of becomings into a succession. And collectivities can be transhumant, semisedentary, sedentary, or nomadic, without by the same token being preparatory stages for the State, which is already there, elsewhere or beside'.[25] History is thus captured as a totalising mechanism to secure a teleological form of being, which overlooks any becoming that materialises outside linear temporality and territorialisation. The following section illustrates how contemporary literature has increasingly instrumentalised storytelling practices as a means of projecting and enabling entangled earthly stories, thus surpassing the exclusionary framework of the modern fantasy. Wary of the violence of this distory, the entangled peace approach intends to speculate over the possibility for a future composed of a multiplicity of worlds, as exposed in the last section.

THE POLITICS OF STORYTELLING

In vein with Deleuzian generative and co-emergent becomings in the world, proliferating practices of story-telling, or what some have called the ethics of story-telling,[26] are expanding across various disciplines as a way of making a different history and speculating over possible futurities.[27] Tsing hints that ' "history" is both a human storytelling practice and that set of reminders from the past that we turn into stories'.[28] Most importantly, the exercise to assemble bits of the past is deemed a determinant possibility to surpass a human-centric cosmovision, by recognising the role of the beyond-the-human as a source of erosion of the apparently almighty Cartesian human subject and its ostensible agential centrality in world history. 'To participate in such entanglement, one does not have to make history in just one way. Whether or not other organisms "tell stories", they contribute to the overlapping tracks and traces that we grasp as history. History, then, is the record of many trajectories of world making, human and not human'.[29] By similarly invoking for the materialisation of a multispecies planet, Haraway uses the notion of 'speculative fabulations' to describe 'stories in which multispecies players, who are enmeshed in partial and flawed translations across difference, redo ways of living and dying attuned to still possible finite flourishing, still possible recuperation'.[30] This author's form of storytelling seeks to enable connections that matter (in both senses).[31] To Haraway, storytelling is underpinned by the practice of 'thinking-with': 'It matters what thoughts think thoughts; it matters what stories tell stories'.[32] Through the fictional Chthulucene character, for example, the author recapitulates how the human, the more-than-human, the other-than-human, the inhuman, the human-as-humus are reconfigured through entangled myriad temporalities, spatialities and assemblages. In her account, 'Practices are activated storytelling'.[33] Ultimately, the Harawayan endeavour concerns itself with entwined forms of living and dying in a planet in the face of threatened habitability.

Without disavowing the radical political breakthrough offered by these storytelling sensitivities, entangled peace intends to move this conversation forward concerned with an element of determinism embedded in the projection of stories of a beyond-the-human, liveable and interconnected world, the limits of which have been exposed in the previous chapter. As Viveiros de Castro suggests, the question here is not to romanticise and anthropomorphise beyond-the-human agencies, but instead to sensitise with a modest understanding of alter perspectiveness to debunk the colonising unidirectionality of anthropocentric forms of knowledge production.[34] Entangled peace as a method of thinking, imagining and projecting peacebuilding events and the broader theatre of the real seeks to enable speculative interventions to configure and materialise forthcoming entwined multiple worlds beyond the elitism and determinism of a future entanglement-sensitive human experience.[35] Instead, far from normative and emancipatory forms of story-telling, the text hints here at a radical openness of the future, an order constituted by the collapse of all possibilities, relational and non-relational, stories and distories.

Storytelling might indeed foster the reconfiguration of space-time framings beyond the teleological and deterministic unfolding of phenomena. 'Events do not just happen one after the other in a random sequence; rather, they are connected to one another, and they affect or cause one another in a range of ways. Story is about the weaving of those connections, either in the recounting of events (storytelling) or simply in one's own "storied experience" of the world',[36] Van Dooren suggests. Entangled peace has sought to argue for the possibility of speculating over war-torn scenarios as processes in which peacebuilders are freed from unreachable linear, goal-oriented strategies and deterministic forms of intervention, which have resulted in limited achievements, stagnated fragility and a generalised anxiety for both external agents and recipients. Grosz shows in her reading of Deleuze that 'problems – the problem of gravity, of living with others, of mortality, of the weather – have no solutions, only ways of living with problems'.[37] Internalising the possibility of not having to solve problems and instead thinking ways of living and staying with them questions the modern understanding of an ever forward and progressive existence on earth, which is a teleological form of seeing progress that goes hand in hand with the hubristic modern historical project.

As an example, the book has also argued how over the recent years, international political actors deeply embedded in the modern coordinates such as the UN are surprisingly showing a growing sensitivity towards non-linear forms of pursuing their strategies. As exposed in chapter 3, the UN recent approach on sustaining peace establishes a new framework for UN peace engagements. Amongst other aspects, peace engagements under the sustaining peace approach would surpass temporary stage-based intervening sequences, meaning that conflict would not be 'temporalised' and divided into pre-, during and post-conflict.[38] In practical terms, this would imply the merging of different departments at the institutional level, such as the DPKO, traditionally associated with interventions in contexts of ongoing violence, and the DPA, most of the time in charge of political and peacebuilding post-conflict programmes. Nonetheless, I have problematised the manner in which the UN is seeking to conceptualise and operationalise sustaining peace as a post-peacebuilding framework of engagement. In short, despite the UN seeming attempt to move towards non-linearity, to the organisation sustaining peace is simply one more strategy ultimately aimed to overcome the complexity of the field, which again presumes a teleological form of being in war-torn scenarios. Rather, entangled peace suggests that non-linear temporality requires a reconfiguration of cause-effect configurations, agential conditions and expectations from the future.

From entangled ontological sensitivities, the linear and teleological idea of history and time is intimately reformulated, which has already been done elsewhere.[39] Similar to Whiteheadian considerations of space, developed in chapter 2, time is not an external property of the extensive continuum, but instead emerges from beings. Whitehead elucidates how 'there is time because there are happenings, and apart from happenings there is nothing'.[40] As 'actual entities' become through intra-actions with other actual entities, 'time would be expressible in terms of the relations of a bit of matter with itself'.[41] He later elaborates on this idea: 'Time is the prevalent misconception that "becoming" involves the notion of a unique seriality for its advance into novelty. Mankind made an unfortunate generalization from its experience of enduring objects'.[42] He goes on to assert that 'recent physical science' (in reference to quantum physics) has abandoned this understanding of time. He follows: 'We dwell critically upon the mass of fables termed history. As a result, we conceive of ourselves as related to past or to future by a mere effort of purely abstract imagination, devoid of direct observation of particular fact. If we admit this conclusion, there is no real evidence that there was a past, or that there will be a future'.[43] As the philosopher goes on, 'The ultimate devil of the temporal world ... lies in the fact that past fades, that time is a "perpetual perishing" [in reference to Locke's concept].... Why should there not be novelty without loss...? In the temporal world it is an empirical fact that process entails loss: the past is present only under an abstraction'.[44] These interventions allow for stories to become in a non-teleological form, thus questioning the sequentiality of time. 'The process of becoming towards novelty is not to be constructed taking for granted a unique seriality for its advance'.[45] Thus, Whitehead stresses the inconsistencies of a deterministic, linear and unique form of understanding time.

In this vein, contemporary authors are increasingly rethinking and repro-ducing non-teleological forms of understanding time. Delanda's reading of Deleuze's Chronos contends: 'Just as objective space is not an inert con-tainer but affects and is affected by massive objects, so objective time is not receptacle for events, but is affected by them'.[46] Most prominently, Barad acknowledges that 'faith in the existence of singular determinate origin and unilinear nature of time itself (the fact that only one movement exists at a time) is waning'.[47] Like Whitehead, Barad argues that 'quantum physics not only deconstructs the strict determinism of Newtonian physics, where the future unfolds predictably from the past, but it also blows away the pro-gressivist notion of time ..., disrupting first-world efforts to harness it as a totalising system on behalf of universalism and its projects, such as imperi-alism'.[48] For humans, linear and teleological historical narratives have been the pretext to a form of progress based on a process of hierarchisation as a result of which earthly resources, organic and inorganic, have been brought to the edge of extinction. In this line of reasoning, as it has been emphasised throughout the book, entangled peace provocatively affirms that there are no goals to be externally reached through rigid external guidance and direction. As Bennet clarifies, 'There is no goal because these directions are themselves created 'along with' the act that runs through them'.[49] In other words, forms of becoming in the world are entangled and mutually constitutive, and never the outcome of a linear, teleological course. For storytelling practices, this has critical implications for the way in which 'time', particularly future time, is speculatively thought of. Drawing on a quantum conception of time, Kirby hints that 'the future isn't so much the unfolding of supplementary moments *in* time, moments whose difference is secured by the distance from an origin now left behind. Rather, the "future" would more accurately reflect the ori-gin's complex identity, its discontinuities or differentiations *with/in itself*'.[50] This messy absence of sequences through which to imagine future stories is embedded in the foundations of the entangled peace approach, which, as exposed in previous chapters, invokes for a reconfiguration of modern space-time framings.

Resonating with accounts on non-modern forms of mediating the theatre of the real, Grosz argues that arts, and all its aesthetic expressions, aim to restore continuities and connections between beings, not aiming to totalise them as religion or modernity would attempt, but enabling them to become, to elaborate their own becomings.[51] Grosz continues to elucidate, through Nietzsche, this argument: 'The more science, especially, the physical sciences, explain matter and its organization in the universe, the more it tends toward art; the more science gains in "truth", the more it loses in objectivity'.[52] While science and reason reveal the world as a set of elements and events in a fixed container evolving constantly and linearly onwards in response to universal deterministic laws and generalised social behaviours, 'indeterminacy also makes life possible'[53] and, beyond positivist science, registers such arts bring in imaginative and speculative possibilities of becoming. As Ruyer would put it, in Grosz's reading of this philosopher, 'Ontoaesthetics address the creativity of the world and the openness of the future'.[54] She continues to argue that the indeterminacy of this directionality to the (yet-to-become) future is precisely what questions the so far unchallenged teleological historical narrative and the linear and limitless path towards human progress: 'Finalism does not articulate a final state or stage, an end or telos but a trajectory of continuing elaboration/transformation, not to something, an ideal, but from something, that is, a becoming'.[55]

Thus, it is suggested that storytelling practices in tune with the aforementioned considerations speak to the cornerstone of entangled peace, a rubric that attempts to surpass celebratory, emancipatory and deterministic constraints. In the book's appreciation of the UN limited results in peacebuilding processes examined in previous chapters, it is suggested that UN problematic performance is not a problem to be solved, but the expression of a potential form of being and becoming based on the awareness that the embedded relationality of actors and processes enable communities and their political ecologies to creatively turn problems into new opportunities, 'a shift to imagining alternative ways of perceiving and responding: understanding problems as emergent and interactive processes that are invitations to grasp the world in richer and more complex ways "from the inside"',[56] as Chandler states. Beyond this, through the entangled peace reading of storytelling practices, these 'problems' the UN encounter are the sign of a call for allowing alter stories to emerge. Thinking with Le Guin, Tsing concludes by recognising that the ultimate ethos of stories is that they should never end, but to lead to further stories.[57] In the following section, the text critically discusses a form of ethics that eschews normative and deterministic formulations, thus suggesting that entangled peace is an invitation to a cosmovision based on the affirmation of the future as the collapse of all possibilities, beyond exclusionary ontological cuts.

THE ETHICS OF ENTANGLED PEACE

The currently expanding transdisciplinary trend towards entanglement fetishism, namely the resolution to tell the story of the world as an outright interconnected wholeness, has been problematised in this book on the basis of similar allegations of determinism against modern, linear and liberal rationalities as well as their forms of being in the planet. As Colebrook suggests, storytelling interventions projecting an entangled world resemble modernity in its attempt to produce a single mode of humanity resulting from a generalisation that only sees relations from a very particular point of view of a very particular history. In her own words, the whole entanglement thinking has 'shored up a quite specific Western, European, rationalist morality of the world: humanity is, properly, that which can recognise itself in all the rich cultural variants that make up one interconnected and self-aware whole'.[58] Along these cautionary lines and modestly sceptical with all-encompassing entangled configurations, entangled peace intends to offer a lens to see the world as the collapse of all possibilities, entangled and non-entangled, relational and non-relational, in other words, stories and distories. In a Whiteheadian mode, this radical openness towards the future is not conceived of here as a surrender to the violence exerted by world distories, but as the affirmation that the world is the composite of an infinite array of possibilities, the atomised divisibility and collision of which cannot be constrained to any normative, deterministic and therefore restrictive force. From this, the determinant endeavour towards projecting and enabling a world of an entangled (and solely entangled) ontogenesis would make the whole framework of entanglements fall under the same exclusionary logic as semiotic-material distories, for instance, modernity. The ethics of entangled peace exposed in the following lines intend to embrace entanglements, relations and collisions beyond these elitist parameters of exclusion.

The ethico-political implications that the text intends to associate with the entangled peace approach are rooted in a long and renowned tradition of thought pioneered by Spinoza, whose popularity resurged in the twentieth century through the comprehensive work of Deleuze. In Spinozist philosophy, as Deleuze dissects, ethics surpasses moral systems of judgement and reactive actions aimed to purposefully transform an 'out-there' world. Instead, ethics assembles immanent modes of existence whose ultimate ethos is to perpetuate their relational processes of becoming, enduring and thriving.[59] Indeed, relations, assemblages, composites and entanglements play a critical role in the Deleuzian reading of Spinozist ethics, for which 'an act is bad whenever it directly decomposes a relation, whereas it is good whenever it directly compounds its relation with other relations'.[60] Therefore, there is not bad in essence but always in reference to the outcome of a relation.[61] In other words, good and bad are always the reflection of encounters.[62] In this vein, Nietzsche declares that all beings instinctively seek for those relational conditions which will allow them to reach an 'optimum' state, and beings will even use their power to overcome any external intrusion or hindrances (in Spinozist terms, 'bad relations') that obstructs the path to this 'optimum' state,[63] which supports the idea of the world as the outcome of the clash between stories and distories. In Spinoza, the moral order, sustained on the attempt to universalise and homogenise a human behaviour and a system of values which are projected from a Eurocentric lens, is overcome by immanent orders that are continuously recomposed through the negotiations between the elements in the world. The philosopher unpacks three human components that constrain the outcome of these negotiations: 'Our singular eternal essence; our characteristic relations (of motion and rest) or our capacities for being affected, which are also eternal truths; the extensive parts, which define our existence in duration and which pertain to our essence insofar as they realize this or that relation of ours (in the same way that the external affections fulfil our capacity for being affected)'.[64] In sum, when modes of existence encounter one another, either one deteriorates the other or they mutually reinforce their own preservation. Resonating with entangled ontologies accounts expounded earlier in the book, to Spinoza ethics have nothing to do with morals. What matters instead are the compositions, forces, speeds, 'capacities for affecting and being affected on this plane of immanence'.[65] The key implication of Spinozist ethics is the impossibility to know beforehand whether an action is good or bad, as this will depend on the outcomes of the relations that the action involves. Hence, Spinoza warns that the fundamental ethical question is the study of the relations, entwinements, assemblages and tensions, which determine the capacities for things to affect or being affected.[66]

In contemporary conversations, particularly in non-anthropocentric new forms of materialisms, Spinozist and Nietzschean ethics have noticeably influenced the so-called affirmative ethics.[67] Illustrative of this ethical intervention, Braidotti defines affirmative ethics as 'a collective practice that acknowledges the passing and dying of multiple universes, grounded in embedded and embodied materialists practices'.[68] This author emphasises that our selves are bonded by ontological relationality and that 'affirmative ethical forces are capable of increasing our relational capacity (*potentia*)'.[69] With the UN peacebuilding endeavour in mind, the text argues that entangled peace is ultimately aimed to speculate over the creativity embedded in the future of conflict-affected scenarios, enabled by infinite possible collisions between actors and processes. In Braidotti's words, 'The ethical idea is to mobilise the active powers of life in the affirmative mode of *potentia*. This actualises the cognitive, affective and sensorial means to cultivate degrees of empowerment and affirmation of one's interconnections to others in their multiplicity'.[70]

Beyond moralistic and universalising formulations, ethico-political disruptions operate from this account as 'experiments with intensities that need to be enacted collectively'.[71] Resonating with the aforementioned annihilating implications of UN-led distories, Braidotti cautiously explains that assemblages as portrayed in the frame of affirmative ethics cannot be equated with colonising encounters or relations that eliminate situated differences. Beyond liberating and emancipatory frameworks, affirmative ethics require an utter reconfiguration of the dealing with pain, vulnerability, weakness and soreness. Negativity is sought to be turned into generative force, not on the basis of a categorical moral imperative, but from the recognition of the co-emergent immanence of human and non-human ecologies.[72]

In vein with this affirmative sensitivities, entangled peace upholds a mode of ethics that neither assumes an external world in which the human can intervene from a separated standing point nor endorses an all-encompassing normative morality of entanglements that should guide the human performance. Rather, the ethics of entangled peace delve into a reconfiguration of action and responsibility. Building on the ethical facet of intra-actions, Barad elucidates that 'ethics is not simply about responsible actions in relation to human experiences of the world; rather, it is a question of material entanglements and how each intra-action matters in the reconfiguring of these entanglements, that is, it is a matter of the ethical call that is embodied in the worlding of the world'.[73] In tune with Spinozist parameters, 'ethics is therefore not about right response to a radically exterior/ised other, but about responsibility and accountability for the lively relationalities of becoming of which we are part'.[74] Interestingly, this author detaches responsibility from the human, not in an exculpatory manner, but as a form of outlining that, first, there are no agents that can deterministically and freely act in the world and, second, 'accountability and responsibility must be thought in terms of what matters and what is excluded from mattering'.[75] Again, reformulating space-time framings and, more specifically, the notion of 'externality within' are crucial in Baradian ethics, where entangled ontology and ethics, both semiotic-material presumptions, blend.[76] ' "Do I dare disturb the universe?" is not a meaningful question.... There is no such exterior possibility where the contemplation of this possibility makes any sense. We are *of* the universe-there is no inside or outside. There is only intra-acting from within and as part of the world in its becoming'.[77] Therefore, the ontology of the world is inextricable from ethicality, as all happenings and process of mattering do not pre-exist the encounters from which they stem. 'The world and its possibilities for becoming are remade with each moment'.[78] The ethical call thus consists of speculating over and materialising lively possibilities of being and becoming. This entwinement between ontology and ethics has been defined by Grosz as onto-ethics. To this author, also inspired by Spinozist ethics, 'good is what is useful to our being and our ability to become more, and evil is what inhibits us to the point of our becoming less'.[79] Again, detouring from moralistic assumptions, good and bad depend on the extent to which an encounter enhances or diminishes the capacity of a thing to exert the power to endure in the world. Accordingly, ethics implies acknowledging that we cannot have control about how we live and die. To Grosz, onto-ethics is not so much about how the world should be but how the world is, and affirming the events with which one is bound.[80] The entangled peace account on speculative ethics hints that being sensitised with entanglements does not entail a normative endeavour towards determining a very exclusive form of (entangled) futures, rather it simply invokes that the world is the arrangement of an infinite multiplicity of colliding possibilities, which hinge on unpredictable and uncertain forces that enact all encounters.

In all, the affirmation of the entangled ontogenesis of beings and processes disables any possibility for intervening *in* the world, for the boundaries between the subject and an 'out-there' world fade. Critically, this withinness of the world renders intrusive and transformatory political action non-sensical, unfeasible. Thinking otherwise entails repositioning the subject in a superior mastery agential level, which would reproduce once again the modern hubris that prompted, among other instances, the UN peacebuilding project since its inception. Along these lines, entangled peace projects conflict-affected scenarios not as a space where a specific desired form of change should happen, but as a space where indeterminate change always unfolds regardless of the illusory existence of an external intervening actor. In her suggestive reading of Levinas, Rose describes 'connectivity ethics' as 'open, uncertain, attentive, participatory and contingent.... Call-and-response, like life and death, are two types of events, co-present, shaping and making each other'. This reconfiguration is 'foundational to world making in a life-affirming awareness of uncertainty and connectivity'.[81] Enlightened by this rather provocative redeployment of ethics and triggered by the observations of UN field missions, the organisation seems to conceive of peacebuilding as an imperative moral that has to be settled by an autonomous and purposeful human actor that can intervene in a given, exteriorised milieu. Mindful of how problematic this might be, in light of all the aforementioned contexts, the text seeks to call for reconsidering that ethics also implies 'let be'.[82] As this form of ethics suggests, the underlaying rationale of ethico-political disruptions invoked by entangled peace responds to letting alter futures be, surpassing and shrinking from the violence of deterministic, normative and exclusionary totalising distories. The above discussion has exposed how the UN peacebuilding system, far from self-reflecting upon its limited field results and more broadly its exclusionary worldview, intends to delegitimise, blame and eventually mould host societies so that these can eventually fit UN's totalising political project, deeply embedded in the foundations of Enlightened modernity. This distory, which erases the possibility for alter, vernacular stories to thrive, has been compared with certain elements within entanglement fetishism positions, from which the world is deterministically portrayed as the outcome of relations between humans and the beyond-the human. As a word of caution, this chapter has hinted that seeing relations and the all-embracing connectivity of the world as the motto for an emancipatory political project reduces entangled forms of storytelling to one more exclusionary and totalising distory. Instead, the notion of entangled peace has attempted to articulate a mode of ethics that embraces the future as the collapse of an endless clash of possibilities, entangled and non-entangled, thus surpassing normative and deterministic ways of being, thinking and becoming in the world.

Conclusion

Along the lines of a growing amount of literature in the discipline of International Relations and beyond, this book has unfolded an exploratory adventure aimed at examining the potential of entangled and relational sensitivities as an analytical framework to capture peacebuilding events. Informed by relevant contemporary debates within the area of Critical Peace and Conflict Studies, the affirmation of the entangled ontogenesis of actors and processes in the war-torn milieu has exposed a particular reading of the UN limits to achieve an essentialised, objectifiable and 'out-there' version of peace. The notion of entangled peace begins with the assumption that beings and events in the peacebuilding setting, and by extension in the broader world, are mutually constituted through their relational condition. Crucially, relations precede the relata, which are not essentialised beings, or what Whitehead calls 'actual entities', but continuous processes of becoming. To be sure, what relates is not beings, but these processes of becoming, or events. This processual ontology through which entangled peace thinks, sees and experiences the world entails, first, a radical reconfiguration of the genealogy of beings, which are actualised through a multiplicity of negotiated unpredictable encounters, and second, a profound reformulation of space-time framings, more specifically, the manner in which events unfold *not in, but with* them. While chapters from 1 to 4 have comprehensively dissected the nuances of entangled peace as a worldview, chapter 5 has reformulated the underlaying ethos of the UN peacebuilding phenomenon as a distory, defined in the book as a story that undoes, erases and obliterates other stories, namely alter world-making possibilities beyond the UN modern totalising endeavour. On top of that, this final chapter has also delved into speculative ethico-political disruptions to be and become in the world in tune with entangled peace formulations. Notwithstanding the valuable contributions of entanglement-sensitive thinking in providing a radical mode of reading earthly events, the text has attempted to push these debates by exposing the limits of what the book has defined as entanglement fetishism, namely the celebratory and rather deterministic projection of the world as an all-encompassing interconnected durable wholeness.

The appreciation of ontology as a condition underpinned by entanglements between beings and processes of the world has been presented as rooted in an extensive tradition of thought. Most significantly, the entangled peace approach draws on the processual philosophy of the English philosopher Alfred North Whitehead and, to a lesser extent, the French philosopher Gilles Deleuze. Beyond these, the book also collects inspiration from contemporary authors who, through their work, have prompted the resurge of entangled ontologies, mainly Bruno Latour, Donna Haraway and Karen Barad. Although the differentiation between these thinkers would require a comprehensively and nuanced scrutiny, the text has intended to outline two common foundations running across these accounts. On the one hand, they question the (human) subject-object Cartesian binary, which untethered a universalising and anthropocentric dualist ontology where reality is, in Heideggerian terms, always present-at-hand. Whitehead and his followers conspicuously dispute that humans, either through positivist science or rational thought, can access reality. Instead, any attempt to portray the world is always an imaginative generalisation or a compilation of fictions, hence the vindication of speculative knowledge production from within these intellectual standpoints. On the other hand, this cluster of thinkers questions the social domain understood as the order of human relations separated and independent from the world. To these authors, the intrinsic relationality of the world is conceived of as the process through which all beings, human and non-human, material and immaterial, become in an entwined mode. Therefore, the entangled ontogenesis of beings and events in the planet twists in weird ways the limits between the material/non-human and the semiotic/human. In all, the fundamental implication of entangled ontologies di-hierarchises human-world relations, and the former is de-centred from the picture and becomes seen as dispossessed from its masterly and dominating position. In line with these assumptions, the claims behind the entangled peace approach have intended to contribute to the reconsiderations about the role of humans in the world, who are unveiled as vulnerable and whose becomings hinge on the processual entanglements with further beings and events.

From these underlaying assumptions of entangled ontologies and through critically reflecting upon field reports, interviews and ethnographic field observations of the blatant limited results of UN peacebuilding endeavours, entangled peace has been unpacked in the book resonating with and discussing three essential debates in contemporary critical peacebuilding literature. First, various UN peacebuilding missions, as illustrated by the Sierra Leonean case, have exposed the ontological limitations of the organisation in knowing and, subsequently, engaging 'the locals' in the peacebuilding enterprise. On the one hand, in seeking to select a representative sample of the local civil society, the UN bumped into what is commonly known in academic debates as the ethnic and rural biases, for which certain groups on society are overrepresented, particularly in political affairs. On the other hand, the text has also problematised that the UN perceives engagement as a process that materialises through highly technical and formal mechanisms of inclusion, which are continuously unmet by the host society. The book argues that these two problematic field developments unveil the ontological limitations of the UN, which sees 'the locals' as an essentialised, objectifiable and 'out-there' body that can be externally grasped, engaged, manipulated and even transformed. Surpassing these ontological flaws, it is suggested, following Barad, that the practice of knowing is a materially entangled process, in which the boundaries between the knower and the known are reconfigured, as both elements constitute each other through intense relations. For example, when thinking and seeking to involve local civil society groups in the peacebuilding programme, as illustrated by the case of the Freetown-based WANEP, the UN enters a process of mutually constitutive material reinvention that transforms the ontology of both the UN and these 'locals'. In other words, once the encounter happens, neither actor remains unmoved, untouched and unaffected. Furthermore, this ontological entanglement cannot be isolated from the immaterial processes which are also part of the ontogenesis of both actors, such as, on the one hand, the modern, liberal and anthropocentric principles embedded in the UN and, on the other hand, the mystical components that bind the local population with the cosmology of 'the bush', black magic and vernacular secret societies. For all this, the first line of argumentation on entangled peace unravels the process of knowing as a material-semiotic and mutually constitutive relational event.

Second, in light of the faulty achievements of UN efforts in pursuit of system-wide coherence as a strategic means to enhance the overall peacebuilding outcome, the text has problematised with a focus on the case of Burundi how the UN assumes that events unfold in the world in a linear, progressive and teleological manner, as if spatial framings are voids waiting to be filled by the human performance. In spite of highly institutionalised protocols, programmatic purposes and technical mechanisms, various field reports and oral accounts have assessed UN system-wide coherence and intra-co-ordination as 'terrible', 'a major problem' and even 'a nightmare'. The book intends to make sense of this controversial aspect by exposing that there are unpredictable events that unexpectedly clash with other events thus troubling any possibility for linear, programmatic and goal-oriented endeavours. For example, Nkuruziza's gesture to expel critical personnel of UN peacebuilding missions from the country, represented a major setback for UN coordination work as well as for the broader peacebuilding project in Burundi. Critically reflecting upon these limitations through authors such as Delanda, entangled peace suggests that events in the world unfold in non-linear, uncertain and messy dynamics. In the book, this assumption entails a radical reconfiguration of Humean cause-effect relations, which cannot be anymore explained through separate sequences from one process to another. Again, what modern terminology defines as cause and effect is here conceived of as mutually enacted in weird formulation. Thus, different to teleological and deterministic worlds, entangled peace radically opens up the future, which hinges on ongoingly negotiated creativeness. In vein with non-linear thinking, the text also discusses the UN failure in achieving a coherent and efficient synergy between the New York-based UN headquarters and the field team. With this goal, the book has brought into question the Euclidean/Newtonian, fix and static conceptualisation of space, noticeably embodied in UN modes of thinking and doing, presuming that the spatial world is a void canvas where the human operates. Rather, through the Whiteheadian notion of 'extensive continuum', the text hints at the concept of 'space' as the expansive outcome of relations between earthly elements. From this account, the fictitious idea of New York and Bujumbura as separated and discontinuous frames becomes obsolete, and the two entities are speculatively projected as intimately inextricable. By seeking to overcome emancipatory goals that seek to transform given and static spatial milieus, the non-fulfilment of which yields a protracted anxiety in peacebuilders, it is suggested that imagining space in this continuous and non-fix fashion has crucial implications, including the refocus on the multiplicity of colliding possibilities between actors and processes beyond normative projects constrained by fix and emancipatory expectances in highly delimited space-time order.

Third, by analysing the unprecedented complexity of war-wrecked scenarios invaded by a plethora of peacebuilding actors, as illustrated by the case of the CAR, the book has intended to articulate how and why the UN has failed in internalising and realising complexity-sensitive field strategies, thus neglecting the effect that inter-actor complex relations have on their agential condition. As a mode of example of these UN efforts, on the one hand, the deployment in 2014 of the MINUSCA was fundamentally aimed to merge multiple peacebuilding dimensions, including the protection of civilians, the facilitation of humanitarian assistance, the promotion of human rights, the protection of UN personnel and the coordination with further peacebuilding actors, amongst others, thus revealing the UN intentionality to disentangle the complex messiness of the ground and fulfil a holistic engagement. On the other hand, the UN sustaining peace approach, resolved in the 2015 report 'The Challenges of Sustaining Peace', expresses an alleged organisational determination to sensitise with the often complexity, intractability and unpredictability of conflict-affected landscapes. What the UN suggests through the sustaining peace approach is a holistic, non-departmentalised and self-organised approach, which is deemed more in tuned with the non-linear reality of peacebuilding settings described earlier. In the book, the entangled peace approach has questioned this UN endeavour for it overlooks that the growing complexity of the CAR stems from the entangled ontogenesis of actors and processes in the particular conflict-affected landscape. By invoking authors such as Law, the text has underlined the critical implications of complexity-thinking, which profoundly transform the idea of agency and free will. It is argued that the affirmation of entangled ontologies reveals that human agency cannot be thought of as autonomous and purposeful. Rather, entangled peace unpacks, in Latourian terminology, a form of distributed agency that reformulates the actor-action circuit by shedding light on the agential weakness of actors, surpassed by the vagueness and unpredictability of entangled beings and events.

Once traced the contours of entangled peace, the book moves forward by stating that, far from unfeignedly self-reflecting upon these operational filed hassles and sensitising with the entangled ontogenesis of actors and processes in the war-torn scenario, the UN holds the host society accountable for the peacebuilding failures and attempts to shape it so that it can eventually fit the UN modern and expansive machinery. For example, the 2015 report on sustaining peace introduced earlier states that societies emerging from conflict are poorly organised, divided, diverse, fragile and ill-capable to articulate their demands. Similarly, various UN peacebuilding officers expressed during interviews, in regard to the role of civil society in peacebuilding processes, things like 'they haven't reached a level of maturity', 'they are weak and difficult to work with' and 'they lack the culture of being organised', among others. In sum, it seems that to the UN is always the host society's 'failure', 'weakness' and 'poor organisation'. Once delegitimised the nature of civil society, I have argued in the book, the UN peacebuilding apparatus, through its strategies, programmes and protocols, intends to mould this host society so that it can fit the UN peacebuilding purposes. Inspired by Morton, the book has defined this UN performance as a totalising process through which the organisation seeks to secure a modern, liberal and anthropocentric worldwide venture. In other words, the UN seeks to taxonomise the world in homogenising and reductionist Kantian categories.

Informed by this totalising endeavour, the text has also introduced and elucidated the concept of 'distory', namely a story that undoes other stories. Distories disregard, displace, erase and obliterate the possibility for alter, entangled, vernacular stories to emerge. It is suggested that the UN peacebuilding enterprise is the mode through which the world's largest international organisation deploys its own distory, thus preventing other stories from thriving. Provocatively, the book has discussed that the UN is therefore doing deathwork, or in Preciado's words, 'necropeace', alluding to the death of those stories that, as a result of the UN peacebuilding ethos, never came into being. Again, through the critical reflection upon the controversial outcomes of observed UN peacebuilding missions, the book hints that the rationale lurking behind the international organisation responds to the burden of securing its modern universalising distory. Following up on this narrative, the text has exposed how increasingly prominent storytelling practices have been instrumentalised by various authors as ethico-political disruptions to enable entwined liveable worlds. Haraway, who has mastered the practice of storytelling to mediate future political ecologies, uses 'speculative fabulations' to portray imaginable stories involving negotiated transactions between human and non-human beings and redoing co-responsible ways of living and dying in the current troubled world. Storytelling thus seeks to reconnect material and immaterial trajectories of world-making beyond a fix notion of space and linear temporalities, embedded in colonising human-centric cosmologies.

Without disavowing the validity of entanglements to provide a meaningful and critical reading of peacebuilding phenomena as well as of the broader world, in the book, the book has also articulated a cautionary word by uncovering the limits of imagining earthly events as deterministically constrained to an all-embracing entangled ontogenesis. Drawing on authors such as Colebrook, it is hinted that entanglement fetishism, namely the increasingly notorious blind and uncritical assumption that all beings and processes in the world are inextricably entwined, risks reproducing the same exclusionary logics as the universalising and expansive project of modernity. Affirming that the future is constrained to the load of entanglements is turning entangled sensitivities into one more distory. To be sure, it is argued that, from the entangled peace account, the entangled ontogenesis of the world is not a condition to be celebrated and enacted through normative emancipatory intrusions in the theatre of the real. Far from these elitist world-making interventions, relations have been depicted as rather oppressive, as a burden that beings and events cannot escape from. In light of this, the suggested ethico-political disruptions in the book point at surpassing this deterministic relational mode of being and becoming the planet. Inspired by contemporary readings of Spinozist ethics, the text has argued in the text that surpassing a universalising moral system of judgement, eventually aimed to transform an 'out-there' world through top-down, masterly and emancipatory interventions, entails the affirmative ethical claim on how the world is over how the world should be. Affirming the withinness of the world, namely the collapsed ontogenesis of beings and events, entails abandoning the idea of an intervenor subject separated from the world. Considering the possibility of wilful liberatory change partly reinforces this violent split, which sets the foundations for intrusive projects such as that of the UN peacebuilding arrangement. Although the theoretical and practical implications of this statement are beyond the scope of this book, the book has invoked Grosz's notion of 'onto-ethics', unfolding the manner in which ontology and ethics become inextricable. To this author, onto-ethics consist of affirming the events with which one is bound. In this vein, entangled peace intends to eschew moralistic claims and appeals instead for a radical openness of the future, which embraces the clash of multiple worlds as the configuration of the theatre of the real. In a Whiteheadian sense, these future possibilities are infinitely atomised, from the particle collision level to the clash of galaxies. Crucially, this radical openness, beyond deterministic versions of entangled thinking, envisions the entangled and the non-entangled as composites of an opened-up world, thus surpassing the violent exclusionary logics of entanglement fetishism. In all, entangled peace is underpinned by the affirmation of a limitless collapse as the prime condition for possibility.

I am aware that entangled peace leaves a substantial number of questions unanswered, thus dissatisfying those theorists and practitioners who expect reflexive clarity and recipes. However, sensitising with uncertainty and equivocality becomes one of the fundamental implications of unveiling entangled peace. Vagueness about the world to come should not necessarily be a source of concern, since the precision of enlightened normative rationalities and their rigid positivist semiotic constructions (e.g. civilisation, race, nation and gender) has mostly unleashed pain and grief, often through the atrocities of violence and war. Entangled peace is an invitation to speculate over alter forms of being and becoming in the everydayness. The unattainability, unpredictability and messiness of peace bequeathed in this book should not be bemoaned as celebratory of the fading of an ultimate heavenly and truthful stage of the world. Instead, entangled peace, through its speculative substratum and beyond the hubris of modern, deterministic and exclusionary distories, has intended to reconfigure the manner in which alter, dissenting worlds can be actualised, worlds that are sensitised with and enabled by a connate, intensive and colliding multiplicity of possible events.

Interviews

Interview I: Albert Caramés, MINUSCA.
  Format in endnote:

  Interview I, anonymous. Freetown, 13/06/2016 (via Skype).
  Interview II: Bishop Josep Humper, Evangelical Church Sierra Leone.
  Interview III, anonymous. Freetown, 27/07/2016.
  Interview IV, anonymous. Freetown, 07/07/2016.
  Interview V, anonymous. Freetown, 01/08/2016.
  Interview VI, anonymous. Barcelona, 16/03/2016 (via Skype).
  Interview VII, anonymous. Freetown, 29/06/2016 (via Skype).
  Interview VIII, anonymous. Barcelona, 07/04/2016 (via Skype).
  Interview IX, anonymous. Barcelona, 14/03/2016 (via Skype).
  Interview X, anonymous. Barcelona, 22/03/2016 (via Skype).
  Interview XI, anonymous. Barcelona, 12/04/2016 (via Skype).
  Interview XII, anonymous. Freetown, 18/07/2016.
  Interview XIII, anonymous. Barcelona, 16/03/2016 (via Skype).
  Interview XIV, anonymous. New York, 01/03/2017
  Interview XV, anonymous. Freetown, 21/07/2016 [via Skype]
  Interview XVI, anonymous. Freetown, 28/07/2016 (via Skype).
  Interview XVII, anonymous. New York, 17/01/2017.

Notes

INTRODUCTION

1 Whitehead, *The Adventure of Ideas*, 368.

2 Whitehead, *The Adventure of Ideas*, 367.

3 Whitehead, *The Adventure of Ideas*, 368.

4 Whitehead, *The Adventure of Ideas*, 369.

5 Stengers, *Cosmopolitics II*, Book VII.

6 Whitehead, *The Concept of Nature*, 24.

7 Although the text draws on Western continental philosophy to elucidate entangled ontologies, non-Western philosophy has also produced accounts examining the relational condition of the human and its environment. For example, Ngcoya argues how in Ubuntu philosophy, shared by numerous communities in the sub-Saharan region, the being of a person is entirely dependent on its relations with other people. In other words, interdependence precedes the being. Similarly, Ling unfolds part-whole relations as the constituency of beings in Daoist philosophy, an ancient Chinese cosmovision. In addition, Malhotra unpacks the interconnectedness and continuity between the spheres of the Self and the Other in Dharmic philosophy, which comprises several Indian systems of thought, including Buddhism and Hinduism. Drawing from Australian indigenous cosmologies, Graham reveals how relations between peoples and land enable and enact social and political configurations. Finally, as illustrative of Caribbean postcolonial thought, Glissant argued that it is the relations amongst cultures that define and affect them. Thus, cultures somehow boundless for the limits are constantly redefined by internal and external relations. For further details on these accounts, see Ngcoya, 'Ubuntu: Toward an Emancipatory Cosmopolitanism?'; Ling, *Imagining World Politics. Sihar & Shenya, A Fable for Our Times*; Malhorta, *Being Different: An Indian Challenge to Western Universalism*; Graham, 'Some Thoughts about the Philosophical Underpinnings of Aboriginal Worldviews'; Glissant, *Poetics of Relation*. See also Nordin et al., 'Towards Global Relational Theorizing: A Dialogue between Sinophone and Anglophone Scholarship on Relationalism'.

8 Devellennes and Dillet, 'Questioning New Materialisms: An Introduction'.

9 See Haraway, *Modest_Witness@Second_Millennium.FemaleMan_Meets_ OncoMouse: Feminism and Technoscience*; Barad, *Meeting the Universe Halfway: Quantum Physics and the Entanglement of Matter and Meaning*; Kirby, *Quantum Anthropologies: Life at Large*; Viveiros de Castro, *Cannibal Metaphysics: For a Post-Structural Anthropology*; Delanda, *Assemblage Theory*.

10 Bergson, *Matter and Memory*.

11 Morton, *Hyperobjects,* 4.

12 See Swyngedouw and Ernstson, 'Interrupting the Anthropo-ObScene: Immuno-Biopolitics and Depoliticizing Ontologies in the Anthropocene'; Harman and Delanda, *The Rise of Realism*; Colebrook, 'A CUT IN RELATIONALITY: Art at the End of the World'.

13 Harman in Harman and Delanda, *The Rise of Realism, 71.*

14 Shaviro, *The Universe of Things. On Speculative Realism.*

15 See Rapoport, *Fights, Games, and Debates*; Boulding, *Conflict And Defense: A General Theory.*

16 Olsen and Ib Martin, 'The Political Functions of Social Research – with Special Reference to Peace and Conflict Research'.

17 See Galtung, 'Violence, Peace, and Peace Research'; Galtung, 'Three Approaches to Peace: Peacekeeping, Peacemaking, and Peacebuilding'.

18 See International Institute for Strategic Studies (IISS), *Armed Conflict Survey 2020.*

19 See Chandler, 'The Uncritical Critique of "Liberal Peace".'

20 Pouligny, *Peace Operations Seen from Below: UN Missions and Local People*; Autesserre, *Peaceland: Conflict Resolution and the Everyday Politics of International Intervention.*

21 See Brigg, 'Relational and Essential: Theorizing Difference for Peacebuilding'; Brigg, 'Relational Sensibility in Peacebuilding: Emancipation, Tyranny, or Transformation?'.

22 See Al-Qaq, *Managing World Order: United Nations Peace Operations and the Security Agenda.*

23 See UN General Assembly, 'Review of the Efficiency of the Administrative and Financial Functioning of the United Nations. Restructuring of the Secretariat of the Organisation'.

24 See UN Secretary General, 'An Agenda for Peace'.

25 See Paris, 'Peacebuilding and the Limits of Liberal Internationalism'; Dillon and Reid, 'Global Governance, Liberal Peace, and Complex Emergency'; Duffield, *Global Governance and the New Wars: The Merging of Development and Security*; Richmond, *A Post-Liberal Peace.*

26 See UN General Assembly, '2005 World Summit Outcome'.

27 Chandler, *Peacebuilding: The Twenty Years' Crisis.*

28 See Bargués-Pedreny, *Deferring Peace in International Statebuilding: Difference, Resilience and Critique*; Millar, 'For Whom Do Local Peace Processes Function? Maintaining Control through Conflict Management'.

29 Advisory Group of Experts, 'The Challenge of Sustaining Peace: Report of the Advisory Group of Experts for the 2015 Review of the United Nations Peacebuilding Architecture'.

30 Grosz, *The Incorporeal: Ontology, Ethics, and the Limits of Materialism*, 153.

31 Oksamytna and Karlsrud, *United Nations Peace Operations and International Relations Theory*.

CHAPTER 1

1 I have more extensively developed this debate in Torrent, 'Problematising UN-Local Civil Society Engagement in Peacebuilding: Towards Non-Modern Epistemes Through Relationality'.

2 For a detailed revision on conceptual approaches from different sensitivities to the concept of civil society, see Chambers and Kymlicka, *Alternative Conceptions of Civil Society*; Lipschutz, 'Reconstructing World Politics: The Emergence of Global Civil Society'; Chandler, *Constructing Global Civil Society*; Alexander, *The Civil Sphere*; Edwards, *Civil Society*.

3 Shepherd, 'Constructing Civil Society: Gender, Power and Legitimacy in United Nations Peacebuilding Discourse', 904.

4 UN General Assembly, 'Report of the World Summit for Social Development', A/CONF.166/9, 37.

5 UN General Assembly, 'Report of the Panel of Eminent Persons on United Nations-Civil Society Relations', A/58/817, 23.

6 See UN General Assembly and UN Security Council, 'Report of the Panel on United Nations Peace Operations', A/55/305-S/2000/809; UN General Assembly, '2005 World Summit Outcome', A/RES/60/1; UN General Assembly and UN Security Council, 'Report of the High-Level Independent Panel on Peace Operations on Uniting Our Strengths for Peace: Politics, Partnership and People', A/70/95-S/2015/446; Advisory Group of Experts, 'The Challenge of Sustaining Peace: Report of the Advisory Group of Experts for the 2015 Review of the United Nations Peacebuilding Architecture'.

7 UN Secretary General, 'An Agenda for Peace', A/47/277.

8 UN General Assembly and UN Security Council, 'Report of the Panel on United Nations Peace Operations', A/55/305-S/2000/809, art. 269.

9 UN Secretary General, 'Peacebuilding in the Immediate Aftermath of Conflict', A/63/881-S/2009/304.

10 UN General Assembly and UN Security Council, 'Review of the United Nations Peacebuilding Architecture', A/64/868-S/2010/393, art. 172.

11 UN General Assembly and UN Security Council, 'Report of the High-Level Independent Panel on Peace Operations on Uniting Our Strengths for Peace: Politics, Partnership and People', A/70/95-S/2015/446.

12 Advisory Group of Experts, 'The Challenge of Sustaining Peace: Report of the Advisory Group of Experts for the 2015 Review of the United Nations Peacebuilding Architecture', art. 128

13 The UN defines the PBC as 'the intergovernmental advisory body that supports peace efforts in countries emerging from conflict'; the PBSO as an entity created to assist and support the PBC, the PBF, and support the SG's efforts to coordinate the UN system in its peacebuilding efforts'; and the PBF as 'the UN's global multi-donor trust fund that provides a critical bridge between conflict and recovery in countries for which no funding mechanism is yet available' (UN Peacebuilding Support Office, 'UN Peacebuilding: An Orientation', 37).

14 Organization for Economic Cooperation and Development, 'Shaping the 21st Century: The Contribution of Development Co-Operation'.

15 United Nations Peacebuilding Support Office, 'UN Peacebuilding: An Orientation', 5.

16 For further discussion on non-state actor participation in International Organisations-led processes aimed to broaden legitimacy, see Barnett and Finnemore, 'The Power of Liberal International Organizations'.

17 Shepherd, 'Constructing Civil Society: Gender, Power and Legitimacy in United Nations Peacebuilding Discourse', 899.

18 Shepherd, 'Constructing Civil Society: Gender, Power and Legitimacy in United Nations Peacebuilding Discourse', 898–9.

19 Shepherd, 'Constructing Civil Society: Gender, Power and Legitimacy in United Nations Peacebuilding Discourse', 904.

20 See Kaldor, *Global Civil Society: An Answer to War*; Lidén, 'Building Peace between Global and Local Politics: On the Cosmopolitan Ethics of Liberal Peacebuilding'.

21 Arnault, 'Legitimacy and Peace Processes'.

22 Nilsson, 'Anchoring the Peace: Civil Society Actors in Peace Accords and Durable Peace'.

23 Street, Mollett, and Smith, 'Experiences of the United Nations Peacebuilding Commission in Sierra Leone and Burundi'.

24 See Williams and Young, 'Civil Society and the Liberal Project in Ghana and Sierra Leone'; Iñiguez de Heredia, 'Escaping Statebuilding: Resistance and Civil Society in the Democratic Republic of the Congo'.

25 The "local turn" and, more broadly, the contentious implications of the entanglement between an essentialised notion of the "internationals" and the "locals" have been extensively and critically covered by a wide range of theoretical sensitivities over the past decade. In addition to the Foucauldian critique, exposed in detail in the text, some of the most renowned interventions in these discussions are Pouligny, *Peace Operations Seen from Below: UN Missions and Local People*; Mac Ginty, *International Peacebuilding and Local Resistance: Hybrid Forms of Peace*; Paffenholz, 'Unpacking the Local Turn in Peacebuilding: A Critical Assessment towards an Agenda for Future Research'; Randazzo, *Beyond Liberal Peacebuilding: A Critical Exploration of the Local Turn*; Jabri, 'Peacebuilding, the Local and the International: A Colonial or a Postcolonial Rationality?'; Millar, 'For Whom Do Local Peace Processes Function? Maintaining Control through Conflict Management'.

26 Chandler, 'Race, Culture and Civil Society: Peacebuilding Discourse and the Understanding of Difference', 371–2.

27 Chandler, 'Race, Culture and Civil Society: Peacebuilding Discourse and the Understanding of Difference', 384.

28 Richmond, 'Resistance and the Post-Liberal Peace', 669.

29 Richmond, 'Resistance and the Post-Liberal Peace', 681.

30 Boyd, *Uncivil Society: The Perils of Pluralism and the Making of Modern Liberalism.*

31 Mac Ginty, *International Peacebuilding and Local Resistance: Hybrid Forms of Peace*; see also Iñiguez de Heredia, 'Escaping Statebuilding: Resistance and Civil Society in the Democratic Republic of the Congo'.

32 Paffenholz, 'Unpacking the Local Turn in Peacebuilding: A Critical Assessment towards an Agenda for Future Research'.

33 Foucault, *The History of Sexuality. Volume 1, An Introduction,* 100.

34 See Randazzo, 'The Paradoxes of the "Everyday": Scrutinising the Local Turn in Peace Building'; Randazzo and Torrent, 'Reframing Agency in Complexity-Sensitive Peacebuilding'.

35 Lewis, 'The Myopic Foucauldian Gaze: Discourse, Knowledge and the Authoritarian Peace', 27–8.

36 For International Relations literature on the material turn, see Grove, *Savage Ecology: War and Geopolitics at the End of the World*; Allan, 'From Subjects to Objects: Knowledge in International Relations Theory'. For literature within Critical Peace and Conflict Studies on the material turn see Aradau, 'Security That Matters: Critical Infrastructure and Objects of Protection'; Smirl, *Spaces of Aid: How Cars, Compounds and Hotels Shape Humanitarianism*; Mac Ginty, 'A Material Turn in International Relations: The 4x4, Intervention and Resistance'; Cudworth and Hobden, 'The Posthuman Way of War'.

37 For International Relations literature on the relational turn, see Kurki, *International Relations in a Relational Universe*; Zanotti, *Ontological Entanglements, Agency and Ethics in International Relations: Exploring the Crossroads.* For literature within Critical Peace and Conflict Studies on the relational turn, see Brigg, 'Relational and Essential: Theorizing Difference for Peacebuilding'; Joseph, 'Beyond Relationalism in Peacebuilding'; Torrent, 'Problematising UN-Local Civil Society Engagement in Peacebuilding: Towards Non-Modern Epistemes through Relationality'.

38 Sabaratnam, 'Avatars of Eurocentrism in the Critique of the Liberal Peace'.

39 Danielsson, 'Transcending Binaries in Critical Peacebuilding Scholarship to Address "Inclusivity" Projects', 1086.

40 Sabaratnam, *Decolonising Intervention: International Statebuilding in Mozambique.*

41 Danielsson, 'Transcending Binaries in Critical Peacebuilding Scholarship to Address "Inclusivity" Projects', 1089.

42 Danielsson, 'Transcending Binaries in Critical Peacebuilding Scholarship to Address "Inclusivity" Projects', 1093.

43 See Weiss, *What's Wrong with the United Nations and How to Fix It.*

44 Bargués-Pedreny, *Deferring Peace in International Statebuilding: Difference, Resilience and Critique*; see also Philipsen, 'When Liberal Peacebuilding Fails: Paradoxes of Implementing Ownership and Accountability in the Integrated Approach'.

45 See Mac Ginty, 'Where Is the Local? Critical Localism and Peacebuilding'; Millar, 'For Whom Do Local Peace Processes Function? Maintaining Control through Conflict Management'.

46 Action Aid, CAFOD, and CARE International, 'Consolidating the Peace?: Views from Sierra Leone and Burundi on the United Nations Peacebuilding Commission – GSDRC'.

47 Interview I, anonymous. Freetown, 13/06/2016 (via Skype).

48 Action Aid, CAFOD, and CARE International, 'Consolidating the Peace?: Views from Sierra Leone and Burundi on the United Nations Peacebuilding Commission – GSDRC'.

49 Jenkins, *Re-Engineering the UN Peacebuilding Architecture. Working Paper: The Future of the Peacebuilding Architecture Project.*

50 UN Peacebuilding Commission, 'Monitoring and Track Mechanism of the Strategic Framework for Peacebuilding in Burundi', PBC/2/BDI/4.

51 UN Peacebuilding Commission, 'Strategic Framework for Peacebuilding in the CAR 2009–2011', PBC/3/CAF/7.

52 Interview II, Bishop Joseph Humper. Freetown, 23/07/2016.

53 Interview III, anonymous. Freetown, 27/07/2016.

54 Interview IV, anonymous. Freetown, 07/07/2016.

55 Interview V, anonymous. Freetown, 01/08/2016.

56 Interview VI, anonymous. Barcelona, 16/03/2016 (via Skype).

57 Graben and Fitz-Gerald, 'Mind the Gap: The Importance of Local Institutional Development in Peace-Building-Funded Security Interventions'.

58 Action Aid, CAFOD, and CARE International, 'Consolidating the Peace?: Views from Sierra Leone and Burundi on the United Nations Peacebuilding Commission – GSDRC'.

59 Does, *Inclusivity and Local Perspectives in Peacebuilding: Issues, Lessons, Challenges*, 7.

60 Vogel, 'Civil Society Capture: Top-Down Interventions from Below?', 475.

61 Barad, *Meeting the Universe Halfway: Quantum Physics and the Entanglement of Matter and Meaning*, 149.

62 Latour, *Reassembling the Social: An Introduction to Actor-Network-Theory.*

63 Haraway, *Staying with the Trouble: Making Kin in the Chthulucene.*

64 Danielsson, 'Transcending Binaries in Critical Peacebuilding Scholarship to Address "Inclusivity" Projects', 1094.

65 Colebrook, 'A CUT IN RELATIONALITY: Art at the End of the World', 175.

66 Colebrook, 'A CUT IN RELATIONALITY: Art at the End of the World', 188.

CHAPTER 2

1 See OECD Observer, 'Policy Coherence: Vital for Global Development'; Sommers, *The Dynamics of Coordination*; Stockton, *Strategic Coordination in*

Afghanistan; Reindorp and Wiles, 'Humanitarian Coordination: Lessons from Recent Field Experience'.

2 De Coning, 'Coherence and Coordination in United Nations Peacebuilding and Integrated Missions – A Norwegian Perspective', 7.

3 Interview VII, anonymous. Freetown, 29/06/2016 (via Skype).

4 UN Secretary General, 'Renewing the UN: A Program for Reform'.

5 UN Secretary General, 'Integrated Missions Planning Process. Guidelines Endorsed by the Secretary General'.

6 UN General Assembly, 'Delivering as One'. Further examples of UN efforts towards coherence include the UN Assistance Development Framework, which helped coordinating UNCT from different countries; the UN Development Group, which led the creation of resident Coordinators; and the creation of the UN Development Operations Coordination Office.

7 See Weiss, *What's Wrong with the United Nations and How to Fix It*; Campbell, 'Governing Globally, Acting Locally: Lessons from Burundi for International Peacebuilding Reform'; Picciotto, 'Evaluating the UN Development System'; Van Beijnum, 'Achievements of the UN Peacebuilding Commission and the Challenges Ahead'; De Coning and Stamnes, *UN Peacebuilding Archit. First 10 Years*.

8 Campbell, 'Governing Globally, Acting Locally: Lessons from Burundi for International Peacebuilding Reform', 86.

9 Jenkins describes three levels of coherence the PBA should achieve. First, the structural level refers to institutional reforms to address the root cause of conflict. Second, the systemic level faces transnational phenomena such as trade, refugees or climate change. Finally, the operational level refers to the first-hand means used on the ground to manage crises (Jenkins, *Re-Engineering the UN Peacebuilding Architecture. Working Paper: The Future of the Peacebuilding Architecture Project, 14.)*. See also Hearn, Bujones, and Kugel, 'The United Nations "Peacebuilding Architecture": Past, Present and Future'.

10 UN General Assembly, '2005 World Summit Outcome', arts. 97–98.

11 More recently, the 2015 AGE report stated: 'Paradoxically, what some would argue is an inherent weakness of the PBC – being limited to an advisory role – can become one of its main and unappreciated strengths, by offering the relevant principal Organs a bridge between them, helping ensure a UN approach to sustaining peace that is coherent, integrated and holistic'. (Advisory Group of Experts, 'The Challenge of Sustaining Peace: Report of the Advisory Group of Experts for the 2015 Review of the United Nations Peacebuilding Architecture', art. 131.)

12 See UN Secretary General, 'Peacebuilding in the Immediate Aftermath of Conflict'.

13 The growing tendency of implementing integrated operations is also visible in the DPKO framework, whose missions have also been operation-alised, to a large extent, in an integrated manner. MINUSCA, the current UN peacekeeping mission deployed in the CAR, illustrates this. See UN General Assembly and UN Security Council, 'Report of the Panel on United Nations

Peace Operations', A/55/305-S/2000/809; United Nations: Department of Peacekeeping Operations, 'Integrated Mission Planning Process Guidelines. Role of the Field'; Hirschmann, 'Organizational Learning in United Nations' Peacekeeping Exit Strategies'.

14 UN Secretary General, 'Note on Guidance on Integrated Missions', art. 4.

15 Petrie and Morrice, 'Scrambling and Pulling Together the UN's Civilian Capacities in Conflict-Prone States', 46.

16 Interview VIII, anonymous. Barcelona, 07/04/2016 (via Skype).

17 UNICEF, 'A Handy Guide on UN Coherence', 68.

18 UN Peacekeeping, 'Report of the Independent High-Level Panel on Peace Operations', art. 142. See also arts. 141, 214, 247.

19 De Coning, 'Coherence and Coordination in United Nations Peacebuilding and Integrated Missions – A Norwegian Perspective', 6.

20 De Coning, 'Coherence and Coordination in United Nations Peacebuilding and Integrated Missions – A Norwegian Perspective', 11.

21 UN Peacekeeping, 'Report of the Independent High-Level Panel on Peace Operations', art. 229.

22 De Coning, 'Coherence and Coordination in United Nations Peacebuilding and Integrated Missions – A Norwegian Perspective', 9.

23 See Körppen, Ropers, and Giessmann, *The Non-Linearity of Peace Processes: Theory and Practice of Systemic Conflict Transformation.*

24 Paris, 'Peacebuilding and the Limits of Liberal Internationalism'.

25 See Lederach, *Building Peace. Sustainable Reconciliation in Divided Societies.*

26 These debates and policy frameworks have been extensively covered on chapter 1.

27 See Mac Ginty, *International Peacebuilding and Local Resistance: Hybrid Forms of Peace*; Richmond, 'Critical Agency, Resistance and a Post-Colonial Civil Society'.

28 Chandler, 'Peacebuilding and the Politics of Non-Linearity: Rethinking "Hidden" Agency and "Resistance"', 25.

29 Chandler, 'Peacebuilding and the Politics of Non-Linearity: Rethinking "Hidden" Agency and "Resistance"', 25.

30 See Advisory Group of Experts, 'The Challenge of Sustaining Peace: Report of the Advisory Group of Experts for the 2015 Review of the United Nations Peacebuilding Architecture', more extensively discussed in chapter 3.

31 See Council of the European Union, 'Council Conclusions on EU Approach to Resilience'.

32 Advisory Group of Experts, 'The Challenge of Sustaining Peace: Report of the Advisory Group of Experts for the 2015 Review of the United Nations Peacebuilding Architecture'.

33 Juncos, 'Resilience in Peacebuilding: Contesting Uncertainty, Ambiguity, and Complexity', 562.

34 For basic literature on resilience in the area of International Relations, see Chandler and Coaffee, *The Routledge Handbook of International Resilience.*

35 Chandler, 'Rethinking the Conflict-Poverty Nexus: From Securitising Intervention to Resilience', 13.

36 Joseph, 'The EU in the Horn of Africa: Building Resilience as a Distant Form of Governance'.

37 Juncos, 'Resilience in Peacebuilding: Contesting Uncertainty, Ambiguity, and Complexity', 568.

38 Juncos, 'Resilience in Peacebuilding: Contesting Uncertainty, Ambiguity, and Complexity', 569.

39 See De Coning, 'Coherence and Coordination in United Nations Peacebuilding and Integrated Missions – A Norwegian Perspective'; De Coning, 'Clarity, Coherence and Context: Three Priorities for Sustainable Peace'; Choedon, 'The United Nations Peacebuilding in Kosovo: The Issue of Coordination'; Hirschmann, 'Organizational Learning in United Nations' Peacekeeping Exit Strategies'; Philipsen, 'When Liberal Peacebuilding Fails: Paradoxes of Implementing Ownership and Accountability in the Integrated Approach'.

40 De Coning, 'Clarity, Coherence and Context: Three Priorities for Sustainable Peace', 9.

41 There are numerous studies discussing problems of coherence and coordination in the UN peacebuilding framework. See Donini, 'The Policies of Mercy: UN Coordination in Afghanistan, Mozambique, and Rwanda'; Dahrendorf, *A Review of Peace Operations: A Case for Change*; Dobbins et al., *The UN's Role in Nation-Building from the Congo to Iraq*; De Coning, 'Coherence and Coordination in United Nations Peacebuilding and Integrated Missions – A Norwegian Perspective'.

42 Boshoff, Vrey, and Rautenbach, *The Burundi Peace Process: From Civil War to Conditional Peace*. For further information on the AMIB, see Peen Rodt, 'The African Union Mission in Burundi'.

43 Adebajo, *UN Peacekeeping in Africa: From the Suez Crisis to the Sudan Conflicts*.

44 UN Security Council, 'Resolution 1719'.

45 This same organisational pattern towards an integrated version of peacebuilding can be observed in further early PBC cases, including Sierra Leone and the CAR. While in the former the DPKO-led United Nations Mission in Sierra Leone (UNAMSIL) was replaced by the DPA-led United Nations Integrated Office in Sierra Leone (UNIOSIL), in the latter the DPKO-led MINURCA was replaced by the DPA-led BONUCA, both integrated missions. The subsequent missions in both countries, namely the United Nations Integrated Peacebuilding Office in Sierra Leone (UNIPSIL) and MINUSCA, respectively, were also of an integrated nature.

46 One interviewee pointed out that the most significant adjustment occurred in terms of staff and mandate was going from 5,000 to 50,000 and from a military component to a completely civilian mission (Interview IX, anonymous. Barcelona, 14/03/2016 [via Skype]).

47 In regard to this transition from BINUB to BNUB, a former external auditor of the UN post-conflict mission in Burundi expressed in an interview that 'they shifted (from BINUB to BNUB) because the government wanted. Because the head of

BINUB was kicked out by the government because they felt he was aligning with the, as far as I understand, with the Independent National Electoral Commission (CENI, in French). So, the government required the shift. And the UN went along with it' (Interview X, anonymous. Barcelona, 22/03/2016 [via Skype]).

48 UN Security Council, 'Resolution 1959', 3.

49 De Coning also identifies negative effects of pursuing coherence. First, in some cases, short-term political and security considerations may over-ride longer-term development considerations and this may undermine the very socio-economic rehabilitation on which sustainable peacebuilding depends. Second, undue pressure on internal actors may materialise when external actors form a coherent block on certain issues. Third, the neutrality, impartiality and independence of humanitarian action may be negatively affected when integrated with political and security activities (De Coning, 'Coherence and Coordination in United Nations Peacebuilding and Integrated Missions – A Norwegian Perspective').

50 See UN General Assembly and UN Security Council, 'Review of the United Nations Peacebuilding Architecture'. One of the interviewees pointed out that when BINUB arrived, intra-co-ordination became problematic because "each UN program had a different hat" (Interview IX, anonymous. Barcelona, 14/03/2016 [via Skype]).

51 Advisory Group of Experts, 'The Challenge of Sustaining Peace: Report of the Advisory Group of Experts for the 2015 Review of the United Nations Peacebuilding Architecture', 26. The report pointed out pitfalls hindering UN peacebuilding action such as the internal fragmentation of the organisation, which hindered successful and effective fieldwork, consistency of delivery, a gender approach, credibility and clear leadership, cooperation with other stakeholders, efficiency of the PBC and PBSO relationship, among other issues. The report also states that the UN mission in Burundi failed in its transition towards to a post-mission stage led by the RC and UNCT structure, which was marked by the absence of clear leadership. This had a negative impact on the UN''s credibility and influence in Burundi. See also Browne and Weiss, *Peacebuilding Challenges for the UN Development System*.

52 Interview XI, anonymous. Barcelona, 12/04/2016 (via Skype).

53 Interview XII, anonymous. Freetown, 18/07/2016.

54 Interview V, anonymous. Freetown, 01/08/2016.

55 Interview I, anonymous. Freetown, 13/06/2016 (via Skype).

56 De Coning, 'Coherence and Coordination in United Nations Peacebuilding and Integrated Missions – A Norwegian Perspective', 7.

57 Zanotti, 'UN Integrated Peacekeeping Operations and NGOs: Reflections on Governmental Rationalities and Contestation in the Age of Risk', 20.

58 Zanotti, 'UN Integrated Peacekeeping Operations and NGOs: Reflections on Governmental Rationalities and Contestation in the Age of Risk', 20.

59 Zanotti, 'UN Integrated Peacekeeping Operations and NGOs: Reflections on Governmental Rationalities and Contestation in the Age of Risk', 28.

60 See Kurki, *Causation in International Relations Reclaiming Causal Analysis*; Lebow, *Constructing Cause in International Relations*; Humphreys, 'Causation in International Relations'.

61 Deleuze and Guattari, *A Thousand Plateaus. Capitalism and Schizophrenia*, 323.

62 Deleuze and Guattari, *A Thousand Plateaus. Capitalism and Schizophrenia*, 8.

63 Deleuze and Guattari, *A Thousand Plateaus. Capitalism and Schizophrenia*, 347.

64 Delanda, *Assemblage Theory*, 12.

65 Deleuze and Guattari, *A Thousand Plateaus. Capitalism and Schizophrenia*, 23.

66 Harman, *Object-Oriented Ontology. A New Theory of Everything*, 165–67.

67 Barad, *Meeting the Universe Halfway: Quantum Physics and the Entanglement of Matter and Meaning*, 129–31.

68 Latour, *Reassembling the Social: An Introduction to Actor-Network-Theory*.

69 Harman, *Object-Oriented Ontology. A New Theory of Everything*, 165–67.

70 Shaviro, *The Universe of Things. On Speculative Realism*, 38.

71 Morton, *Hyperobjects*, 65.

72 See Chandler, 'A World without Causation: Big Data and the Coming of Age of Posthumanism'.

73 Bouka, 'Status and Dynamics of the Political Situation in Burundi'.

74 Interview XIII, anonymous. Barcelona, 16/03/2016 (via Skype). See also Wilén and Chapaux, 'Problems of Local Participation and Collaboration with the UN in a Post-Conflict Environment: Who Are the "Locals"?'

75 There are numerous reports and accounts underlining the correlation between strong leadership and coherence and intra-coordination. See Centre on International Cooperation and International Peace Institute, 'Taking Stock, Looking Forward: A Strategic Review of the Peacebuilding Commission'; UN Secretary General, 'Peacebuilding in the Immediate Aftermath of Conflict'; UN Peacebuilding Commission, 'The Peacebuilding Commission: New York-Based, Field-Oriented'.

76 See Choedon, 'The United Nations Peacebuilding in Kosovo: The Issue of Coordination', 52. Personality traits have also been noticed by different accounts as affecting coherence and intra-coordination. A DPA Policy Coordination Officer working on Sierra Leone recalled during an interview that usually coherence and coordination rely on personal relationships (Interview XIV, anonymous. New York, 01/03/2017). In this vein, another interviewed expert on the case of the CAR expressed: "I think a lot depends on particular individuals we talk about. Some people get along and we"ll work well together, and some people don't get along and don't work very well together, and some people don't get along but are still able to work together during emergencies … Overall it's all really difficult…" (Interview XV, anonymous. Freetown, 21/07/2016 [via Skype]).

77 Delanda, *A Thousand Years of Nonlinear History*, 17.

78 See UN General Assembly and UN Security Council, 'Review of the United Nations Peacebuilding Architecture'. See also Rugumamu, 'Does the UN Peacebuilding Commission Change the Mode of Peacebuilding in Africa?', 6; Wyeth, 'Peacebuilding at the UN over the Last 10 Years', 5. Asked about ONUB-BINUB transition in Burundi, a policy expert commented: "there were still turf battles under the same headings, so they did not really diminish the turf battle at least in the beginning" (Interview IX, anonymous. Barcelona, 14/03/2016 [via Skype]).

79 Barad, *Meeting the Universe Halfway: Quantum Physics and the Entanglement of Matter and Meaning*, 178.

80 Delanda, *A Thousand Years of Nonlinear History*, 373.

81 See Murithi, 'Peacebuilding or "UN-Building"? African Institutional Responses to the Peacebuilding Commission', 90; Jenkins, *Re-Engineering the UN Peacebuilding Architecture. Working Paper: The Future of the Peacebuilding Architecture Project, 22*; NYU Centre on International Cooperation and International Peace Institute, 'Taking Stock, Looking Forward: A Strategic Review of the Peacebuilding Commission'; Does, *Inclusivity and Local Perspectives in Peacebuilding: Issues, Lessons, Challenges*; McCandless and Tschirgi, 'Strategic Frameworks That Embrace Mutual Accountability for Peacebuilding: Emerging Lessons in PBC and Non-PBC Countries', 33.

82 Rugumamu, 'Does the UN Peacebuilding Commission Change the Mode of Peacebuilding in Africa?', 6.

83 A former ONUB officer for the SSR unit commented during an interview on how the lack of protocols to engage on the ground as a UN family is a major barrier for UN intra-co-ordination. Moreover, he added that achievements in coordination usually depend very much on the area programmes such as SSR or DDR have long been implemented by the UN, so they might achieve better results (Interview XIII, anonymous. Barcelona, 16/03/2016 [via Skype]).

84 See Barad, *Meeting the Universe Halfway: Quantum Physics and the Entanglement of Matter and Meaning*; Wendt, *Quantum Mind and Social Science. Unifying Physical and Social Ontology*; Arfi and Kessler, 'Forum Introduction: Social Theory Going Quantum-Theoretic? Questions, Alternatives and Challenges'.

85 Barad, *Meeting the Universe Halfway: Quantum Physics and the Entanglement of Matter and Meaning*, 64.

86 Kirby, *Quantum Anthropologies Life at Large*, 31.

87 In Whitehead, *Process and Reality*, 209; see Bergson, *Time and Free Will. An Essay on the Immediate Data of Consciousness*.

88 Whitehead, *The Concept of Nature*, 44.

89 Whitehead, *The Concept of Nature*, 24.

90 Whitehead, *Process and Reality*, 66–67.

91 Morton, *Hyperobjects*, 56.

92 Harman and Delanda, *The Rise of Realism*, 123.

93 Barad, 'Troubling Time/s and Ecologies of Nothingness: Re-Turning, Re-Membering, and Facing the Incalculable', 83.

94 Kirby, *Quantum Anthropologies: Life at Large*, XI.

95 Kirby, *Quantum Anthropologies: Life at Large*, 39.

96 Kirby, *Quantum Anthropologies: Life at Large*, 39.

97 Kirby, *Quantum Anthropologies: Life at Large*, 61.

98 Kirby, *Quantum Anthropologies: Life at Large*, 76.

99 Kirby, *Quantum Anthropologies: Life at Large*, 84.

100 Kirby, *Quantum Anthropologies: Life at Large*, 96.

101 Zanotti, 'Reorienting IR: Ontological Entanglement, Agency, and Ethics', 370.

102 See Wendt, *Quantum Mind and Social Science. Unifying Physical and Social Ontology*.

CHAPTER 3

1 I have more extensively developed this debate in Randazzo and Torrent, 'Reframing Agency in Complexity-Sensitive Peacebuilding'.

2 UN General Assembly, '2005 World Summit Outcome', art. 98.

3 UN General Assembly and UN Security Council, 'Report of the High-Level Independent Panel on Peace Operations on Uniting Our Strengths for Peace: Politics, Partnership and People', art. 55.

4 See De Coning and Stamnes, *UN Peacebuilding Archit. First 10 Years*; Weiss, *What's Wrong with the United Nations and How to Fix It*; Browne and Weiss, *Peacebuilding Challenges for the UN Development System*; De Coning and Peter, *United Nations Peace Operations in a Changing Global Order*.

5 De Coning, 'How UN Peacekeeping Operations Can Adapt to a New Multipolar World Order', 537.

6 See Carayannis and Fowlis, 'Lessons from African Union – United Nations Cooperation in Peace Operations in the Central African Republic'.

7 See Carayanis and Lombard, *Making Sense of the Central African Republic*.

8 For a more detailed account on the implications of the UN-led liberal peace endeavours in the CAR, see Maiangwa and Suleiman, 'Liberal Peace Intervention in the Central African Republic: Limitations and Reworking a "Hybrid" Order'.

9 See McFarlane and Malan, 'Crisis and Response in the Central African Republic: A New Trend in African Peacekeeping?'

10 UN Security Council, 'Resolution 1159', 3.

11 UN Security Council, 'Resolution S/1999/1235', 2.

12 Interview VII, anonymous. Freetown, 29/06/2016 (via Skype).

13 Center on International Cooperation, 'Annual Review of Global Peace Operations 2009'.

14 Center on International Cooperation, 'Annual Review of Global Peace Operations 2010'; See also Meyer, 'Regional Conflict Management in Central Africa: From FOMUC to MICOPAX'.

15 International Institute for Strategic Studies, 'Central African Republic: Instability and Intervention'.

16 De Coning, 'Peace Enforcement in Africa: Doctrinal Distinctions between the African Union and United Nations', 146.

17 Makinda, Okumu and Mickler, *The African Union Addressing the Challenges of Peace, Security, and Governance*.

18 De Coning, 'Peace Enforcement in Africa: Doctrinal Distinctions between the African Union and United Nations', 155.

19 International Institute for Strategic Studies, 'Central African Republic: New UN Mission'.

20 See Kane, 'Interreligious Violence in the Central African Republic'.

21 See International Crisis Group, 'The Central African Republic's Hidden Conflict'.

22 Carvalho and Lucey, 'Fractured Peacebuilding in the Central African Republic: Lessons for African Union Engagement'.

23 See Dillon and Reid, 'Global Governance, Liberal Peace, and Complex Emergency'; Joseph, 'The EU in the Horn of Africa: Building Resilience as a Distant Form of Governance'.

24 See Moe, 'The Strange Wars of Liberal Peace: Hybridity, Complexity and the Governing Rationalities of Counterinsurgency in Somalia'; Tamminen, 'Challenges: EU Civilian Crisis Management and the Objective of Impact Assessment – Kosovo as an Example of Complexity'.

25 See Brusset, Coning, and Hughes, *Complexity Thinking for Peacebuilding Practice and Evaluation*; Cilliers and Preiser, *Complexity, Difference and Identity*; Geyer and Pickering, 'Applying the Tools of Complexity to the International Realm: From Fitness Landscapes to Complexity Cascades'.

26 Coleman, 'Conflict, Complexity, and Change: A Meta-Framework for Addressing Protracted, Intractable Conflicts – III'.

27 Different to the fields of computational power or big data, where complexity is a defining quality of the field of study, the chapter's approach to complexity focuses instead on frameworks for which complexity presents ontological as well as epistemological challenges to the notion of mastery of the social and the political. This perspective is chosen as it features prominently in peacebuilding literature, and also as it shares foundational assumptions with many post-liberal frameworks of inquiry into peacebuilding theory.

28 Other approaches, also consistent with post-liberal frameworks, include emphasis on the iterative processes that shape the local context. See Richmond, 'Becoming Liberal, Unbecoming Liberalism: Liberal-Local Hybridity via the Everyday as a Response to the Paradoxes of Liberal Peacebuilding'; Shinko, 'Agonistic Peace: A Postmodern Reading'; Björkdahl and Höglund, 'Precarious Peacebuilding: Friction in Global-Local Encounters'; Tom, 'In Search for Emancipatory Hybridity: The Case of Post-War Sierra Leone'; Visoka, 'Peace Is What We Make of It? Peace-Shaping Events and "Non-Events"'.

29 Urry, 'The Complexity Turn', 5. See also Law, *After Method: Mess in Social Science Research*.

30 Körppen, 'Space beyond the Liberal Peacebuilding Consensus – A Systemic Perspective'.

31 Burns, 'Facilitating Systemic Conflict Transformation through Systemic Action Research'.

32 Kavalski, 'The Fifth Debate and the Emergence of Complex International Relations Theory: Notes on the Application of Complexity Theory to the Study of International Life', 449.

33 De Coning, 'Adaptive Peacebuilding', 302.

34 De Coning, 'Adaptive Peacebuilding', 303.

35 De Coning, 'Adaptive Peacebuilding', 305.

36 Schwartz and Nichols, *After Collapse: The Regeneration of Complex Societies*, 10.

37 De Coning, 'Adaptive Peacebuilding', 305.

38 See Bargués, 'Realising the Post-Modern Dream: Strengthening Post-Conflict Resilience and the Promise of Peace'; Randazzo, 'The Paradoxes of the "Everyday": Scrutinising the Local Turn in Peace Building'.

39 See Hirblinger and Simons, 'The Good, the Bad, and the Powerful: Representations of the "Local" in Peacebuilding'.

40 Hendrick, 'Complexity Theory and Conflict Transformation: An Exploration of Potential and Implications'.

41 Lemke, 'Discourse, Dynamics, and Social Change'.

42 Torrent, 'Problematising UN-Local Civil Society Engagement in Peacebuilding: Towards Non-Modern Epistemes Through Relationality'; Visoka, 'Peace Is What We Make of It? Peace-Shaping Events and "Non-Events"'.

43 Vimalarahaj and Nadarajah, 'Thinking Peace: Revisiting Analysis and Intervention in Sri Lanka'.

44 See Coole and Frost, *New Materialisms: Ontology, Agency and Politics*; Cudworth and Hobden, 'The Posthuman Way of War'; De Vries and Rosenow, 'Opposing the Opposition? Binarity and Complexity in Political Resistance'; Delanda, *Assemblage Theory*.

45 Besides the UN, widely developed in this section, other international agencies such as the World Bank, the OCDE and the EU are also gradually shifting towards non-linear, complexity-sensitive policy frameworks (for the World Bank, see Hallegatte et al., *Shock Waves Managing the Impacts of Climate Change on Poverty*; for the OCDE, see Mitchell, 'Risk and Resilience: From Good Idea to Good Practice'; for the EU, see Juncos, 'Resilience in Peacebuilding: Contesting Uncertainty, Ambiguity, and Complexity').

46 See UN Chief Executive Board for Coordination, 'Bringing the UN System Together to Support Conflict Prevention and Peacebuilding within the Broader 2030 Agenda for Sustainable Development'.

47 Randazzo and Torrent, 'Reframing Agency in Complexity-Sensitive Peacebuilding'.

48 For further literature on results of recent UN peacebuilding endeavours, see Campbell, 'Governing Globally, Acting Locally: Lessons from Burundi for International Peacebuilding Reform'; Picciotto, 'Evaluating the UN Development System'; De Coning and Stamnes, *UN Peacebuilding Archit. First 10 Years*.

49 Advisory Group of Experts, 'The Challenge of Sustaining Peace: Report of the Advisory Group of Experts for the 2015 Review of the United Nations Peacebuilding Architecture', 7.

50 De Coning, 'From Peacebuilding to Sustaining Peace: Implications of Complexity for Resilience and Sustainability'.

51 Advisory Group of Experts, 'The Challenge of Sustaining Peace: Report of the Advisory Group of Experts for the 2015 Review of the United Nations Peacebuilding Architecture', 12.

52 See UN Security Council, 'Resolution 2149'.

53 Interview I, anonymous. Freetown, 13/06/2016 (via Skype).

54 Juncos, 'Resilience in Peacebuilding: Contesting Uncertainty, Ambiguity, and Complexity'.

55 De Coning, 'From Peacebuilding to Sustaining Peace: Implications of Complexity for Resilience and Sustainability'.

56 Initially, the DPA and the new PBA were tasked with conflict prevention and peacebuilding, and the DPKO and the Department of Field Support (DFS) were tasked with peacekeeping and peace enforcement competencies.

57 See Advisory Group of Experts, 'The Challenge of Sustaining Peace: Report of the Advisory Group of Experts for the 2015 Review of the United Nations Peacebuilding Architecture'.

58 See Haraway, *Staying with the Trouble: Making Kin in the Chthulucene*; Latour, *Reassembling the Social: An Introduction to Actor-Network-Theory*.

59 See Chadwick, Debiel, and Gadinger, *Relational Sensibility and the "Turn to Local": Prospects for the Future of Peacebuilding*; Brigg, 'Relational and Essential: Theorizing Difference for Peacebuilding'; Joseph, 'Beyond Relationalism in Peacebuilding'.

60 Brigg, 'Relational and Essential: Theorizing Difference for Peacebuilding'.

61 Martin de Almagro, 'Hybrid Clubs: A Feminist Approach to Peacebuilding in the Democratic Republic of Congo', 321.

62 See Richmond, 'A Pedagogy of Peacebuilding: Infrapolitics, Resistance, and Liberation'; Mac Ginty, 'Between Resistance and Compliance: Non-Participation and the Liberal Peace'; Kappler, 'Coping with Research: Local Tactics of Resistance against (Mis-)Representation in Academia'.

63 Moe, 'The Strange Wars of Liberal Peace: Hybridity, Complexity and the Governing Rationalities of Counterinsurgency in Somalia', 103.

64 Loode, 'Peacebuilding in Complex Social Systems', 73.

65 See Bennet, *Vibrant Matter: A Political Ecology of Things*; Randazzo and Torrent, 'Reframing Agency in Complexity-Sensitive Peacebuilding'.

66 See Kappler, 'Coping with Research: Local Tactics of Resistance against (Mis-)Representation in Academia'; Mac Ginty, 'Between Resistance and Compliance: Non-Participation and the Liberal Peace'; Richmond, 'A Pedagogy of Peacebuilding: Infrapolitics, Resistance, and Liberation'; Chandler, 'Peacebuilding and the Politics of Non-Linearity: Rethinking "Hidden" Agency and "Resistance"'.

67 See Sabaratnam, 'IR in Dialogue ... but Can We Change the Subjects? A Typology of Decolonising Strategies for the Study of World Politics'; Jabri, 'Peacebuilding, the Local and the International: A Colonial or a Postcolonial Rationality?'

68 Jabri, 'Peacebuilding, the Local and the International: A Colonial or a Postcolonial Rationality?', 6.

69 De Coning, 'Peace Enforcement in Africa: Doctrinal Distinctions between the African Union and United Nations', 154.

70 Zanotti, 'UN Integrated Peacekeeping Operations and NGOs: Reflections on Governmental Rationalities and Contestation in the Age of Risk', 25.

71 Zanotti, 'UN Integrated Peacekeeping Operations and NGOs: Reflections on Governmental Rationalities and Contestation in the Age of Risk', 28.

72 Delanda elucidates this point: 'When we think that the majority of equations used in science are linear and that a linear conception of causality dominated Western thought for over two millennia, we may be inclined to think that our lack of familiarity with questions of self-organized heterogeneity and our tendency to think about complexity in terms of homogeneous hierarchies derive from the way we represent the world to ourselves. (...) Western societies transformed the objective world (or some areas of it) into the type of structure that would "correspond" to their theories, so that the latter became, in a sense, self-fulfilling prophecies'. Delanda, *A Thousand Years of Nonlinear History,* 273.

73 Law and Urry, 'Enacting the Social', 402.

74 Zanotti, 'Reorienting IR: Ontological Entanglement, Agency, and Ethics', 363.

75 Zanotti, 'Reorienting IR: Ontological Entanglement, Agency, and Ethics', 370.

76 Wendt, *Quantum Mind and Social Science. Unifying Physical and Social Ontology,* 266.

77 Zanotti, 'Reorienting IR: Ontological Entanglement, Agency, and Ethics', 373.

78 Latour, *Reassembling the Social: An Introduction to Actor-Network-Theory*, 46.

79 Latour, *Reassembling the Social: An Introduction to Actor-Network-Theory*, 46.

80 Barad, *Meeting the Universe Halfway: Quantum Physics and the Entanglement of Matter and Meaning*, 172.

81 De Coning, 'Adaptive Peacebuilding'.

82 See Devere, Te Maihāroa, and Synott, *Peacebuilding and the Rights of Indigenous Peoples.*

CHAPTER 4

1 Shaviro, *The Universe of Things. On Speculative Realism,* 34.

2 Whitehead, *Process and Reality,* 148.

3 Colebrook, 'A CUT IN RELATIONALITY: Art at the End of the World', 178.

4 Although the text draws on Western continental philosophy to elucidate entangled ontologies, non-Western philosophy has also produced accounts examining the relational condition of the human and its environment. See endnote 7 in 'Introduction' chapter.

5 Heidegger, 'Being and Time', 53.

6 Whitehead, *Process and Reality*, 7.

7 See Harman, *Object-Oriented Ontology. A New Theory of Everything*; Bogost, *Alien Phenomenology, or What's It like to Be a Thing.*

8 Whitehead, *Process and Reality*, 88.

9 Whitehead, *Process and Reality*, 222.

10 Whitehead, *Process and Reality*, 148.

11 Whitehead, *Process and Reality*, 158.

12 Whitehead, *The Concept of Nature*, 24.

13 See Whitehead, *Process and Reality*, 24, 148 and 312.

14 For a discussion about the dialectics between critical realism and assemblage theory, see Rutzou and Elder-Vass, 'On Assemblages and Things: Fluidity, Stability, Causation Stories, and Formation Stories'.

15 Deleuze, *Spinoza: Practical Philosophy*, 114.
16 Deleuze, *Spinoza: Practical Philosophy*, 77.
17 Deleuze, *Spinoza: Practical Philosophy*, 123.
18 Deleuze, *Spinoza: Practical Philosophy*, 125.
19 Deleuze, *The Fold. Leibniz and the Baroque*, 46.
20 Deleuze, *The Fold. Leibniz and the Baroque*, 52.
21 Deleuze, *The Fold. Leibniz and the Baroque*, 58.
22 Deleuze, *The Fold. Leibniz and the Baroque*, 81.
23 Deleuze, *The Fold. Leibniz and the Baroque*, 81.
24 Deleuze and Guattari, *A Thousand Plateaus. Capitalism and Schizophrenia*, 292.
25 Deleuze and Guattari, *A Thousand Plateaus. Capitalism and Schizophrenia*, 280.
26 Deleuze and Guattari, *A Thousand Plateaus. Capitalism and Schizophrenia*, 504.
27 For Grosz, beyond the ideal-material divide, Deleuze's 'the plane of immanence is the condition for their emergence, their opposition and any rethinking of their relations'. Grosz, *The Incorporeal: Ontology, Ethics, and the Limits of Materialism*, 139.
28 Deleuze and Guattari, *A Thousand Plateaus. Capitalism and Schizophrenia*, 255.
29 Deleuze and Guattari, *A Thousand Plateaus. Capitalism and Schizophrenia*, 255.
30 Beyond Latour, Haraway and Barad, deemed in this book the pioneers of the contemporary entangled ontological turn, accounts on materialist entangled ontologies are numerous. Delanda manifests that "becoming and multiplicity are the same thing" (Delanda, *Intensive Science and Virtual Philosophy*, 75). To this author, becoming is a molecular and intensive relation that operates beyond ontological equilibrium and that is populated by real multiplicities. Similarly, Steven Shaviro markedly inspired by Whitehead, affirms "both the deep interrelatedness of all things and the ways that their interactions and variations continually lead to consequences that are new and unforeseen" (Shaviro, *The Universe of Things. On Speculative Realism*, 4). Still through Whitehead, he goes on to explain the unexpected processes of becoming of things through the concept of creativity, which in Whitehead''s speculative metaphysics explains self-causation. Elaborating on corporeal and incorporeal materialist ontologies, Grosz, drawing on Stoic philosophy, affirms that "bodies are bodies only to the extent that they are capable of acting on each other through collective relations" (Grosz, *The Incorporeal: Ontology, Ethics, and the Limits of Materialism*, 27). To this author, the fate of all bodies in the universe is causally connected in her account and causation is associated with deterministic convergence of things, which carries them with it, thus perpetuating the iterative unfolding of future universes. Finally, in their seminal edited collection on new materialisms, Coole and Frost conceive of "materiality in a relational, emergent sense as contingent materialisation – a process within which more or less enduring structures and assemblages sediment and congeal" (Coole and Frost, *New Materialisms: Ontology, Agency and Politics*, 29). Furthermore, the authors insist that relational materialist ontologies might be the result of intrinsic inertia but can also manifest a clash of power relations underlying opposing interests. Coole also exposes that this relational, processual and non-static ontology "is not about Being, but becoming: crucially, what is invoked is a process not a state, a process of materialisation in which matter literally matters itself" (Coole, 'Agentic Capacities and Capacious Historical Materialism: Thinking with New Materialisms in the Political Sciences', 453). The author depicts a world

in which interactions produce self-organising processes of change and emergence revealing an ontology of becoming, which gives primacy to process in a notoriously Whiteheadinan fashion. For further details on this scholarly work, see also Connolly, *Facing the Planetary: Entangled Humanism and the Politics of Swarming*; Dolphjin and Van der Turin, *New Materialism: Interviews & Cartographies*; Stengers, *Thinking with Whitehead: A Free and Wild Creation of Concepts*.

31 Latour, *Reassembling the Social: An Introduction to Actor-Network-Theory*, 34.

32 Mol, 'Ontological Politics. A Word and Some Questions', 75.

33 Mol, 'Ontological Politics. A Word and Some Questions', 85.

34 Haraway, *When Species Meet*, 163.

35 Haraway, *When Species Meet*, 287.

36 Haraway, *Staying with the Trouble: Making Kin in the Chthulucene*, 13.

37 Haraway, *Staying with the Trouble: Making Kin in the Chthulucene*, 97.

38 See Barad, *Meeting the Universe Halfway: Quantum Physics and the Entanglement of Matter and Meaning*.

39 As an example of the instrumentalisation of new materialism within International Relations, see Srnicek, Fotou, and Arghand, 'Introduction: Materialism and World Politics'. For new materialist accounts engaging with Critical Peace and Conflict and Security Studies see Aradau, 'Security That Matters: Critical Infrastructure and Objects of Protection'; Mac Ginty, 'A Material Turn in International Relations: The 4x4, Intervention and Resistance'.

40 Aradau, 'Security That Matters: Critical Infrastructure and Objects of Protection'.

41 Gregory, 'The Natures of War', 39.

42 Weizman, *Hollow Land*.

43 For a discussion on the relational account in International Relations, see Kurki, *International Relations in a Relational Universe*; Zanotti, *Ontological Entanglements, Agency and Ethics in International Relations: Exploring the Crossroads*. For a discussion on relationality in peacebuilding see Chadwick, Debiel, and Gadinger, *Relational Sensibility and the 'Turn to the Local': Prospects for the Future of Peacebuilding*; Joseph, 'Beyond Relationalism in Peacebuilding'; Brigg, 'Relational and Essential: Theorizing Difference for Peacebuilding'; Torrent, 'Problematising UN-Local Civil Society Engagement in Peacebuilding: Towards Non-Modern Epistemes Through Relationality'; Richmond, 'The Green and the Cool: Hybridity, Relationality and Ethnographic-Biographical Responses to Intervention'.

44 Brigg, 'Relational Sensibility in Peacebuilding: Emancipation, Tyranny, or Transformation?', 14.

45 Brigg.

46 Brigg, 'Relational and Essential: Theorizing Difference for Peacebuilding'.

47 Zanotti, 'Reorienting IR: Ontological Entanglement, Agency, and Ethics'.

48 See Torrent, 'Problematising UN-Local Civil Society Engagement in Peacebuilding: Towards Non-Modern Epistemes Through Relationality'.

49 See Garcia, *Form and Object. A Treatise on Things*.

50 See Action Aid, CAFOD, and CARE International, 'Consolidating the Peace?: Views from Sierra Leone and Burundi on the United Nations Peacebuilding Commission – GSDRC'.

51 See Action Aid, CAFOD, and CARE International.

52 See Weiss, *What's Wrong with the United Nations and How to Fix It*.

53 Jenkins, *Re-Engineering the UN Peacebuilding Architecture. Working Paper: The Future of the Peacebuilding Architecture Project*.

54 See the following interview bits in chapter 1: Interview II, Interview III, Interview IV and Interview VI.

55 Interview II, Bishop Joseph Humper. Freetown, 23/07/2016.

56 Barad, *Meeting the Universe Halfway: Quantum Physics and the Entanglement of Matter and Meaning*, 342.

57 See Danielsson, 'Transcending Binaries in Critical Peacebuilding Scholarship to Address "Inclusivity" Projects'.

58 Barad, *Meeting the Universe Halfway: Quantum Physics and the Entanglement of Matter and Meaning*, 136.

59 Barad, *Meeting the Universe Halfway: Quantum Physics and the Entanglement of Matter and Meaning*, 342.

60 Barad, *Meeting the Universe Halfway: Quantum Physics and the Entanglement of Matter and Meaning*, 342.

61 Barad, *Meeting the Universe Halfway: Quantum Physics and the Entanglement of Matter and Meaning*, 393.

62 Criticising the quantum-inspired space-time conceptualisation, Arfi comments: 'Our natural languages and discourses rarely offer us notions and ideas that are suitable to explicating the subtleties of sophisticated mathematical theories that are not wired in classical physics. Speaking, for example, of spacetime warping or quantum entanglement simply defies any expression in terms of our everyday language except by resorting to analogies and metaphors, which then gives the wrong presentation of the "weirdness" of the issues at stake. And the idea of no background – that is, not even empty space – is just impossible to portray in human natural language'. Arfi and Kessler, 'Forum Introduction: Social Theory Going Quantum-Theoretic? Questions, Alternatives and Challenges', 103.

63 Barad, *Meeting the Universe Halfway: Quantum Physics and the Entanglement of Matter and Meaning,* 393.

64 See bits from Interview XIII, anonymous. Barcelona, 16/03/2016 (via Skype). See also Wilén and Chapaux, 'Problems of Local Participation and Collaboration with the UN in a Post-Conflict Environment: Who Are the "Locals"?'

65 See Jenkins, *Peacebuilding From Concept to Commission*; Rugumamu, 'Does the UN Peacebuilding Commission Change the Mode of Peacebuilding in Africa?'; Wyeth, 'Peacebuilding at the UN over the Last 10 Years'.

66 Chandler, 'Peacebuilding and the Politics of Non-Linearity: Rethinking "Hidden" Agency and "Resistance"'.

67 See Rugumamu, 'Does the UN Peacebuilding Commission Change the Mode of Peacebuilding in Africa?'; Street, Mollett, and Smith, 'Experiences of the United Nations Peacebuilding Commission in Sierra Leone and Burundi'.

68 Whitehead, *Process and Reality*, 66–67.

69 See Harman and Delanda, *The Rise of Realism*, 123; Morton, *Hyperobjects*, 56.

70 See Randazzo and Torrent, 'Reframing Agency in Complexity-Sensitive Peacebuilding'.

71 Urry, 'The Complexity Turn', 3–5.

72 See Torrent, 'Problematising UN-Local Civil Society Engagement in Peacebuilding: Towards Non-Modern Epistemes through Relationality'; Delanda, *Assemblage Theory*; De Vries and Rosenow, 'Opposing the Opposition? Binarity and Complexity in Political Resistance'.

73 Juncos, 'Resilience in Peacebuilding: Contesting Uncertainty, Ambiguity, and Complexity'.

74 See Advisory Group of Experts, 'The Challenge of Sustaining Peace: Report of the Advisory Group of Experts for the 2015 Review of the United Nations Peacebuilding Architecture'.

75 Interview I, anonymous. Freetown, 13/06/2016 (via Skype).

76 Zanotti, 'UN Integrated Peacekeeping Operations and NGOs: Reflections on Governmental Rationalities and Contestation in the Age of Risk', 27.

77 Zanotti, 'UN Integrated Peacekeeping Operations and NGOs: Reflections on Governmental Rationalities and Contestation in the Age of Risk', 28.

78 Tsing, *The Mushroom at the End of the World: On the Possibility of Life in Capitalist Ruins*; see also Crutzen, 'Geology of Mankind'.

79 Chandler, *Ontopolitics in the Anthropocene: An Introduction to Mapping, Sensing and Hacking*.

80 See Morton, *Hyperobjects*; Haraway, *Staying with the Trouble: Making Kin in the Chthulucene*; Connolly, *Facing the Planetary: Entangled Humanism and the Politics of Swarming*.

81 See endnote 39 in the present chapter.

82 Serres, *The Natural Contract*, 25.

83 Serres, *The Natural Contract*, 33.

84 Bennett, *Vibrant Matter: A Political Ecology of Things,* 23.

85 Bennett, *Vibrant Matter: A Political Ecology of Things,* 23.

86 Stengers, *In Catastrophic Times: Resisting the Coming Barbarism,* 45.

87 Kurki, *International Relations in a Relational Universe*, 123.

88 Harman in Harman and Delanda, *The Rise of Realism,* 30–31. See also Harman, *Object-Oriented Ontology. A New Theory of Everything*, 134–135.

89 Harman in Harman and Delanda, *The Rise of Realism,* 71.

90 Harman in Harman and Delanda, *The Rise of Realism,* 57.

91 Harman, *Object-Oriented Ontology. A New Theory of Everything*, 107.

92 Harman, *Object-Oriented Ontology. A New Theory of Everything*, 12.

93 Harman, *Object-Oriented Ontology. A New Theory of Everything*, 107. For a similar account, see Morton, *Being Ecological*.

94 Bargués, 'From Critique to Affirmation in International Relations', 8.

95 Bargués, 'From Critique to Affirmation in International Relations', 8.

96 Bargués, 'From Critique to Affirmation in International Relations', 8.

97 Joseph, 'Beyond Relationalism in Peacebuilding'. For similar accounts, see Swyngedouw and Ernstson, 'Interrupting the Anthropo-ObScene: Immuno-Biopolitics and Depoliticizing Ontologies in the Anthropocene'; Malm, *The Progress of This Storm: Nature and Society in a Warming World*. Dissenting with this first line of argumentation, which perceives entangled ontologies as yielding a power-blind analysis, Latour, sceptical with Foucauldian post-structuralist analysis, warns that 'we

have to be very scrupulous in checking whether power and domination are explained by the multiplicity of objects given a central role and transported by vehicles which should be empirically visible – and we will not be content to have power and domination themselves be the mysterious container that holds inside of it that which makes the many participants in the action move'. Latour, *Reassembling the Social: An Introduction to Actor-Network-Theory*, 83.

98 Shaviro, *The Universe of Things. On Speculative Realism*, 33.

99 Shaviro, *The Universe of Things. On Speculative Realism*, 34.

100 Colebrook, 'A CUT IN RELATIONALITY: Art at the End of the World', 177.

101 Colebrook, 'A CUT IN RELATIONALITY: Art at the End of the World', 189.

102 For similar cautionary arguments on relationality see Puig de la Bellacasa, *Matters of Care. Speculative Ethics in More than Human Worlds*.

103 Whitehead, *Process and Reality*, 148.

CHAPTER 5

1 Advisory Group of Experts, 'The Challenge of Sustaining Peace: Report of the Advisory Group of Experts for the 2015 Review of the United Nations Peacebuilding Architecture', 22. See also Micinski, 'NGO Frequent Flyers: Youth Organizations and the Undermining of Reconciliation in Bosnia and Herzegovina'.

2 Interview XVI, anonymous. Freetown, 28/07/2016 (via Skype).

3 Interview XVII, anonymous. New York, 17/01/2017.

4 Interview XVII, anonymous. New York, 17/01/2017.

5 Interview XVII, anonymous. New York, 17/01/2017.

6 Interview IX, anonymous. Barcelona, 14/03/2016 (via Skype).

7 UN General Assembly and UN Security Council, 'Review of Progress in the Implementation of the Strategic Framework for Peacebuilding in Burundi'; UN Peacebuilding Commission, 'Report of the Peacebuilding Commission Mission to the Central African Republic, 10–15 October 2011'.

8 See Boyd, *Uncivil Society: The Perils of Pluralism and the Making of Modern Liberalism*; Mac Ginty, *International Peacebuilding and Local Resistance: Hybrid Forms of Peace*.

9 Vogel, 'Civil Society Capture: Top-Down Interventions from Below?', 473.

10 The process through which international actors transfer their modern parameters, it is suggested, is gradual and subtle. For example, although Sierra Leoneans had generally maintained respect for traditional roles, alternative dispute mechanisms created by donors were becoming more trusted (see Vincent, 'A Village-Up View of Sierra Leone''s Civil War and Reconstruction: Multilayered and Networked Governance'). This societal shift requires moving away from communalist obligations and traditional structures towards individualist thinking and respect for a modern state and modern social structures (see Spagnoli, *Homo-Democraticus: On the Universal Desirability and the Not So Universal Possibility of Democracy and Human Rights)*. Nowadays, Sierra Leone functions on the basis of a hybrid system, which some have deemed a

destabilising element due to the local difficulties in finding the balance between the traditional and modern modus operandi (Harris, *Sierra Leone: A Political History*).

11 Wark, *Molecular Red: Theory for the Anthropocene,* 131.

12 Morton, *Hyperobjects,* 19.

13 Scott, *Seeing like a State: How Certain Schemes to Improve the Human Condition Have Failed.*

14 Haraway, 'A Cyborg Manifesto: Science, Technology, and Socialist-Feminism in the Late Twentieth Century', 118.

15 Vogel, 'Civil Society Capture: Top-Down Interventions from Below?'.

16 See Robinson, *The Complete Mars Trilogy.*

17 See Bogost, *Alien Phenomenology, or What's It like to Be a Thing*; Harman, *Object-Oriented Ontology. A New Theory of Everything.*

18 Beier, 'Dispatch from the Future: Science Fictioning (in) the Anthropocene', 262.

19 See Whitehead, *Process and Reality, 5. See also* Heidegger, 'Being and Time', 53.

20 Preciado, *An Apartment on Uranus.*

21 Deleuze and Guattari, *A Thousand Plateaus. Capitalism and Schizophrenia,* 292.

22 Deleuze and Guattari, *A Thousand Plateaus. Capitalism and Schizophrenia,* 393.

23 Deleuze and Guattari, *A Thousand Plateaus. Capitalism and Schizophrenia,* 418.

24 Deleuze and Guattari, *A Thousand Plateaus. Capitalism and Schizophrenia,* 292.

25 Deleuze and Guattari, *A Thousand Plateaus. Capitalism and Schizophrenia,* 430.

26 Giraud, *What Comes after Entanglement? Activism, Anthropocentrism, and an Ethics of Exclusion,* 49.

27 See Haraway, *Staying with the Trouble: Making Kin in the Chthulucene*; Tsing, *The Mushroom at the End of the World: On the Possibility of Life in Capitalist Ruins*; Van Dooren, *Flight Ways. Life and Loss at the Edge of Extinction*; Rose, *Wild Dog Dreaming. Love and Extinction*; Puig de la Bellacasa, *Matters of Care. Speculative Ethics in More than Human Worlds.*

28 Tsing, *The Mushroom at the End of the World: On the Possibility of Life in Capitalist Ruins,* 168.

29 Tsing, *The Mushroom at the End of the World: On the Possibility of Life in Capitalist Ruins,* 168.

30 Haraway, *Staying with the Trouble: Making Kin in the Chthulucene,* 10.

31 Haraway, *Staying with the Trouble: Making Kin in the Chthulucene,* 10.

32 Haraway, *Staying with the Trouble: Making Kin in the Chthulucene,* 39.

33 Haraway, *Staying with the Trouble: Making Kin in the Chthulucene,* 132.

34 Viveiros de Castro, *Cannibal Metaphysics: For a Post-Structural Anthropology.*

35 See Grove, *Savage Ecology: War and Geopolitics at the End of the World.*

36 Van Dooren, *Flight Ways. Life and Loss at the Edge of Extinction,* 69.

37 Grosz, *Becoming Undone: Darwinian Reflections on Life, Politics and Art,* 78.

38 See Advisory Group of Experts, 'The Challenge of Sustaining Peace: Report of the Advisory Group of Experts for the 2015 Review of the United Nations Peacebuilding Architecture'.

39 See Barad, 'Quantum Entanglements and Hauntological Relations of Inheritance: Dis/Continuities, SpaceTime Enfoldings, and Justice-to-Come'; Bertrand, Goettlich, and Murray, 'The Politics of Time in International Relations'.

40 Whitehead, *The Concept of Nature*, 66.

41 Whitehead, *The Concept of Nature*, 24.

42 Whitehead, *Process and Reality*, 35.

43 Whitehead, *The Adventure of Ideas*, 246.

44 Whitehead, *The Adventure of Ideas*, 336.

45 Whitehead, *The Adventure of Ideas*, 336.

46 Delanda in Harman and Delanda, *The Rise of Realism*, 130. See also Smolin, *Time Reborn: From the Crisis in Physics to the Future of the Universe*.

47 Barad, 'Troubling Time/s and Ecologies of Nothingness: Re-Turning, Re-Membering, and Facing the Incalculable', 57.

48 Barad, 'Troubling Time/s and Ecologies of Nothingness: Re-Turning, Re-Membering, and Facing the Incalculable', 61.

49 Bennet, *Vibrant Matter: A Political Ecology of Things*, 79.

50 Kirby, *Quantum Anthropologies Life at Large*, 30.

51 Grosz, *The Incorporeal: Ontology, Ethics, and the Limits of Materialism*. See also Bleiker, 'In Search of Thinking Space: Reflections on the Aesthetic Turn in International Political Theory'.

52 Grosz, *The Incorporeal: Ontology, Ethics, and the Limits of Materialism*, 104.

53 Tsing, *The Mushroom at the End of the World: On the Possibility of Life in Capitalist Ruins*, 20.

54 Grosz, *The Incorporeal: Ontology, Ethics, and the Limits of Materialism*, 211.

55 Grosz, *The Incorporeal: Ontology, Ethics, and the Limits of Materialism*, 212.

56 Chandler, 'Intervention and Statebuilding beyond the Human: From the "Black Box" to the "Great Outdoors"', 81.

57 Tsing, *The Mushroom at the End of the World: On the Possibility of Life in Capitalist Ruins*, 287.

58 Colebrook, 'A CUT IN RELATIONALITY: Art at the End of the World', 189.

59 Deleuze, *Spinoza: Practical Philosophy*, 23.

60 Deleuze, *Spinoza: Practical Philosophy*, 35.

61 Deleuze, *Spinoza: Practical Philosophy*, 37.

62 Deleuze, *Spinoza: Practical Philosophy*, 71.

63 Nietzsche, 'On the Genealogy of Morals', 543.

64 Deleuze, *Spinoza: Practical Philosophy*, 41.

65 Deleuze, *Spinoza: Practical Philosophy*, 125.

66 Deleuze, *Spinoza: Practical Philosophy*, 125.

67 See Braidotti, *Posthuman Knowledge*; Grosz, *The Incorporeal: Ontology, Ethics, and the Limits of Materialism*; Puig de la Bellacasa, *Matters of Care. Speculative Ethics in More than Human Worlds*.

68 Braidotti, *Posthuman Knowledge*, 158.

69 Braidotti, *Posthuman Knowledge*, 50.

70 Braidotti, *Posthuman Knowledge*, 158.

71 Braidotti, *Posthuman Knowledge*, 158.

72 Braidotti, *Posthuman Knowledge*, 169.

73 Barad, *Meeting the Universe Halfway: Quantum Physics and the Entanglement of Matter and Meaning*, 160.

74 Barad, *Meeting the Universe Halfway: Quantum Physics and the Entanglement of Matter and Meaning*, 393.

75 Barad, *Meeting the Universe Halfway: Quantum Physics and the Entanglement of Matter and Meaning*, 394.

76 Haraway also elucidates this point: "With this kind of material – semiotic tool as companion, the past, present, and future are all very much knotted into one another, full of what we need for the work and play of habitat restoration, less deadly curiosity, materially entangled ethics and politics, and openness to alien and native kinds symbiogenetically linked" (Haraway, *When Species Meet*, 292).

77 Barad, *Meeting the Universe Halfway: Quantum Physics and the Entanglement of Matter and Meaning*, 396.

78 Barad, *Meeting the Universe Halfway: Quantum Physics and the Entanglement of Matter and Meaning*, 396.

79 Grosz, *The Incorporeal: Ontology, Ethics, and the Limits of Materialism*, 81.

80 Grosz, *The Incorporeal: Ontology, Ethics, and the Limits of Materialism*, 153.

81 Rose, *Wild Dog Dreaming. Love and Extinction*, 143–44.

82 Rose, *Wild Dog Dreaming. Love and Extinction*, 149.

Bibliography

Action Aid, CAFOD, and CARE International. 'Consolidating the Peace?: Views from Sierra Leone and Burundi on the United Nations Peacebuilding Commission – GSDRC', 2007.

Adebajo, Adekeye. *UN Peacekeeping in Africa: From the Suez Crisis to the Sudan Conflicts*. Boulder, CO: Lynne Rienner Publishers, 2011.

Advisory Group of Experts. 'The Challenge of Sustaining Peace: Report of the Advisory Group of Experts for the 2015 Review of the United Nations Peacebuilding Architecture', 2015.

Al-Qaq, Richard Kareem. *Managing World Order: United Nations Peace Operations and the Security Agenda*. London: I. B. Tauris & Co., 2009.

Alexander, Jeffrey C. *The Civil Sphere*. Oxford: Oxford University Press, 2006.

Allan, Bentley B. 'From Subjects to Objects: Knowledge in International Relations Theory'. *European Journal of International Relations* 24, no. 4 (November 23, 2017): 841–64.

Aradau, Claudia. 'Security That Matters: Critical Infrastructure and Objects of Protection'. *Security Dialogue* 41, no. 5 (October 1, 2010): 491–514.

Arfi, Badredine, and Oliver Kessler. 'Forum Introduction: Social Theory Going Quantum-Theoretic? Questions, Alternatives and Challenges'. *Millenium: Journal of International Studies* 47, no. 1 (2018): 67–73.

Arnault, Jean. 'Legitimacy and Peace Processes'. *Conciliation Resources* 25 (2014): 21–5.

Autesserre, Séverine. *Peaceland: Conflict Resolution and the Everyday Politics of International Intervention*. Cambridge: Cambridge University Press, 2014.

Barad, Karen. *Meeting the Universe Halfway: Quantum Physics and the Entanglement of Matter and Meaning*. Durham, NC: Duke University Press, 2007.

———. 'Quantum Entanglements and Hauntological Relations of Inheritance: Dis/Continuities, SpaceTime Enfoldings, and Justice-to-Come'. *Derrida Today* 3, no. 2 (November 2010): 240–68.

————. 'Troubling Time/s and Ecologies of Nothingness: Re-Turning, Re-Membering, and Facing the Incalculable'. *New Formations: A Journal of Culture/Theory/Politics*, no. 92 (2017): 56–86.

Bargués, Pol. *Deferring Peace in International Statebuilding: Difference, Resilience and Critique*. London: Routledge, 2018.

————. 'From Critique to Affirmation in International Relations'. *Global Society* 33, no. 1 (2019): 1–11.

————. 'Realising the Post-Modern Dream: Strengthening Post-Conflict Resilience and the Promise of Peace'. *Resilience* 3, no. 2 (May 4, 2015): 113–32.

Barnett, Michael, and Martha Finnemore. 'The Power of Liberal International Organizations'. In *Power in Global Governance*, edited by Michael Barnett and Raymond Duvall, 161–84. Cambridge: Cambridge University Press, 2005.

Beier, Jessie. 'Dispatch from the Future: Science Fictioning (in) the Anthropocene'. In *Interrogating the Anthropocene Ecology, Aesthetics, Pedagogy, and the Future in Question*, edited by Jan Jagodinski, 359–400. London: Palgrave Macmillan, 2018.

Beijnum, Mariska Van. 'Achievements of the UN Peacebuilding Commission and the Challenges Ahead'. In *The UN Peacebuilding Architecture: The First 10 Years*, edited by Cedric De Coning and Eli Stamnes, 77–95. New York, NY: Routledge Global Institutions, 2016.

Bennet, Jane. *Vibrant Matter: A Political Ecology of Things*. Durham, NC: Duke University Press, 2010.

Bergson, Henri. *Matter and Memory*. Eastford, CT: Martino Fine Books, 2011.

————. *Time and Free Will: An Essay on the Immediate Data of Consciousness*. New York, NY: Dover Publications, 2003.

Bertrand, Sarah, Kerry Goettlich, and Christopher Murray. 'The Politics of Time in International Relations'. *Millennium: Journal of International Studies* 46, no. 3 (June 22, 2018): 251–52.

Björkdahl, Annika, and Kristine Höglund. 'Precarious Peacebuilding: Friction in Global-Local Encounters'. *Peacebuilding* 1, no. 3 (September 1, 2013): 289–99.

Bleiker, Roland. 'In Search of Thinking Space: Reflections on the Aesthetic Turn in International Political Theory'. *Millennium: Journal of International Studies* 45, no. 2 (January 20, 2017): 258–64.

Bogost, Ian. *Alien Phenomenology, or What's It like to Be a Thing*. Minneapolis, MN: University of Minnesota Press, 2012.

Boshoff, Henri, Waldemar Vrey, and George Rautenbach. *The Burundi Peace Process: From Civil War to Conditional Peace*. Pretoria: Institute for Security Studies, 2010.

Bouka, Yolande. 'Status and Dynamics of the Political Situation in Burundi'. *ISS Central African Report* 1 (2014): 1–16.

Boulding, Kenneth Ewart. *Conflict and Defense: A General Theory*. Whitefish, MT: Literary Licensing, 2012.

Boyd, Richard. *Uncivil Society: The Perils of Pluralism and the Making of Modern Liberalism*. Oxford: Lexington Books, 2004.

Braidotti, Rosi. *Posthuman Knowledge*. Cambridge: Polity Press, 2019.

Brigg, Morgan. 'Relational and Essential: Theorizing Difference for Peacebuilding'. *Journal of Intervention and Statebuilding* 12, no. 3 (July 3, 2018): 352–66.

———. 'Relational Sensibility in Peacebuilding: Emancipation, Tyranny, or Transformation?' In *Relational Sensibility and the 'Turn to the Local': Prospects for the Future of Peacebuilding*, edited by W. Chadwick, T. Debiel, and F. Gadinger, 12–18. Duisburg: Käte Hamburger Kolleg/Centre for Global Cooperation Research, 2013.

Browne, Stephen, and Thomas Weiss, eds. *Peacebuilding Challenges for the UN Development System*. New York, NY: Future United Nations Development System, 2015.

Brusset, Emery, Cedric de Coning, and Bryn Hughes, eds. *Complexity Thinking for Peacebuilding Practice and Evaluation*. London: Palgrave Macmillan, 2016.

Burns, Danny. 'Facilitating Systemic Conflict Transformation through Systemic Action Research'. In *The Non-Linearity of Peace Processes: Theory and Practice of Systemic Conflict Transformation*, edited by D. Körrpen, N. Ropers, and H.J. Giessmann, 97–110. Opladen: Barbara Budrich Publishers, 2011.

Campbell, Susanna. 'Governing Globally, Acting Locally: Lessons from Burundi for International Peacebuilding Reform'. In *Peacebuilding Challenges for the UN Development System*, edited by Stephen Browne and Thomas Weiss, 81–92. New York, NY: Future United Nations Development System, 2015.

Carayanis, Tatiana, and Louisa Lombard, eds. *Making Sense of the Central African Republic*. London: Zed Books, 2015.

Carayannis, Tatiana, and Mignonne Fowlis. 'Lessons from African Union – United Nations Cooperation in Peace Operations in the Central African Republic'. *African Security Review* 26, no. 2 (April 3, 2017): 220–36.

Carvalho, Gustavo de, and Amanda Lucey. 'Fractured Peacebuilding in the Central African Republic: Lessons for African Union Engagement'. *Policy Brief* 87, (2016): 1–12. Pretoria: Institute for Security Studies.

Center on International Cooperation. 'Annual Review of Global Peace Operations 2009', 2009.

———. 'Annual Review of Global Peace Operations 2010', 2010.

Chadwick, Wren, Tobias Debiel, and Frank Gadinger, eds. *Relational Sensibility and the 'Turn to the Local': Prospects for the Future of Peacebuilding*. Duisburg: Käte Hamburger Kolleg/Centre for Global Cooperation Research, 2013.

Chambers, Simone, and Will Kymlicka. *Alternative Conceptions of Civil Society*. Princeton, NJ: Princeton University Press, 2002.

Chandler, David. 'A World without Causation: Big Data and the Coming of Age of Post-humanism'. *Millenium: Journal of International Studies* 43, no. 3 (2015): 833–51.

———. *Constructing Global Civil Society: Morality and Power in International Relations*. Basingstoke: Palgrave Macmillan, 2004.

———. 'Intervention and Statebuilding Beyond the Human: From the "Black Box" to the "Great Outdoors"'. *Journal of Intervention and Statebuilding* 12, no. 1 (January 2, 2018): 80–97.

———. *Ontopolitics in the Anthropocene: An Introduction to Mapping, Sensing and Hacking*. Abingdon: Routledge, 2018.

———. *Peacebuilding: The Twenty Years' Crisis*. Basingstoke: Palgrave Macmillan, 2017.

———. 'Peacebuilding and the Politics of Non-Linearity: Rethinking "Hidden" Agency and "Resistance"'. *Peacebuilding* 1, no. 1 (March 1, 2013): 17–32.

———. 'Race, Culture and Civil Society: Peacebuilding Discourse and the Understanding of Difference'. *Security Dialogue* 41, no. 4 (August 1, 2010): 369–90.

———. 'Rethinking the Conflict-Poverty Nexus: From Securitising Intervention to Resilience'. *Stability: International Journal of Security and Development* 4, no. 1 (2015): 1–14.

———. 'The Uncritical Critique of "Liberal Peace"'. *Review of International Studies* 36, no. S1 (2010): 137–55.

Chandler, David, and Jon Coaffee, eds. *The Routledge Handbook of International Resilience*. Abingdon-on-Thames: Routledge, 2020.

Choedon, Yeshi. 'The United Nations Peacebuilding in Kosovo: The Issue of Coordination'. *International Studies* 47, no. 1 (January 1, 2010): 41–57.

Cilliers, Paul, and Rika Preiser, eds. *Complexity, Difference and Identity*. London & New York: Springer, 2010.

Colebrook, Claire. 'A CUT IN RELATIONALITY: Art at the End of the World'. *Angelaki* 24, no. 3 (May 4, 2019): 175–95.

Coleman, Peter T. 'Conflict, Complexity, and Change: A Meta-Framework for Addressing Protracted, Intractable Conflicts – III'. *Peace and Conflict: Journal of Peace Psychology* 12, no. 4 (December 1, 2006): 325–48.

De Coning, Cedric. 'Adaptive Peacebuilding'. *International Affairs* 94, no. 2 (March 1, 2018): 301–17.

———. 'Clarity, Coherence and Context: Three Priorities for Sustainable Peace'. Working Paper 31, 2010. Oslo: NUPI.

———. 'Coherence and Coordination in United Nations Peacebuilding and Integrated Missions – A Norwegian Perspective'. NUPI Report, Security in Practice 5, 2007. Oslo: NUPI.

———. 'From Peacebuilding to Sustaining Peace: Implications of Complexity for Resilience and Sustainability'. *Resilience* 4, no. 3 (September 1, 2016): 166–81.

———. 'How UN Peacekeeping Operations Can Adapt to a New Multipolar World Order'. *International Peacekeeping* 26, no. 5 (October 20, 2019): 536–39.

———. 'Peace Enforcement in Africa: Doctrinal Distinctions between the African Union and United Nations'. *Contemporary Security Policy* 38, no. 1 (January 2, 2017): 145–60.

De Coning, Cedric, and Mateja Peter, eds. *United Nations Peace Operations in a Changing Global Order*. London: Palgrave Macmillan, 2019.

De Coning, Cedric, and Eli Stamnes, eds. *The UN Peacebuilding Architecture: The First 10 Years*. New York, NY: Routledge Global Institutions, 2016.

Connolly, William. *Facing the Planetary: Entangled Humanism and the Politics of Swarming*. Durham, NC: Duke University Press, 2017.

Coole, Diana. 'Agentic Capacities and Capacious Historical Materialism: Thinking with New Materialisms in the Political Sciences'. *Millennium: Journal of International Studies* 41, no. 3 (June 19, 2013): 451–69.

Coole, Diana, and Samanta Frost, eds. *New Materialisms: Ontology, Agency and Politics*. Durham, NC: Duke University Press, 2010.

Council of the European Union. 'Council Conclusions on EU Approach to Resilience', 2013. https://www.consilium.europa.eu/uedocs/cms_data/docs/pressdata/en/foraff/137319.pdf

Crutzen, Paul J. 'Geology of Mankind'. *Nature* 415, no. 23 (2002).

Cudworth, Erika, and Steve Hobden. 'The Posthuman Way of War'. *Security Dialogue* 46, no. 6 (2015): 513–29.

Dahrendorf, Nicola. *A Review of Peace Operations: A Case for Change*. London: King's College, 2003.

Danielsson, Anna. 'Transcending Binaries in Critical Peacebuilding Scholarship to Address "Inclusivity" Projects'. *Third World Quarterly* 41, no. 7 (July 2, 2020): 1085–1102.

Delanda, Manuel. *A Thousand Years of Nonlinear History*. New York, NY: Swerve Editions, 2000.

———. *Assemblage Theory*. Edinburgh: Edinburgh University Press, 2016.

———. *Intensive Science and Virtual Philosophy*. London: Continuum, 2002.

Deleuze, Gilles. *Spinoza: Practical Philosophy*. San Francisco, CA: City Lights Books, 1988.

———. *The Fold. Leibniz and the Baroque*. Minneapolis, MN: University of Minnesota Press, 1993.

Deleuze, Gilles, and Felix Guattari. *A Thousand Plateaus. Capitalism and Schizophrenia*. Minneapolis, MN: University of Minnesota Press, 1987.

Devellennes, Charles, and Benoît Dillet. 'Questioning New Materialisms: An Introduction'. *Theory, Culture & Society* 35, no. 7–8 (December 29, 2018): 5–20.

Devere, Heather, Kelli Te Maihāroa, and John P. Synott, eds. *Peacebuilding and the Rights of Indigenous Peoples*. London & New York: Springer, 2017.

Dillon, Michael, and Julian Reid. 'Global Governance, Liberal Peace, and Complex Emergency'. *Alternatives: Global, Local, Political* 25, no. 1 (January 1, 2000): 117–43.

Dobbins, James, Seth G. Jones, Keith Crane, Andrew Rathmell, Brett Steele, Richard Teltschik, and Anga R. Timilsina. *The UN's Role in Nation-Building from the Congo to Iraq*. Washington, DC: Rand Corporation, 2005.

Does, Antonia. *Inclusivity and Local Perspectives in Peacebuilding: Issues, Lessons, Challenges*. New York, NY: Dag Hammarskjold Foundation, 2013.

Dolphjin, Rick, and Iris Van der Turin. *New Materialism: Interviews & Cartographies*. Ann Arbor, MI: Open Humanities Press, 2012.

Donini, Antonio. 'The Policies of Mercy: UN Coordination in Afghanistan, Mozambique, and Rwanda'. Occasional Paper 22, 1996. Providence, RI: The Thomas J. Watson Jr. Institute for International Studies.

Dooren, Thom Van. *Flight Ways. Life and Loss at the Edge of Extinction*. New York, NY: University of Columbia Press, 2014.

Duffield, Mark. *Global Governance and the New Wars: The Merging of Development and Security*. London: Zed Books, 2001.

Edwards, Michael. *Civil Society*. Cambridge: Polity, 2014.

Foucault, Michel. *The History of Sexuality. Volume 1, An Introduction.* New York, NY: Vintage, 1990.

Galtung, Johan. 'Three Approaches to Peace: Peacekeeping, Peacemaking, and Peacebuilding'. *Impact of Science on Society* 1, no. 2 (1976): 25–9.

———. 'Violence, Peace, and Peace Research'. *Journal of Peace Research* 6, no. 3 (December 1969): 167–91.

Garcia, Tristan. *Form and Object. A Treatise on Things.* Edinburgh: Edinburgh University Press, 2014.

Geyer, Robert, and Steve Pickering. 'Applying the Tools of Complexity to the International Realm: From Fitness Landscapes to Complexity Cascades'. *Cambridge Review of International Affairs* 24, no. 1 (March 1, 2011): 5–26.

Ginty, Roger Mac. 'A Material Turn in International Relations: The 4x4, Intervention and Resistance'. *Review of International Studies* 43, no. 5 (2017): 855–74.

———. 'Between Resistance and Compliance: Non-Participation and the Liberal Peace'. *Journal of Intervention and Statebuilding* 6, no. 2 (June 1, 2012): 167–87.

———. *International Peacebuilding and Local Resistance: Hybrid Forms of Peace.* Basingstoke: Palgrave Macmillan, 2011.

———. 'Where Is the Local? Critical Localism and Peacebuilding'. *Third World Quarterly* 36, no. 5 (May 4, 2015): 840–56.

Giraud, Eva Haifa. *What Comes after Entanglement? Activism, Anthropocentrism, and an Ethics of Exclusion.* Durham, NC: Duke University Press, 2019.

Glissant, Édouard. *Poetics of Relation.* Ann Arbor, MI: University of Michigan Press, 1997.

Graben, Sari, and Ann Fitz-Gerald. 'Mind the Gap: The Importance of Local Institutional Development in Peace-Building-Funded Security Interventions'. *Conflict, Security & Development* 13, no. 3 (2013): 285–316.

Graham, Mary. 'Some Thoughts about the Philosophical Underpinnings of Aboriginal Worldviews'. *Worldviews: Global Religions, Culture, and Ecology* 3, no. 2 (n.d.): 105–18.

Gregory, Derek. 'The Natures of War'. *Antipode* 48, no. 1 (2016): 3–56.

Grosz, Elisabeth. *Becoming Undone: Darwinian Reflections on Life, Politics and Art.* Durham, NC: Duke University Press, 2011.

———. *The Incorporeal: Ontology, Ethics, and the Limits of Materialism.* New York, NY: Columbia University Press, 2017.

Grove, Jairus Victor. *Savage Ecology: War and Geopolitics at the End of the World.* Durham, NC: Duke University Press, 2019.

Hallegatte, Stephane, Mook Bangalore, Laura Bonzanigo, Marianne Fay, Tamaro Kane, Ulf Narloch, Julie Rozenberg, David Treguer, and Adrien Vogt-Schilb. *Shock Waves: Managing the Impacts of Climate Change on Poverty.* Washington: International Bank for Reconstruction and Development/World Bank, 2016.

Haraway, Donna. *A Cyborg Manifesto: Science, Technology, and Socialist-Feminism in the Late Twentieth Century.* Minneapolis and London: University of Minnesota Press, 2007.

———. *Modest_Witness@Second_Millennium.FemaleMan_Meets_OncoMouse: Feminism and Technoscience.* Abingdon-on-Thames: Routledge, 1997.

―――. *Staying with the Trouble: Making Kin in the Chthulucene*. Durham, NC: Duke University Press, 2016.

―――. *When Species Meet*. Minneapolis, MN: University of Minnesota Press, 2007.

Harman, Graham. *Object-Oriented Ontology. A New Theory of Everything*. London: Pelican Books, 2018.

Harman, Graham, and Manuel Delanda. *The Rise of Realism*. Malden, MA: Polity Press, 2017.

Harris, David. *Sierra Leone: A Political History*. London: C Hurst & Co Publishers Ltd., 2013.

Hearn, Sarah, Alejandra Kubitschek Bujones, and Alischa Kugel. 'The United Nations "Peacebuilding Architecture": Past, Present and Future'. New York, 2014.

Heidegger, Martin. 'Being and Time'. In *Martin Hidegger, Basic Writings*, edited by David Farrell Krell. London: Harper Collins, 2008.

Hendrick, Diane. 'Complexity Theory and Conflict Transformation: An Exploration of Potential and Implications'. Working Paper 17, 2009. Bradford: Department of Peace Studies, University of Bradford.

Hirblinger, Andreas T., and Claudia Simons. 'The Good, the Bad, and the Powerful: Representations of the "Local" in Peacebuilding'. *Security Dialogue* 46, no. 5 (October 20, 2015): 422–39.

Hirschmann, Gisela. 'Organizational Learning in United Nations' Peacekeeping Exit Strategies'. *Cooperation and Conflict* 47, no. 3 (August 22, 2012): 368–85.

Humphreys, Adam. 'Causation in International Relations'. In *Oxford Bibliographies in International Relations*, edited by Patrick James. Oxford: Oxford University Press, 2020.

Iñiguez de Heredia, Marta. 'Escaping Statebuilding: Resistance and Civil Society in the Democratic Republic of the Congo'. *Journal of Intervention and Statebuilding* 6, no. 1 (2012): 75–89.

International Crisis Group. 'The Central African Republic's Hidden Conflict'. Briefing 105, 2014. Brussels: International Crisis Group.

International Institute for Strategic Studies, ed. *Armed Conflict Survey 2020*. Abingdon-on-Thames: Routledge, 2020.

International Institute for Strategic Studies. 'Central African Republic: Instability and Intervention'. *Strategic Comments* 19, no. 9 (October 16, 2013): ix–x.

―――. 'Central African Republic: New UN Mission'. *Strategic Comments* 20, no. 6 (October 7, 2014): x–xi.

Jabri, Vivienne. 'Peacebuilding, the Local and the International: A Colonial or a Postcolonial Rationality?' *Peacebuilding* 1, no. 1 (March 1, 2013): 3–16.

Jenkins, Rob. 'Re-Engineering the UN Peacebuilding Architecture'. Working Paper, 2010. Oslo: Norwegian Institute of International Affairs.

Jenkins, Rob. *Peacebuilding from Concept to Commission*. Abingdon-on-Thames: Routledge, 2013.

Joseph, Jonathan. 'Beyond Relationalism in Peacebuilding'. *Journal of Intervention and Statebuilding* 12, no. 3 (July 3, 2018): 425–34.

————. 'The EU in the Horn of Africa: Building Resilience as a Distant Form of Governance'. *Journal of Common Market Studies* 52, no. 2 (March 1, 2014): 285–301.

Juncos, Ana E. 'Resilience in Peacebuilding: Contesting Uncertainty, Ambiguity, and Complexity'. *Contemporary Security Policy* 39, no. 4 (October 2, 2018): 559–74.

Kaldor, Mary. *Global Civil Society: An Answer to War*. Cambridge: Cambridge Polity Press, 2003.

Kane, Mouhamadou. 'Interreligious Violence in the Central African Republic'. *African Security Review* 23, no. 3 (September 22, 2014): 312–17.

Kappler, Stefanie. 'Coping with Research: Local Tactics of Resistance against (Mis-) Representation in Academia'. *Peacebuilding* 1, no. 1 (March 1, 2013): 125–40.

Kavalski, Emilian. 'The Fifth Debate and the Emergence of Complex International Relations Theory: Notes on the Application of Complexity Theory to the Study of International Life'. *Cambridge Review of International Affairs* 20, no. 3 (September 1, 2007): 435–54.

Kirby, Vicki. *Quantum Anthropologies: Life at Large*. Durham, NC: Duke University Press, 2011.

Körppen, Daniela. 'Space Beyond the Liberal Peacebuiling Consensus – A Systemic Perspective'. In *The Non-Linearity of Peace Processes: Theory and Practice of Systemic Conflict Transformation*, 77–96. Opladen: Verlag Barbara Budrich, 2011.

Körppen, Daniela, Norbert Ropers, and Hans J. Giessmann, eds. *The Non-Linearity of Peace Processes: Theory and Practice of Systemic Conflict Transformation*. Opladen: Verlag Barbara Budrich, 2011.

Kurki, Milja. *Causation in International Relations Reclaiming Causal Analysis*. Cambridge: Cambridge University Press, 2008.

————. *International Relations in a Relational Universe*. Oxford: Oxford University Press, 2020.

Latour, Bruno. *Reassembling the Social: An Introduction to Actor-Network-Theory*. Oxford: Oxford University Press, 2005.

Law, John. *After Method: Mess in Social Science Research*. London: Routledge, 2004.

Law, John, and John Urry. 'Enacting the Social'. *Economy and Society* 33, no. 3 (2004): 390–410.

Lebow, Richard Ned. *Constructing Cause in International Relations*. Cambridge: Cambridge University Press, 2014.

Lederach, John Paul. *Building Peace. Sustainable Reconciliation in Divided Societies*. Washington, DC: United States Institute of Peace Press, 1997.

Lemke, J. L. 'Discourse, Dynamics, and Social Change'. *Cultural Dynamics* 6, no. 1–2 (March 1, 1993): 243–75.

Lewis, David. 'The Myopic Foucauldian Gaze: Discourse, Knowledge and the Authoritarian Peace'. *Journal of Intervention and Statebuilding* 11, no. 1 (January 2, 2017): 21–41.

Lidén, Kristoffer. 'Building Peace between Global and Local Politics: On the Cosmopolitan Ethics of Liberal Peacebuilding'. *International Peacekeeping* 16, no. 5 (2009): 616–34.

Ling, L.H.M. *Imagining World Politics. Sihar & Shenya: A Fable for Our Times*. London: Routledge, 2014.

Lipschutz, Ronnie D. 'Reconstructing World Politics: The Emergence of Global Civil Society'. *Millennium* 21, no. 3 (1992): 389–420.

Loode, Serge. 'Peacebuilding in Complex Social Systems'. *Journal of Peace, Conflict & Development* 4, no. 18 (2011): 68–82.

Maiangwa, Benjamin, and Muhammad Dan Suleiman. 'Liberal Peace Intervention in the Central African Republic: Limitations and Reworking a "Hybrid" Order'. *African Security* 10, no. 1 (2017): 1–24.

Makinda, Samuel M., F. Wafula Okumu, and David Mickler. *The African Union Addressing the Challenges of Peace, Security, and Governance*. Abingdon-on-Thames: Routledge, 2016.

Malhorta, Rajiv. *Being Different: An Indian Challenge to Western Universalism*. India: Harper Collins, 2013.

Malm, Andreas. *The Progress of This Storm: Nature and Society in a Warming World*. London: Verso, 2018.

Martin de Almagro, María. 'Hybrid Clubs: A Feminist Approach to Peacebuilding in the Democratic Republic of Congo'. *Journal of Intervention and Statebuilding* 12, no. 3 (July 3, 2018): 319–34.

McCandless, Erin, and Necla Tschirgi. 'Strategic Frameworks That Embrace Mutual Accountability for Peacebuilding: Emerging Lessons in PBC and Non-PBC Countries'. *Journal of Peacebuilding & Development* 5, no. 2 (June 1, 2010): 20–46.

McFarlane, Fiona, and Mark Malan. 'Crisis and Response in the Central African Republic: A New Trend in African Peacekeeping?' *African Security Review* 7, no. 2 (January 1, 1998): 48–58.

Meyer, Angela. 'Regional Conflict Management in Central Africa: From FOMUC to MICOPAX'. *African Security* 2, no. 2–3 (November 30, 2009): 158–74.

Micinski, Nicholas R. 'NGO Frequent Flyers: Youth Organizations and the Undermining of Reconciliation in Bosnia and Herzegovina'. *Journal of Peacebuilding & Development* 11, no. 1 (2016): 99–104.

Millar, Gearoid. 'For Whom Do Local Peace Processes Function? Maintaining Control through Conflict Management'. *Cooperation and Conflict* 52, no. 3 (September 5, 2017): 293–308.

Mitchell, Andrew. 'Risk and Resilience: From Good Idea to Good Practice'. Working Papers 13, 2013. Paris: OECD.

Moe, Louise Wiuff. 'The Strange Wars of Liberal Peace: Hybridity, Complexity and the Governing Rationalities of Counterinsurgency in Somalia'. *Peacebuilding* 4, no. 1 (January 2, 2016): 99–117.

Mol, Annemarie. 'Ontological Politics. A Word and Some Questions'. *The Sociological Review* 47, no. 1 (1999): 74–89.

Morton, Timothy. *Being Ecological*. London: Pelican Books, 2018.

———. *Hyperobjects*. Minneapolis, MN: University of Minnesota Press, 2013.

Murithi, Tim. 'Peacebuilding or "UN-Building"? African Institutional Responses to the Peacebuilding Commission'. *Journal of Peacebuilding & Development* 4, no. 2 (January 2, 2008): 89–94.

Ngcoya, Mvuselelo. 'Ubuntu: Toward an Emancipatory Cosmopolitanism?' *International Political Sociology* 9, no. 3 (2015): 248–62.

Nietzsche, Friedrich. 'On the Genealogy of Morals'. In *Basic Writings*, edited by Walter Kaufmann, 437–600. New York, NY: Modern Library, 2000.

Nilsson, Desirée. 'Anchoring the Peace: Civil Society Actors in Peace Accords and Durable Peace'. *International Interactions* 38, no. 2 (April 1, 2012): 243–66.

Nordin, Astrid H.M., Graham M. Smith, Raoul Bunskoek, Chiung-chiu Huang, Yih-jye Hwang, Patrick Thaddeus Jackson, Emilian Kavalski, et al. 'Towards Global Relational Theorizing: A Dialogue between Sinophone and Anglophone Scholarship on Relationalism'. *Cambridge Review of International Affairs* 32, no. 5 (2019): 570–81. Routledge, September 3, 2019.

NYU Centre on International Cooperation, and International Peace Institute. 'Taking Stock, Looking Forward: A Strategic Review of the Peacebuilding Commission', 2008. New York, NY: Center on International Cooperation, and International Peace Institute.

Oksamytna, Kseniya, and John Karlsrud, eds. *United Nations Peace Operations and International Relations Theory*. Manchester: Manchester University Press, 2020.

Olsen, Ole Jess, and Jarvad Ib Martin. 'The Political Functions of Social Research – with Special Reference to Peace and Conflict Research'. *International Peace Research Association*, 1970, 92–109.

Organization for Economic Co-operation and Development. 'Shaping the 21st Century: The Contribution of Development Co-Operation', 1996. Paris: Organisation for Economic Cooperation and Development.

———. 'Policy Coherence: Vital for Global Development', 2003. Paris: Organisation for Economic Cooperation and Development.

Paffenholz, Thania. 'Unpacking the Local Turn in Peacebuilding: A Critical Assessment towards an Agenda for Future Research'. *Third World Quarterly* 36, no. 5 (May 4, 2015): 857–74.

Paris, Roland. 'Peacebuilding and the Limits of Liberal Internationalism'. *International Security* 22, no. 2 (1997): 54–89.

Peen Rodt, Annemarie. 'The African Union Mission in Burundi'. *Civil Wars* 14, no. 3 (September 1, 2012): 373–92.

Petrie, Charles, and Adrian Morrice. 'Scrambling and Pulling Together the UN's Civilian Capacities in Conflict-Prone States'. In *Peacebuilding Challenges for the UN Development System 2*, edited by Stephen Browne and Thomas Weiss, 2015: 39–53. New York, NY: Future United Nations Development System.

Philipsen, Lise. 'When Liberal Peacebuilding Fails: Paradoxes of Implementing Ownership and Accountability in the Integrated Approach'. *Journal of Intervention and Statebuilding* 8, no. 1 (2014): 42–67.

Picciotto, Robert. 'Evaluating the UN Development System'. In *Post-2015 UN Development: Making Change Happen?*, edited by Stephen Browne and Thomas Weiss, 112–26. New York, NY: Routledge Global Institutions, 2014.

Pouligny, B. *Peace Operations Seen from Below: UN Missions and Local People*. London: Hurst & Co, 2006.

Preciado, Paul B. *An Apartment on Uranus*. London: Fitzcarraldo Editions, 2019.

Puig de la Bellacasa, María. *Matters of Care. Speculative Ethics in More than Human Worlds*. Minneapolis, MN: University of Minnesota Press, 2017.

Randazzo, Elisa. *Beyond Liberal Peacebuilding: A Critical Exploration of the Local Turn*. Abingdon: Routledge, 2017.

———. 'The Paradoxes of the "Everyday": Scrutinising the Local Turn in Peace Building'. *Third World Quarterly* 37, no. 8 (August 2, 2016): 1351–70.

Randazzo, Elisa, and Ignasi Torrent. 'Reframing Agency in Complexity-Sensitive Peacebuilding'. *Security Dialogue*, April 16, 2020, 096701062090430. https://doi.org/10.1177/0967010620904306.

Rapoport, Anatol. *Fights, Games, and Debates*. Ann Arbor, MI: University of Michigan Press, 1974.

Reindorp, Nicola, and Peter Wiles. *Humanitarian Coordination: Lessons from Recent Field Experience*. London: Overseas Development Institute, June 2001.

Richmond, Oliver. 'The Green and the Cool: Hybridity, Relationality and Ethnographic-Biographical Responses to Intervention'. *Mediterranean Politics* 23, no. 4 (October 2, 2018): 479–500.

———. *A Post-Liberal Peace*. Abingdon-on-Thames: Routledge, 2011.

———. 'A Pedagogy of Peacebuilding: Infrapolitics, Resistance, and Liberation'. *International Political Sociology* 6, no. 2 (June 1, 2012): 115–31.

———. 'Becoming Liberal, Unbecoming Liberalism: Liberal-Local Hybridity via the Everyday as a Response to the Paradoxes of Liberal Peacebuilding'. *Journal of Intervention and Statebuilding* 3, no. 3 (November 1, 2009): 324–44.

———. 'Critical Agency, Resistance and a Post-Colonial Civil Society'. *Cooperation and Conflict* 46, no. 4 (December 1, 2011): 419–40.

———. 'Resistance and the Post-Liberal Peace'. *Millennium* 38, no. 3 (May 1, 2010): 665–92.

Robinson, Kim Stanley. *The Complete Mars Trilogy*. London: Harper Voyager, 2015.

Rose, Deborah Bird. *Wild Dog Dreaming. Love and Extinction*. Charlottesville, VA: University of Virginia Press, 2011.

Rugumamu, Severine. 'Does the UN Peacebuilding Commission Change the Mode of Peacebuilding in Africa?'. FES Briefing Papers 8, 2009. Bonn: Friedrich Ebert Stiftung.

Rutzou, Timothy, and Dave Elder-Vass. 'On Assemblages and Things: Fluidity, Stability, Causation Stories, and Formation Stories'. *Sociological Theory* 37, no. 4 (December 17, 2019): 401–24.

Sabaratnam, Meera. 'Avatars of Eurocentrism in the Critique of the Liberal Peace'. *Security Dialogue* 44, no. 3 (June 2013): 259–78.

———. *Decolonising Intervention: International Statebuilding in Mozambique*. London & New York: Rowman & Littlefield, 2017.

———. 'IR in Dialogue … but Can We Change the Subjects? A Typology of Decolonising Strategies for the Study of World Politics'. *Millennium* 39, no. 3 (April 27, 2011): 781–803.

Schwartz, Glenn M., and John J. Nichols. *After Collapse: The Regeneration of Complex Societies*. Tucson, AZ: University of Arizona Press, 2010.

Scott, James C. *Seeing Like a State: How Certain Schemes to Improve the Human Condition Have Failed*. New Haven, CT: Yale University Press, 2020.

Serres, Michel. *The Natural Contract*. Ann Arbor, MI: The University of Michigan Press, 1995.

Shaviro, Steven. *The Universe of Things. On Speculative Realism*. Minneapolis, MN: University of Minnesota Press, 2014.

Shepherd, Laura J. 'Constructing Civil Society: Gender, Power and Legitimacy in United Nations Peacebuilding Discourse'. *European Journal of International Relations* 21, no. 4 (December 16, 2015): 887–910.

Shinko, Rosemary E. 'Agonistic Peace: A Postmodern Reading'. *Millennium* 36, no. 3 (May 1, 2008): 473–91.

Smirl, Lisa. *Spaces of Aid: How Cars, Compounds and Hotels Shape Humanitarianism*. London: Zed Books, 2015.

Smolin, Lee. *Time Reborn: From the Crisis in Physics to the Future of the Universe*. New York, NY: Mariner Books, 2013.

Sommers, Marc. *The Dynamics of Coordination*. Providence: Thomas J. Watson, Jr. Institute for International Studies, 2000.

Spagnoli, Filip. *Homo-Democraticus: On the Universal Desirability and the Not So Universal Possibility of Democracy and Human Rights*. Cambridge: Cambridge Scholars Publishing, 2003.

Srnicek, Nick, Maria Fotou, and Edmund Arghand. 'Introduction: Materialism and World Politics'. *Millennium: Journal of International Studies* 41, no. 3 (June 7, 2013): 397–97.

Stengers, Isabelle. *Cosmopolitics II*. Minneapolis, MN: University of Minnesota Press, 2011.

———. *In Catastrophic Times: Resisting the Coming Barbarism*. London: Open Humanities Press, 2015.

———. *Thinking with Whitehead: A Free and Wild Creation of Concepts*. Cambridge, MA: Harvard University Press, 2011.

Stockton, Nicholas. *Strategic Coordination in Afghanistan*. Kabul: Afghanistan Research and Evaluation Unit, 2002.

Street, Anne M., Howard Mollett, and Jennifer Smith. 'Experiences of the United Nations Peacebuilding Commission in Sierra Leone and Burundi'. *Journal of Peacebuilding and Development* 4, no. 2 (2008): 33–46.

Swyngedouw, Erik, and Henrik Ernstson. 'Interrupting the Anthropo-ObScene: Immuno-Biopolitics and Depoliticizing Ontologies in the Anthropocene'. *Theory, Culture & Society* 35, no. 6 (November 13, 2018): 3–30.

Tamminen, Tanja. 'Challenges: EU Civilian Crisis Management and the Objective of Impact Assessment – Kosovo as an Example of Complexity'. In *Complexity Thinking for Peacebuilding Practice and Evaluation* edited by Emery Brusset, Cedric De Coning and Bryn Hughes, 2016: 111–39. London: Palgrave Macmillan.

Tom, Patrick. 'In Search for Emancipatory Hybridity: The Case of Post-War Sierra Leone'. *Peacebuilding* 1, no. 2 (June 1, 2013): 239–55.

Torrent, Ignasi. 'Problematising UN-Local Civil Society Engagement in Peacebuilding: Towards Non-Modern Epistemes Through Relationality'. *Journal of Intervention and Statebuilding* 13, no. 5 (2019): 618–37.

Tsing, Anna. *The Mushroom at the End of the World: On the Possibility of Life in Capitalist Ruins*. Princeton, NJ: Princeton University Press, 2015.

UN Chief Executive Board for Coordination. 'Bringing the UN System Together to Support Conflict Prevention and Peacebuilding within the Broader 2030 Agenda for Sustainable Development', 2016. New York, NY: United Nations System.

UN Department of Peacekeeping Operations. 'Integrated Mission Planning Process Guidelines. Role of the Field', 2010.

UN Department of Peacekeeping Operations. 'Report of the Independent High-Level Panel on Peace Operations', 2015. https://www.un.org/en/ga/search/view_doc.asp?symbol=S/2015/446.

UN General Assembly. '2005 World Summit Outcome', 2005. https://www.un.org/womenwatch/ods/A-RES-60-1-E.pdf.

———. 'Delivering as One', 2006. http://www.un.org/en/ga/search/view_doc.asp?symbol=A/61/583.

———. 'Report of the Panel of Eminent Persons on United Nations-Civil Society Relations', 2004. https://www.unog.ch/80256EDD006B8954/%0D(httpAssets)/09916F545454357BC1256F5C005D4352/$file/A-58-817.pdf.

———. 'Report of the World Summit for Social Development', 1995. https://undocs.org/A/CONF.166/9.

———. 'Review of the Efficiency of the Administrative and Financial Functioning of the United Nations. Restructuring of the Secretariat of the Organisation', 1992.

UN General Assembly, and UN Security Council. 'Report of the High-Level Independent Panel on Peace Operations on Uniting Our Strengths for Peace: Politics, Partnership and People', 2015. https://www.un.org/en/ga/search/view_doc.asp?symbol=S/2015/446.

———. 'Report of the Panel on United Nations Peace Operations', 2000. http://www.un.org/en/%0Dga/search/view_doc.asp?symbol=A/55/305.

———. 'Review of Progress in the Implementation of the Strategic Framework for Peacebuilding in Burundi', 2011.

———. 'Review of the United Nations Peacebuilding Architecture', 2010. http://www.un.org/ga/search/view_doc.asp?symbol=A/64/868.

UN Integrated Missions Planning Process. 'Guidelines Endorsed by the Secretary-General on 13 June 2006'. *International Peacekeeping*, 15:4, 588–607.

UN Peacebuilding Commission. 'Monitoring and Track Mechanism of the Strategic Framework for Peacebuilding in Burundi', 2007. https://digitallibrary.un.org/record/%0D613396/files/PBC_2_BDI_4-EN.pdf.

———. 'Report of the Peacebuilding Commission Mission to the Central African Republic, 10–15 October 2011', n.d. https://www.un.org/ga/search/view_doc.asp?symbol=PBC/5/CAF/1.

———. 'Strategic Framework for Peacebuilding in the CAR 2009–2011', n.d. https://www.un.org/ga/search/view_doc.asp?symbol=PBC/3/CAF/7.

———. 'The Peacebuilding Commission: New York-Based, Field-Oriented', 2013. http://www.un.org/en/peacebuilding/pdf/oc/Field-based interface- workshop summary-12Jul13-FINAL.pdf.

UN Peacebuilding Support Office. 'UN Peacebuilding: An Orientation', 2010. https://www.un.org/peacebuilding/sites/www.un.org.peacebuilding/files/documents/peacebuilding_orientation.pdf.

UN Secretary General. 'An Agenda for Peace', 1992. http://www.un-documents.net/a47-277.htm.

———. 'Note on Guidance on Integrated Missions', 2006. http://reliefweb.int/report/world/secretary-generals-note-guidance-integrated-missions.

———. 'Peacebuilding in the Immediate Aftermath of Conflict', 2009. http://www.un.org/en/peacebuilding/pbso/pdf/s2009304.pdf.

———. 'Renewing the UN: A Program for Reform', 1997. https://www.unicef.org/about/execboard/files/A-51-950_Renewing_the_UN-ODS-English.pdf.

UN Security Council. 'Resolution 1159', 1998. https://www.securitycouncilreport.org/atf/cf/%7B65BFCF9B-6D27-4E9C-8CD3-CF6E4FF96FF9%7D/CAR SRES1159.pdf.

———. 'Resolution 1719', 2006. http://unscr.com/en/resolutions/doc/1719.

———. 'Resolution 1959', 2010. http://unscr.com/en/resolutions/doc/1959.

———. 'Resolution 2149', 2014.

———. 'Resolution S/1999/1235', 1999. https://undocs.org/S/1999/1235.

UNICEF. 'A Handy Guide on UN Coherence', 2015. New York, NY: United Nations System.

Urry, John. 'The Complexity Turn'. *Theory, Culture & Society* 22, no. 5 (October 1, 2005): 1–14.

Vimalarahaj, Luxshi, and Suthaharan Nadarajah. 'Thinking Peace: Revisiting Analysis and Intervention in Sri Lanka'. In *The Non-Linearity of Peace Processes: Theory and Practice of Systemic Conflict Transformation*, edited by Daniela Körppen, Norbert Ropers and Hans J. Giessmann, 2011: 129–45. Opladen: Verlag Barbara Budrich.

Vincent, James B. M. 'A Village-Up View of Sierra Leone's Civil War and Reconstruction: Multilayered and Networked Governance'. *IDS Research Report*. Brighton: IDS, 2012.

Visoka, Gëzim. 'Peace Is What We Make of It? Peace-Shaping Events and "Non-Events"'. *Peacebuilding* 4, no. 1 (January 2, 2016): 54–70.

Viveiros de Castro, Eduardo B. *Cannibal Metaphysics: For a Post-Structural Anthropology*. Minneapolis, MN: Univocal, 2014.

Vogel, Birte. 'Civil Society Capture: Top-Down Interventions from Below?' *Journal of Intervention and Statebuilding* 10, no. 4 (October 1, 2016): 472–89.

Vries, Leonie Ansems De, and Doerthe Rosenow. 'Opposing the Opposition? Binarity and Complexity in Political Resistance'. *Environment and Planning D: Society and Space* 33, no. 6 (December 10, 2015): 1118–34.

Wark, McKenzie. *Molecular Red: Theory for the Anthropocene*. London: Verso, 2016.

Weiss, Thomas. *What's Wrong with the United Nations and How to Fix It*. Cambridge: Polity Press, 2016.

Weizman, Eyal. *Hollow Land*. London: Verso, 2017.

Wendt, Alexander. *Quantum Mind and Social Science. Unifying Physical and Social Ontology*. Cambridge: Cambridge University Press, 2015.

Whitehead, Alfred. *Process and Reality*. New York, NY: Free Press, 1979.

———. *The Adventure of Ideas*. London: Macmillan Publishers, 1969.

———. *The Concept of Nature*. Project Gutenberg, 2006.

Wilén, Nina, and Vincent Chapaux. 'Problems of Local Participation and Collaboration with the UN in a Post-Conflict Environment: Who Are the "Locals"?' *Global Society* 25, no. 4 (October 2011): 531–48.

Williams, David, and Tom Young. 'Civil Society and the Liberal Project in Ghana and Sierra Leone'. *Journal of Intervention and Statebuilding* 6, no. 1 (March 1, 2012): 7–22.

Wyeth, Vanessa. 'Peacebuilding at the UN over the Last 10 Years'. Essay Series 6, 2011. Bonn: FriEnt.

Zanotti, Laura. *Ontological Entanglements, Agency and Ethics in International Relations: Exploring the Crossroads*. Abingdon-on-Thames: Routledge, 2019.

———. 'Reorienting IR: Ontological Entanglement, Agency, and Ethics'. *International Studies Review* 19, no. 3 (September 1, 2017): 362–80.

———. 'UN Integrated Peacekeeping Operations and NGOs: Reflections on Governmental Rationalities and Contestation in the Age of Risk'. *International Peacekeeping* 17, no. 1 (February 1, 2010): 17–31.

Index

Note: Page numbers in *italics* denotes tables on corresponding page.

adaptive peacebuilding, 54
Advisory Group of Experts (AGE), xxi,
    48–49, 114n51
affirmative ethics, 91–92
African Union (AU), 26; peacebuilding
    initiatives led by, 40
African Union Mission in Burundi
    (AMIB), 26
AGE. *See* Advisory Group of Experts
agency: action and, 53–54; in Central
    African Republic peacebuilding, 55;
    in entangled complexity, 50–56; in
    entangled peace, 50–56; hybrid, 51–52;
    of local citizens, in peacebuilding
    initiatives, 7; non-deterministic forms
    of, 53
Agenda for Prosperity, in Sierra Leone, 12
Albania, 21
Almagro, Martin de, 51
alternative dispute mechanisms, in Sierra
    Leone peacebuilding initiatives, 126n10
AMIB. *See* African Union Mission in
    Burundi
Anthropocene, 73–74, 82
anthropocentric modernity, xii;
    knowledge production and, 86
assemblages: in complexity-sensitive
    peacebuilding, 38–45; components of,

74; Deleuze on, 30, 60–61; of external
    peace missions, 38–45; Gaia concept
    and, 74; Latour on, 62–63; linear
    causality and, 30–31;
    semiotic-material flows in, 30
assistentialism, 5
AU. *See* African Union
autonomy, in civil society, 7

Ban Ki-Moon, 3
Barad, Karen, xiv, 1, 62–63, 96; on
    causality, 69; on externalities, 35, 53
Bennet, Jane, xiv
Bergson, Henri, xiv, 19
BINUB. *See* United Nations Integrated
    Office in Burundi
BINUCA. *See* United Nations Integrated
    Peacebuilding Support Office in the
    Central African Republic
BNUB. *See* United Nations Office in
    Burundi
BONUCA. *See* Support Office in the
    Central African Republic
Bosnian war, xx
Boutros-Ghali, Boutros, xix–xx, 3
Brahimi report. *See* Panel on United
    Nations Operations
Braidotti, Rosi, xiv

147